I0024256

Williams Winters

The History of the Ancient Parish of Waltham Abbey

Williams Winters

The History of the Ancient Parish of Waltham Abbey

ISBN/EAN: 9783744690072

Printed in Europe, USA, Canada, Australia, Japan

Cover: Foto ©ninafisch / pixelio.de

More available books at **www.hansebooks.com**

THE HISTORY

OF THE

Ancient Parish

OF

WALTHAM ABBEY

OR

Holy Cross,

BY

W. WINTERS, F.R., Hist. Soc.,

*Author of Select Passages in the Life of King Harold ; Ecclesiastical Works
of the Middle Ages ; Our Parish Registers ; Queen Eleanor
Memorial, Waltham Cross, etc., etc.*

" Of noble actes auncyenlly enrolde,
Of famous Princes and Lords of Estate,
By thy report are wonte to be extold
Registeringe trewly every former date."

Skelton, on " The Dolorous Death," &c.

PUBLISHED BY THE AUTHOR,
CHURCH YARD, WALTHAM ABBEY, ESSEX,
1888.

CONTENTS.

INTRODUCTION.

WALTHAM, for many centuries, has been regarded by English historiographers as a place of importance, principally on account of its cathedral-like Abbey,—the history of which, says Dr. Fuller, "is the history of the Church of England."

From the number of fragments of ancient pottery, coins, &c. (see page 184), which have been discovered in this parish at different times, it is quite evident that prior to the Saxon rule in Waltham, the locality was familiar to the Romans, and other warlike men of Britain who ranged the primeval wilds of Essex,* and whose trackways are traceable from Ambresbury Banks across the ancient Lea to Cheshunt, the *Durolitum* of the Romans.†

The early history of the Abbey Church is established by reliable documents, such as the *Great Charter (Cartæ Antiquæ) of Waltham* and the *Cottonian* and *Harleian MSS.*, in which appear Edward the Confessor's gifts to Harold and the various lands given by Harold to his Church. A copy of the original deed, of contemporary date, (1062,) is preserved in the Public Record Office. Domesday Book is another splendid document extant, which contains notices in brief of everything belonging to the parish at that period.‡ Every acre of land is there recorded, also all houses, fisheries, mills, woods, cattle, together with the names of their owners, &c. The Abbey of Waltham being a royal foundation it was not subject to episcopal jurisdiction, but only to the "See of Rome and the King." The superior was one of the twenty-eight mitred Abbots of England, and ranked the twentieth. These mitred Abbots were called "Abbots General " or "Abbots Sovereign," and sat as Lords in Parliament, four of which were denominated "Abbots exempt," viz., the Abbots of Waltham, Bury, St. Albans and Evesham. The Abbey of

---

* Warlies, and its surroundings, by W. Winters.

† Salmon's History of Hertfordshire, p. 7, 1728.

‡ *Doomsday Book* consists of two volumes, a greater and a less. The first called the " Winchester Book " was made A.D. 1148; and the second known as the " Bolden Book " was compiled A.D. 1183.

Waltham had continued (from its foundation by Harold in 1060) for 480 years under several Deans and twenty-seven Abbots.* The list of the Abbots of Waltham, from the time of Henry II., to the dissolution of the Abbey in 1540, inserted in this volume, has been carefully compiled from the *Harleian* and *Cottonian MSS.*, compared with the works of Dugdale, Willis, Stevens, Newcourt and others; and the ministers of the Abbey from the Reformation to the present time have been principally arranged according to the Repertorium of Newcourt and the Parish Registers. The clergy in charge of the Abbey since the dissolution were until recently designated either incumbents or curates. The late Rev. James Francis, M.A., was the last *Incumbent* and the first *Vicar* of the parish. By an Act passed some time ago called "The District Church Amendment Act," the ecclesiastical living of Waltham became a Vicarage in August, 1868. The Abbey was not under episcopal jurisdiction until 1854.

An original document discovered in the Public Record Office a few years ago by J. Burtt, Esq., has thrown much light upon the architectural alterations made in the Abbey in the reign of Edward I. This notorial instrument setting forth a mandate for the repair of the church is in Latin, and was issued September 6th, 1286, by Abbot Reginaldi. (See page 97.)

OLD ENGRAVINGS OF THE ABBEY CHURCH.

Many engravings of the Abbey Church have been published in works of history, but none of them are of great antiquity. There may be earlier private drawings and paintings which have not come before our notice. Our private collection of plates of the Abbey is as follows:—(1) John Farmer, 1735, south view; (2) 1750 south east view; (3) a similar drawing, by James Peak, 1763; (4) north view, 1779, shows the Abbot's refectory, re-published September 15th, 1783, by J. Hooper; (5) east view; (6) 1798, south view; the tower was then in course of re-erection;

---

* The privilege of being exempt from all episcopal jurisdiction was granted to the first Abbot, Wido or Guido, by Pope Lucius III., who was the first Pope elected by Cardinals, A.D. 1181. The Abbots of Waltham were indulged with the use of Pontificals by Pope Celestine III., A.D. 1191. In the November of 1197 the Archbishop of Canterbury visited the Abbey of Waltham and expressed his confidence in the Abbot's mode of government. *Vide* Chron. Rich. I. (*Stubbs.*)

(7) south view, by S. Rawle, Nov. 1st, 1804; (8) north view, by
J. Greig, July 1st, 1804; exterior view, by Greig, Dec.,
1804, also Abbey gates, from a drawing by C. Arnald; (9)
distant view of the Abbey by Ellis, for Dr. Hughson's
description of London, 1805; (10) north-east view, by
F. Calvert; (11) south-west view (small); (12) south-east
view, by George Shepherd, engraved by W. Woolnorth,
March 1st, 1805, also a view of the Abbey gates; (13) nave
and great arch, by Barlow, September 20, 1807; (14) small
north view, by Greig, April 1st, 1808; (15) small interior view, by
Greig; (16) west front, as it appeared before the erection
of the western tower, by J. Carter, May 1st, 1810, also
architectural details of the Abbey Church, by J. Carter,
1807; (17) north view with Abbey gates, by John Harris,
November 4, 1812; (18) interior view with seals, Abbey gates, &c.,
by E. Ogbourn (Hist. Essex), 1814; (19) interior and exterior,
views by John Coney, 1817—1818, showing royal arms on the
front of the mill near the "Factory Stones"; (20) south-east
view, by C. H. Campion; (21) "Baker's Entry," by H. Bartlett;
(22) two plates of the church, by Brayley, 1834; (23) north
view, by G. F. Sargent, August 1st, 1842; (24) an engraving
by Mr. Salmons, of Cheshunt. Various views of the church were
taken during its restoration, in 1859-60. J. E. Thompson published a ground plan of the church, engraved by E. Rolfe.
T. Morris made a drawing of the Elizabethan Market House,
Waltham Abbey, showing the old whipping-post, 1598, engraved
by G. Hollis. A much better view of the Market House was
made by the late Joseph Upton, a native of this town. In our
collection of Views of the Abbey we have an engraving of a
13th century seal from the Abbot of Waltham to Hugh Nevil.
Also two counter seals of the Abbot of Waltham, dated A.D.
1253; Views of Copt Hall, &c.

NOTED PERSONS OF THE NEIGHBOURHOOD.

Most of the Kings of England, from Harold to Charles II.,
as also many ecclesiastical dignitaries, have at different times
visited Waltham Abbey. Harold no doubt visited Waltham
many times during the erection of his college. His last visit
was shortly before the Battle of Hastings. Henry II. made
his last Will and Testament under the shadow of the Abbey

in 1182. Henry III. frequently visited the Abbey in 1270; and numerous are the writs that were signed in Waltham at various periods by Royal hands.

The body of Queen Eleanor rested here in 1291-2; and the body of Edward I. was brought from Scotland in 1307, and rested within the precincts of the Abbey for fifteen weeks. Here Richard III. took shelter for a short time during the insurrection of Wat Tyler; and later on, Archbishop Cranmer resorted to the house of Master Cressey in the Romeland, when the plague raged at Cambridge. Thomas Tallis was precentor for some time in the Abbey Church, *temp.* Henry VIII. The Bassanœ family of Waltham were great musicians; and received Royal patronage from Henry VIII., Edward VI., Queen Elizabeth, James I., Charles I. and Charles II. Sir Anthony Denny, Chamberlain to King Henry VIII., possessed nearly the whole of the eccclesiastical property of Waltham. He resided near the Abbey, and afterwards at Cheshunt, where he died and was buried. The Denny's intermarried with the Earls of Carlisle, Bedford, Exeter, Kennoul, Manchester and other notable families, most of whom resided in the parish of Waltham; as also the Lords Brook, Grevill and Buckhurst. In the time of James I. and Charles I., as many as five knights resided in Waltham Abbey, besides the noble families of Cressey, Colte, Bassanoe, Vavassor, Sackville Dorset, Foxe, Wollaston, Swift and others.*

Sir Anthony Denny received many noble gifts from Henry VIII. and Edward VI. and later monarchs. Sir Edward Denny possessed a pair of mittens presented by Queen Elizabeth to Margaret, his mother, wife of Sir Edward Denny and lady-in-waiting to the Queen. Sir Edward Denny possessed

---

* In the Harl. MSS. 2,240, fol. 44, occur the names of the Freeholders of Waltham, "on whose lands issues might be levied" in 1633. Those for Waltham *Township* were: Edward Cooke, gent., Henry Blott, Edward Turner, William Nash, Rolland Patterson, John Golding, John Vavassor, gent. and Francis Greene, gent. For *Upshire*: Ralph Hodge, John Derrington, Thomas Huntley, Henry Williams and Edward Palmer, gent. *Arm.* For *Hallifield*, Thos. Brewett, Henry Curle, Henry Wollaston, gent. For *Sewardstone*, Edward Fullham, William Cramphorn, Richard Stock, and William Reynolds. An account was rendered about this period of persons chargeable in Waltham, for what was called "*The Essex Loan*," viz., "*Township.*"—John Tanner in *bonus* x li —xx li.; John Standish in *bonus* x li.—xx li.; Upshire and Hallifield Robert Hall, gent in terr. (land) x li.—xx li.

also a magnificent scarf given by King Charles I. to Adam.
Hill, of Huntingdon (whose daughter married Peter Denny),
for rallying his troops of horses at the battle of Edghill. His
Majesty wore the scarf on that memorable day. Sir E. Denny
also owned a pair of gloves given to Edward Denny, Esq.,
by King James I.

The names of several pilgrims who sailed to New England
between the years 1630 and 1640 occur in the Registers of
Waltham Abbey and Nazing. At this period, and for a
century later, Waltham was infested with the " Essex Gang "
and " Waltham Blacks," who ranged the neighbourhood,
committing all kinds of depredations. After awhile ·the
notorious highwayman, Dick Turpin, resided in the outskirts
of the parish, and on the 4th of May, 1737, he wilfully shot
Thomas Morris, servant to Henry Thompson, keeper of the
Forest; an entry of which occurs in the Parish Registers
thus : " Thomas Morrise, servant to Mr. Henry Thompson,
shot upon ye Forest, Bur. May 7th, 1737." The King
offered £200 reward for the apprehension of Turpin on
account of this murder (See " Our Parish Registers," p. 77).

EARLY NAMES OF PERSONS DERIVED FROM THE PLACE OF THEIR NATIVITY.

In very early times many persons were named after the
locality in which they were born, or the trade they followed.
Hence we have Hugh of Waltham, common clerk of the
City of London, in 1312. William of Waltham appears in the
list of persons connected with the transfer and valuation of
pledges, taken for arrears of tallage in 1314—" From William
de Waltham, one posuet, value 12d." John of Waltham, a
native of this town, temp. Richard II., died Bishop of
Salisbury in 1395, and was buried in the Royal Chapel,
Westminster Abbey. Roger Waltham, a native of Waltham,
was Canon of St. Paul's and a learned author. In 1316 the
Abbot of Waltham appointed as one of his attorneys Peter
de Waubham, with a view to claim his franchise in the
Exchequer. On the 15th July, 1429, Robert Waltham, son
and heir of Walter Waltham, of Waltham Holy Cross,
received for the term of his life, in fee simple, three
tenements in Waltham near the " Cimitermni Pynest "

(Green), High Beech.   John of Cestrehunte and Richard of
Cestrehunte (Cheshunt), " Plumers and Fethermongers," resided
in Cheshunt in 1281.   Feathers at this early period were
used exclusively for cushions and beds of the most wealthy;
the middle and humbler classes slept upon straw.

ANCIENT DEEDS AND CHARTERS RELATING TO WALTHAM.*

Chief of the early MSS. relating to the Abbey Church are
preserved in the British Museum, viz., Harleian—*Liber Niger*,
3766 ; *Liber Rebrus*, 3766 ; *Registra*, 391, 3,739, 4,809 ;
Chartæ and Extractæ Chartarum, 6,748 ; *Abbatum Nomina*
3,776, 7,520 ; *Taxationes*, 1,850 ; *Fundatio*, 692 ; *De
Inventione Crucis*, 3,776 ; *Miracula* and *Reliquiæ*, 3,776 ;
Waltham Forest, 6,839, 6,853, and 6,705. Cottonion MSS.
—*Register*, Tib. C. ix.; *De cruce ibi deducta*, Jul. D. vi.;
Carta Fund. Claud D. ii ; *Waltham (de terris apud)* Nero,
C. iii.; *Roger Waltham*, Vesp. B. xxi. Lansd. MSS. 763,
Church music, used in the Abbey, in the fifteenth century.
(See " Ecclesiastical works of the middle ages," by W.
Winters, p. 53).   The *Carta Antique* of Waltham, in the
Public Record Office, is of great value. We have, at various
times, and at great expense, collected many ancient deeds of
interest, in which occur the early names of persons, lands,
and domestic buildings in the parish of Waltham.   In the
collection of *Ancient Deeds* and *Charters* preserved in the
Record Office, are several relating to lands, buildings, etc., in
this town, and from which we have taken extracts for this
work.

NAMES OF ANCIENT PLACES IN WALTHAM.

(1) *Highbridge Street* (or West Street).—Brihtuff Foht conveyed to John Foht, his son, one tenement, with ·a quantity
of arable land in *Manneland* (Honey Lane) one croft in
Siwordston called *Herdcroft*, two acres in *Westsote*, with a
tenement held in trust by the Abbot of Waltham, rent
" *tres solid.*"   Signed in the presence of Heni de Wermel,
Rob. de Hertford, Gal. de Langrich, Manigod Napp, Simœ
le Guc^d, Thme de Halifeld, Abraham fil Thom, Will, Pulier

* Many of these deeds are in the author's possession.

and Alan Clico. (2) John Foot in 1314, conveyed to his son "Dauye," one messuage in the *ville* of Waltham in "*Haye Strate*" (High Street) abutting a messuage and gardens on the west, and land of John Fross on the east. 7 Ed. II., 1314. (3) Two "shopis" in *West Street*, belonging to Johan Poley de Waltham, 13, Richard II., 1390. John de Poley with four others held a religious appointment in St. Sepulchre's Chapel, Waltham, founded A.D. 1346. (4) 1395, John Perkyns, son of John Perkyns of Waltham, conveyed, by deed, two shops in *West Street*, in the tenure of Richard Hosiere and Thomas Frankside, to Thomas Wolmersty, Bobt. Ferour, Walto Cuffle, and John Gladwyne. John Perkyns sold to the said persons a garden situate in *Spaineshaw* in *Frosshenlane*, Waltham, adjoining the premises of Elene Byffayn, John Sabrichford, and a cottage and garden in "*Bowyers*," 18, Ric. II. (5) John Perkys granted a garden in *West Street*, called "*Bowyers*," to Walter Enfield and John Gladwyn, 19, Ric. II. (6) William Stephens conveyed a tenement in *West Street* on the *Marsh Bank* with a garden near the "*Fullingmell Streme*" and "*Austin & le Pynfolde*," to Walter More, John Balitre, and William Henry of Waltham, 3, Hen. IV., 1402. This garden belonged to John Ive, rector of St. Michael's *Wood Street, London* 23 Ric. II. In 1477 these premises fell into the possession of Robert Shambrook, John Audley, and Richard Ram of Waltham. (7) Agreement between William Somer, Robert atte Lee (Robert at the Lee) and Robert Curson, respecting the sale of a tenement in *West Street*, 1 Hen. VI., 1422 (Red Seal). This MS. is in the British Museum (Add. MSS., 6012), and was purchased, January 23, 1844, of J. Graham, Leverton School-master. (8) Richard Swarston, February 14, 2 Rich. III., 1485, conveyed to Robto Norton of Waltham one tenement and garden situate in "*Hie stret*," near the premises of John Pomante on the West, the "*Officm Pilant de Waltham*" on the East, abutting on the north the land of Walteri Harberd, and the land formerly belonging to the Mandevilles on the south. (9) A transfer of property in *High strete* belonging to the late John Swarston of Waltham, to Walto Swarston, Robto Suttell, Willo Pagrym, John Drawsword and John Sawnden (3 Hen. VIII) 1512. (10) A narrow slip of parchment of the same date signed "Cressy" — being an agreement between Agnes King, of London widow of Richard King, grocer, and Thomas Elscy, relative to the sale of land, &c., in Waltham. (11) Walter Swarston, late of Waltham, sold to John Champney, his half tent. &c. in *High-strete* for the sum of £5 13s. 4d. (18 Hen. VIII), 1518 (Red Seal). (12) Alice Champney widow of John Champney sold her property in *Hygh Strete* to Thomas Melowe, Tho. Saunders, Tho. Clendon, and John Breteyne, and which formerly belonged to John Wren of Waltham, "Bryke lyre," 1528 (Red Seal). John Champney of Leyton sold the said property to John Wren for £10. This MS (English) is dated 13 Oct. (19 Hen. VIII) 1528. (13) John Wren (who is called a "tyler" residing at Nazing in 1535) sold his premises in *Hygh Strete* to John Dedyngton; these premises were near the house of William Haleworth, (Red Seal). (14) In 1545, John Wren "Bryckleyar" *de Nasyng* sold his property in *Highestreate* called *Resing* [Risings] formerly in the possession of Walter Herbert and William Corbyn, Dated, Nazing, 20 Jan., 36 Hen. VIII, (Red Seal). (15) British Museum MS. (Add. Charter 6013). An agreement between Will. Browne of Waltham, and Agness and Robert Porter concerning a tenement in *Westrete de Waltham* belonging to "the Guild" of the "B. Mariæ de Waltham." 11 Jan. (3 Ed. VI.) 1550. (16) John Corbet granted his house and orchard called "*Poynts*" in *Hyestreate* to John Derrington for the sum of £20. (17) The "Crosse Keys," House was granted by Thomas Parnell "Baker of Waltham" to Thomas Camp, Jun., of Nazing, Yeoman, Dec. 15, 1609. This building situate in *West Street* was formerly occupied by William Hare and afterwards by John Biggs. It stood near the tenement belonging to John Goldsborough, gent. then occupied by Wm. Nokes, tailor, and "a yard and cart-way of Sir W. Wade, Knt., held by John Wetherhead, 14 June, 1611. (18) 1638, Richard Dawson, gent., surrendered all his copyhold property in *West Streete* "nere to the *Highebridge*," with a close called *Brick-hill-close*, late in the tenure of Edward Liverland to John Chomeley of Crowhurst co. Surrey. (19) 1638 Edward May surrendered to his daughter Mary Duchat, widow, two houses adjoining the *Church Yard*, one of which was in the occupation of Henry Wood "Body Maker." (20) This MS. contains Court Leet admittances from 1691 to 1695.

The Romeland.—(1) Richard Mascoll and Maria his wife, surrendered (to Henry Denny Lord of the Manor) a house and garden in the *Romeland* occupied by John Reed and

Tho. Wilkenson to the use of Thomas Milles, 22 May, 1567.
(2) MSS. dated 1567, 1576, 1593 and 1610 relate to the transfer
of the same property belonging to John Hudson. (3) 1614.
Elizabeth Collop surrendered a cottage in the *Romeland* near
the house of W. Ward [Sir W. Wade, Knt.] to Phillippi Fuller
and Christiance Bayford. (4) 1615. Richard Payne surrendered
a house in the *Romeland*, in the occupation of Margaret Warner.
(5) 1628. *"Frankpledge"* respecting Elizabeth Collop, Thomas
Brewett, Henrici Hermqman and several tenements in the *Romeland*. (6) 1662. At this period the manor of Waltham was
possessed by Margretto Countess Carlisle. Tho. Mezant
surrendered his premises in the *Romeland* to Abraham Hudson.
(7) A similar deed occurs under date 1660 in which are the
names of William Earl of Bedford, Margaret Countisso
Carlisle, Christopher Davenport, Abraham Hudson, Jacobi
Stringer, Tho. Mezant, Christopher Wright, Thoms Monk,
and Ambrose Sumpner. (8) 1686. Willio Countis Bedford
Lord of the Manor. On the death of Thomas Monk three
houses in the *Romeland* were surrendered to the use of John
Bell, yeoman.

*Sun Street** (or East Street).—(1) The earliest document
relating to *Sun Street*, dates back to 1447. Tenements in
Est Stret formerly belonged to William Orgon and Alice his
wife, were transferred by Walter Lok, of Waltham, to John
Gladwyn of *London*, Draper, and William Treue, of Waltham.
(2) 1447, relates to the property of Wm. Orgon, in *Est Stret*,
situated between the house of Thos. Lok, "plomer," and the
houses formerly held by John Arke, Walter More and the
"cimitu Abbathie de Waltham." (3) 1516. Property in
Trykkeryslane or *Cryketleslane* in *Estrete* in which occurs the
names of Richard Lynton, Geo. Jackson (Brewer), John Baker,
John Drawswerd, Wm. Orgore, Geo. Salt, Robt. Farethwatte
(Brown Seal, " R," within a wreath). (4) 1531. A house sold
by Aleyn Keys to William Bereman for £5. The premises
connected with this house were situated betweene the *kyngs
high way* on the south partie, and the walle of the *"nowe
Chircheyourd* (new Churchyard) of the Abbot of Waltham on

---

* Early in the present century an old thatched house stood on the site
of Mr. Richards' house, Sun Street. The straw eaves of this house were
very low and in the way of foot passengers. Mr. Jurdan, pig dealer,
occupied the house last.

the north partie. This was the old "White Horse" beerhouse, demolished in 1851. (5) 1531, Bereman's *Release to Allyn Keyes*, (Latin), (Seven red seals), signed, W. Bereman (*Weaver*), W. Mugg, T. Bereman, R. Walenger, J. Pecok, J. Collop, A. Keys (*Baker*), W. Cressy, gent., J. Blunt (*Miller*), J. Bretyn, *Peynter* [painter], R. Alexander de Weston, in com. *Hertford*, J. Alexander de villa *Hertford* (*Bocher*) [Butcher], and R. Orgon. The situation of the property is described as in *East-strete* on the south of the *Noui Cemeterii Abbatis de Waltham*, new churchyard, (now the *old one.*) (6) 1555. xxxth Julie, sale of a house in *Eststrete*, by John Kayes to John Tanner alias Adamps, for £12, "abbutange upon the wall of the late dissolved Monasterie of Waltham holli crosse." This was the "White Horse" property, Sun Street. (7) 1562. A house in *Est Strete* (late the property of W. Waller) sold by J. Humphrey of *Southwell*, yeoman, to W. Norman, Lynnen Draper of Waltham, for £18 10s. (Red Seal). (8) 1563. Sale of Property in *Tryckery-lane* alias *Creketts-lane*, *Estrete*, by J. Waterer to Andrew Warner de *Cowpsald* [Coopersale.] (9) 1564. Grant of a house in *Estreate*, to W. Norman, by W. Pond, W. Iverye, J. King (of *Cheshen*) and J. Barnard. Signed, W. Pond, J. Dennet clic. de *Eppinge*, and J. Legge. (10) 1565. Sale of property by Andrew Warner of *Epping* to Giles Brett of *Stortford*, situated in *Trickrisse Lane*, alias *Creketts Lane*, *Estrett*, near the house of W. Orgore. Signed, J. Vavasor and others. (11) 1569. Sale of the same premises by Giles Brett to Geo. Wilsdon. (12) 1577. Sale of three shops and a piece of land in *East Street*, the property of Edward Maplesdon and Jasper Nicolls (the latter was host of the Old Cock Inn). These Shops were situated south of the monastery, near the "White Horse" in *Sun Street*. (13) Same deed refers to Jasper Nicholls and Richard Willinson (Williamson) "Basketmaker." Property situated in "*Creeks Lane*" or "*Cricket Lane*," dated October 30th, 1578. (14) Law suit between Henry Breton and Ellen Towers, widow, of Waltham. Jan. 23rd 1579. Anne Breton by her will dated June 14, 1541, bequeathed certain property in Waltham to W. Towers, late husband of the defendant, and to his heirs after the decease of John Stickney &c. (15) Court of request P. R. Off. 23 Eliz. 1581. To the Queen's moste excellent matie. Plaintiff Thomas Hare, defendant William Howe, certain premises in Waltham called "*Chequer*"

belonging to Rob. and Joan Hare, of Waltham, and afterwards to their son Thomas Hare, of *Smythfield nere London*,
Boocher, and which was formerly possessed by Walter Rand,
was unlawfully entered upon by William Howe, "Collier" (a man
of greate welthe and well frended and allied in the said
county of Essex) who possessed the deeds of the said property.
(16) June 1st, 1589. Sale of a house called "Reasons'* in
Est Strete, belonging to Richard Derryington, carpenter. (17)
surrender of property in *East Street* from 1615 to 1623. (18)
1623, John Beebie of Waltham, Blacksmith, sold his house
(then in the occupation of James Cliborne glazier) known as the
"White Horse," to Thomas Stocke of *Sewardstone*, yeoman for
£9 10s. Signed J. Leverton, J. Smyth, and Giles Knight.
(19) 1633. Surrender of property in *Carbuncles Dunghill
Fountain Square* and *East Street*.

The Market Place.—(1) Feb 13, 1622. Surrendered by
Peter Humble a house near the Market Place, and adjoining
a tenement belonging to Lord Denny, to Mary Nicolls, widow of
Jasper Nicolls of the "Cock Inn," This house is called in the
deed "*Church Gate House*," and appears to be the one owned
and occupied by the writer. Peter Humble was the son of Richard
Humble, Alderman of London, who married the daughter of
John Pierson, of Nazing. (2) 28 Eliz. Surrender of a cottage
in the *Corn Market* neere *Catebrigg Donghill* in *Scole Streete*
(School Street). Admission of Samuel Fox, gent. (son of the
martyrologist), to a meadow called "*Suffield*," &c., 28 May,
2 James I. (3) 1636. Surrender of a house in the *Market-
place*, occupied by John Bennett, also a tenement near the
"Cock Inn" *East Street*. Certain fines presented at the Court
Leet respecting *Town Meade*, &c.

Ancient Deeds relating to Waltham (exact locality not
given).—(1) 1404. The property in Waltham belonging to
Johes Wodrowe and Walto Moor was sold to W. Skynner,
J. Finch, mason, J. Reygner, carpenter, W. Syndlesham,
bocher, and J. Lowe, bocher, 5 Hen. IV., 1404 (Two red
seals). (2) 1448. Johannis Friday of *London*, and Willi
Friday, her son of Waltham; property released to Georgio
Brown, of Waltham, situated near the property of Rici
Rysynges; Signed, Willo. Wake, and others. Nov. 15,
26 Hen. VI. (red seal). (3) 1570. Transfer of Land be-

---

* Probably the same property as belonged to Richard Rysynges in 1448.

longing to William Merick "now beinge buylded upon wth shoppes or houses in the towne of Waltham," to Katherine Willesdon. (Small black seal). (4) Lawsuit between Laurence Biggins and Margaret his wife, John Powell and Elizabeth his wife, and Alice Lambert, widow, respecting property in Waltham. Signed, "Cesar." Oct. 30, 1619, (white seal, broken). Sir Julius Cæsar, born at Tottenham in 1557, died 1636, was Master of the Rolls. (5) Court Leet, June 3rd, 1639. Fine of Five Pounds for any person receiving a stranger into the town. (6) 1697. Elizabeth Bell, widow of John Bell, disposed of all her rights of Waltham Turnpike, which she held of James, Earle of Kennoule, and his predecessors, to James Travers, of Waltham, Feb. 18, 1697. *Sewardstone Street* (otherwise *Sheepcote Street, Eldford Street* and *South Street*). (1) 1326. Laurence de Scykeneye conveyed to Simon his son two acres of land in *Eldworth-field.* One acre near the land of R. Forshim, east of *Town mead.* Witness Gilbert de Camera, John Fot, Barcho Palfreyman, John Hok, John ate Wode, Barcho Scot, Roger de Kingstone, W. le Marchal, W. Frosshenlane and Simon de Doittone. (Oval Seal). (2) John Foots granted to John Hoks property in *Fotys lane* Waltham, 1339. (3) John Golde and Cadnia his wife granted a parcel of land to John Alisauner of Waltham called *Eldfordefeld.* 1341. (4) John Golde and Catina sold John Alisauner of Waltham one piece of land called *Eldefordefeld* between *Town-mede* and *Eldefordestrate,* 1342 (red seal). (5) John Foot granted to Walter Bret citizen of *London,* 3 acres of land in *Eldeworth lane* near the land of John Loord and John Froyssch, 1348. (6) John Dysaundri of *Enfield* granted to John Bret arable land formerly belonging to John Goolde situated in *Eldworth.* Signed, John Mandeville and others, 1352. (7) Walter Bret granted to Henry Webbe three pieces of land adjoining the land of the Abbot of Waltham, and that of John Roger and John Stringer, 1365 (seal). (8) Elina Henesfield, widow of Waltham, sold land called *Eldworth fell,* 1376. (9) Henry le Webbe released to Roger Herras, William Skynner, John Trylle and John Sewale 7 acres of land in *Eldworthweye,* near *Fledlondys* and *Tonmed (Floodlands* and *Town mead*), 1391. (10) John Baldock and John Stock of Waltham granted to Walter Waltham all their land in *Eldworth feld,* 1392. (11) John Hay, son of Godwin Hay, granted to

John Foot his lands in *Yanneland* (or *Manneland*) and *Edineford* in Waltham, 1392. (12) Roger Herras, W. Skynne, J. Trille, J. Sewale of Waltham, disposed of seven acres of land in *Eldworthfeldi*, 1392. (*Floodlands* belonged to the Abbot of Waltham). (13) Nicho. de Kent granted Richard Warle and John Taylor one tenement in *Oldefordestrete* in Waltham, 1394. (14) Willim Fallam disposed of his tenements, &c., in *Eldeworth strett* with land in *Pynest grove* in *Vpschire*, 1431 (seal broken). (15) Deed relating to land near the tenement of Alice Holts and *Town Mead*, 1473. (16) Land in *Town Mead* near *Ilfordfeld* in *Shepcot-lane* and *Fotes-lees* and *Mannelond* on the north of *Honey-lane*, 1473. (Small seal.)

Sheepcote Street or *Sewardstone Street.*—(1) John Frosch, mercer of London, granted to Robt. atte How de Waltham his messuage in *Schepecote-stret*, near the house of Johis Chege-welle, 1333. (2) William Breggis, Rector of *Gestmyngthorp** granted to John Foot and Emma his wife a tenement in *Ham stret (Hammond Street)* with land called *Munlond* in *Cobhyge*, eight acres called *Herefeld*, one croft called *Maystris Croft* in *Schepecote stret*, two crofts called *Holecroftes* near *Honey Lane* and *Puchisland*, 1356. (3) Walter Bret of *London* and Christina his wife released to Thomas Poydras a tenement in *Clousebregge* with 3 acres of arable land adjoining *Potterishelle*, *Childrenedoune*, *Bekebrokysdoune*, *Primhisfeld* and *Westfeld*, in Waltham, 1365. (4) Thomas Poydras granted to John Hood of *Upshire* in Waltham and Agneti his wife a tenement near *Clousebregg* which he bought of Walter Bret, 1367. (5) Johes May, Tho. Derby, Radus Palmer, Walter Sherery, Johes Sadeler, Johes Balytre and Walta atte More, confirmed to Roger Herof, Walto Shercy, Bocher and Walto Enfield of Waltham the rental of certain premises in *Shepcote strete* formerly belonging to Willi Mannying de Waltham (16 Ric.) 1393, (six seals.) (6) John Hood granted to John Martyn a tenement in *Shepcote strete* near the garden of W. Foot, 1397. (7) Anderus the son of Henry (Fitz Aucher) of *Copped halle* granted to Henry de Bougeye and Roesis his wife twelve acres of (arable) land and two acres of wood in *Schepcotstrete*, 1399. (8) John Vync of Waltham, and Willim Thurston granted

* Everard, the son of Sir Ralph de Geist or Geisthorp, co. Norfolk, gave the lordship of the manor of Geisthorp or Gestmyngthorp with the advowson of the church to the Abbots of Waltham, *temp* Hen. II.

to John Foot and Margery His wife property near *Holecroft*, Waltham, 1341. (9) Robt. Smyth, of Waltham, Yeoman, Robt. Bardesey, gent. and Tho. Lyffyn, citizen of *London*, granted land and a tenement in Waltham, 1483. (10) Court of Request, *temp* Elizabeth, a lawsuit between Margaret Golding, widow, and Margaret Carter respecting three acres of land in *Cobmead*. (11) Particulars for grants 7 Ed. VI. Property of Lady Joan Denney, widow of Sir Anthony Denny, 1553. (12) Deed between Sir Henry Bosvile of *Eynsford*, *Kent*, and Robert Newman relating to the rental of 16 acres of land in *Sheepwak-feilds* at £14 per annum 1689. (13) Deed relating to John Farmer, the historian of Waltham Abbey. At the time this deed was written, John Farmer resided at *Cheshunt*. The deed refers to the sale of copyhold property to Jeremiah Bentham, of Algate, London, gent. 1720—1750.

School Street or Silver Street.—(1) Walter de Cokham, John, son of Ralph, the Cowherd, of Waltham, granted certain messuages formerly called *Curtilagio*, in *Skolestrate*, in Villa de Waltham, Signed, Barcho de Rangrich, Simon de Duncon, John Hook, Thomas Saxpe, Johne Fot, Walto *de Frossthenlane*. Johne atte Down, Roger de Middleton and others. 15 Ed. iii. 1342. (2) Richard Yong of Waltham granted to Richard Wheler his premises in *Clowesbruggestrete* between the property of John Martyn and the abbot of Waltham in *Estfeld*, 1427. (3) John Sabrichford, and John *de Ware* respecting property in *Frosthenlane*, Waltham Abbey. (4) Deed between Nicholas Burman and John Colyn, relating to the sale of a cottage in *School Street* in the occupation of Andrew Bright (one of the ancestors of the Brights of New England) April 8, 1455. (5) A parchment in which occurs the name of *Francisco Harvye*, the owner of "*Frank Harvye's Field*," situated at the lower end of *Sewardstone Street*, 1625. (6) Surrender of property at the Court Leet in 1633, 1637 and 1638. (7) Sale of cottages and land in *Carbuncle-Dunghill* in the occupation of Robt. Sparkes, Elizbeth Clay, and John Aylett, 1712. (8) Respecting the property of Nathaniel Kilhog, and Susannah Smith, 1739. Early in the last century *Silver Street* was called "*Kilhogs Lane*." (9) Court Leet. Property called "*Goddard's*" *in School Street*, otherwise *Silver Street*, 1708 to 1831. (10) A list of persons who subscribed towards the purchase of Bells for the Abbey Church 16th cent. (See "Our Parish Registers" p. 136. (11) (Printed) Table of Surplice and Parochial Fees 1824.

Notices of property belonging to the Abbey situated in Arlsey co. Beds will be found in "*Collectane Typographica et Genealogica*" Vol. vi. (see "Ecclesiastical works of the Middle Ages," by W. Winters.) For MSS. respecting the River Lea *circa* 1482, see Lansd. Coll. I. fol. 42. Rights of pasturage in Waltham Marshes (*circa* 1574) see Hunter Collection of MSS. 25, 289. Suits in Chancery relating to property in Waltham see "Proceedings in Chancery" *temp.* Elizabeth (printed).

A LIST OF THE NAMES OF SOME OF THE EARLY RESIDENTS OF WALTHAM ABBEY.

(From the Parish Registers.)

Richard Brown, of *High Bridges*, [High Bridge] 1564; Tawney at *Copthall*, 1567; Myles Apryce of *Sewardstone*, 1568; John Stoke of *Sewardstone*, 1569; Lawrens Greene of *Copthallgreane*, 1569; Robt. Paydly of *Sewardstone*, 1569; Robert Carter of *Pynest*, 1570; Tho. Browne of the *hey bregeds* [High Bridge], 1571; John Preclow of *Halowfeld* [Holyfield], 1571; John Poore, *Sewardstone*, 1571; Roger Somers of *Upcheare* [Upshire] 1572; Peter Shelly, taller [Tailor] of *Waltham*, 1573; George Wright *leberts hell* [Lippetts Hill] 1573; Ralf Daniel of *Pinest*, 1578; Mr. Tho. Hall of *Claverhambury*, 1580; Tho. Coleman of *olyfield* 1590; Thomas Stocke of *Reves Gate*, 1591; Robert Lowen of *Ames Green*, carpenter. 1591; William Harrison of *Walth. Town*, 1596; Henry Cook of *Mott Street*, 1599; Ralf Gardener, of *Mott Street*, 1599; Eliz. Smith of *Pynest*, 1599; Ann Peacock of *Honey Lane*. 1599; Will Green of *Dallants*, 1599; John Carter of *Pynest*, 1600; Thomas Whitehead of *Holyfield*, 1600; Xristopher Peacock of *Cobbinend*, 1600; Henry Boult, gent., dwelling at *Sewardstone*, 1600; Will. Poole of *Pynest*, 1600; Robert Case of *Leopards Hill*, 1600; Henry Hadowaye of *Mott Street*, 1601; Nicholas Wesden of *Mott Street*, 1601; Geo. Peacock, dwelling at *Copt Hall*, 1602; Tho. Quick of *Pynest*, 1603; John White of *Harold's Park*, 1613; Henry Lowen, *Fairmead*, 1700; Richard Farmer, *Pinest*, 1729; Mrs. Burr, *Dallants*, 1737; Ben. Stevens, *King's Oak*, 1746; John Harding, *Quinton Hill*, 1752.

NAMES OF A FEW OF THE GENTRY AND TRADESMEN OF WALTHAM, EXTRACTED FROM AN OLD ACCOUNT BOOK BELONGING TO THE PIGBONE FAMILY OF WALTHAM ABBEY, DATE 1703—1760:—Madam Bruce, 1723; John Sharp, *Govener*, 1726-7; W. Adams, glazier, of Waltham, 1731; Richard Farmer, *Piness Green*, neare *Waltham*, 1732; Richard Stracy, att *Cobben end*, 1732; R. Rutter, at *Dallants Farm*, 1733; Charles Chesher, att ye *Harrow*, 1733; George Beavis Higler, at *Sewardstone* 1733; Robert Druce, *Waltham*, Hatter, 1733; Tho. Dew Farmer, *Sewardstone*, 1733; John Evans, Crown at *Waltham*, 1733; Thomas Freeman at ye Boar's

Head, *Waltham*, 1733; Thomas Judd att *Holyfield*, Farmer, 1733; Mr. Pearce, gentleman, *Waltham*, 1733; William Taylor, Blacksmith, 1733; John Cass, *Leather Bottle*, 1734; John Farmer, attorney, att *Waltham*, 1734; W. Hill, carpenter, *Waltham* 1734; Ambrose Keys, Daysman at Copt Hall Green, 1734; John Lyntall att *Sewardstone*, ye Blackhorse and Cock, 1734; W. Miller at ye Crocked Billet, *Forest Side*, 1734; Mr. Pigbone, sen., at *High Beech* 1734; W. Pigbone, jun., Farmer, *Sewardstone*, 1734; Henry Thompson, at *Fair Mead Bottom*, Keeper 1734 (his servant, Mr. Mason, was shot by Dick Turpin); John Clark, *Sewardstone Bury*, Farmer, 1734; Mrs. Eliz. Hitchen, widow and Butcher att *Waltham*, 1734; Charles Jones, Esq., att ye *Abbey*, 1734; John Beard, *Copthall Green*, 1734; Ralph Dell, att *Loughton*, 1734; Thomas Stubberfield att *Holyfield*, 1734; George Gill at *Hayse Hill, Holyfield*, Farmer, 1734; John Aylbury, Tylekiln Farm, 1735; Widow Burr att *Dallants*, 1739; John Hunt, Wheelwright at *Waltham*, 1740; Will. Peirce, Blacksmith, 1742; Nowel Thompson, Carpenter, 1747; Miss Harding of *Quinton Hill*, 1758; Mr. Cowell, *Dallants*, 1758; Mr. Johnson, Starchman, 1758; Sir William Wake, 1758; John Conyers, Esq., 1758; Mrs. Preston, *Cobbin*, 1758; W. Sargant at *Dallance*, 1758; Mrs Walker to a Womans *Wool Shrowd*, 1758 (for the dead); Mrs. Mainard, Copt Hall Green, 1759; Burrell, *puddin gwoman*, 1759; Mrs. Burgh, Harold's Park, 1759; Mrs. Sanders, *Cold Hall*, 1759; Mr. Pomphrey, to *Shroud and Pillow* 6s. 10d. 1759; Mrs. Grant 1oz. *of Tea*, 6¾d., 1759; Mrs. Letchworth to 1oz. of *Bloom Tea* 11d., 1759; Mr. Purnell, *Cheshunt*, 1759; Richard Fuller, *Leopards Hill*.

ACCOUNT BOOK, 1760.—Mr. Cowell at the *Crown*, 1760; Miss Sukey Auther, Miss Polly Auther, 1760; (these were daughters of John Auther the first Baptist Minister in *Waltham Abbey*); Mrs. Childs at the *Owl*, 1760; Mrs. Sanders at ye *Compasses*, 1760; Mr. Greenwood at ye *Oyll Mills*, 1760; Mr. Fuller, *Piners Green*, 1760; Mr Hervey at *Skillets*, [Hill], 1760; Mrs. Clark *Shopkeeper*, 1760; Mrs. Eaton, *Galley Hill*, 1760; Mrs. Sanders at the Horseshoes, 1760; Lady Cesars, 1762; Workhouse, 1762; Will. Ford, *Holyfield*, 1762; Francis Harvey, 1769. We possess many interesting MSS. relating to the Manor of Sewardstone, &c.

LIST OF PLACES, BUILDINGS, &c., IN WALTHAM ABBEY, FROM THE ORDNANCE SURVEY OF 1871.

Abbey Church, Abbey Farm and Gardens, Ames Green, and Farm. Araben House, Aldergrove Lodge, Aldergrove Wood, Avey Lane, and Farm, Almshouse Plain, Almshouses (Highbridge-street.)

Buffey's Farm, Blackbush Plain, Buttonseed Corner, Blind-lane, Beaulieu, Beech-hill-park, Bathing-pond, Boutwell Farm, Breach Barns, Breaches, Broomstick Hall, Burgess Farm, Burry Road, Bury Wood, Barn Hill, Broadgate, Broadgate Springs, Balcony-house.

Cuckoo-pits, Claypit-hall, Cemetery, Coneybury Wood, Cold Hall, Church lands (Copt Hall), and Churchyard and Road, Cornmill and Stream, Cobbin-brook, Cobbinend Farm, Crook-mile Clapgate-lane, Cashfield House, Coleman's-lane, Carrall's Farm, Clavenhambury-road and Farm, Claypit-hill, Copt-hall, Copthall-green, Copthall School, Chandler's Farm, Crown-hill.

Dalance Farm, Deer-park-wood, Dawshill, Day's Farm.

Earl's-path, Edmondsey Mead, Epping or Waltham Forest, Epping-road.

Farm Hill, Fir-tree-cottage, Forest-side, Forest Lodge, Fernhall Farm, Fisher's Green and Farm, Fair Mead Bottom.

Gillwell-park and Farm, Grubs Hill, Galley-hill-green, Galley-hill-wood, Great Riddens Pond, Golden Row, Green Yard, Great Hoppit.

Holyfield Hamlet, Holyfield Hall and Farm, High Beech, Horseshoe Hill, Home Farm, Honey Lane, Honey Lands, Honey Lane Plain, Horse-mill Island, Homefield Wood, Hook's Marsh, Hall Marsh, Haye's Hill, Harold's Park and Farm, Hillwood, Hawksmouth Farm, Highbridge-street, Hume's Farm.

Long-street, Long-hills, Ludgate Plain, Ludgate House, Lippit's Hill, Lippitt's Hill Lodge, Lovet's Mead, Lower Island, Little Hoppit, Lodge-lane, Longfield Shaw, Louse Hall Lane, Luther's Farm, Longcroft-grove, Lodge Farm, Limes.

Manor House, Marshall's Farm, Mott Street, Martletts, Maynard's Farm, Mongham's Hill, Manning's Cottage, Magpie Hill, Maple Springs.

Newton's Pool, Nazing Cottage, Nursery High Beech, Netherhouse, Nether House Farm, Obelisk Farm, Obelisk Wood, Old Gravel Pit, Oxleys Wood.

Poplar Shaw, Pear Tree Farm, Pear Tree Plain, Paynes Island, Pick Hill, Pick Hill Farm, Pattypool, Puck-lane, Potkiln Shaw, Piper's Farm, Pinner's Green, Pepper Alley, Park Farm, Petensary Farm, Paternoster Hill, Prince Field Farm, Powder Mill-lane.

Quinton Hill and Farm, Queen Meads.

Royal Gunpowder Factory, River Lea Navigation, Rookery Lane, Rookery, Ravens Farm, Rugged-lane, Round Thicket, Rifle Range, Reeves Gate, Romeland.

Sewardstone Hamlet, Sewardstone-street and Road, Shatterbushes Wood, Spratt's Hedgerow Wood, Stocking Grove, Sewage, Sewardstone Green, Sewardstone Bury, Sewardstone Mills, Sudbury House, St. Paul's Church (High Beech), Springfield House, Skillit Hill, Southend Farm, Sergeant's Green, Stoney Bridge, Small Lea River, Spencer's Farm, Stubbing-hall Farm, Sun Street, Silver-street, Township of Waltham, Town Mead, The Warren, The Grange, The Cheshnuts, Thompson's Wood, Thompson's-lane, Thrift Hall.

Upshire Hamlet, Upshire Hall.

Waltham Holy Cross, Waltham Lane, Waltham Marsh, Warlies Park, Wood Green Farm, Wood Green Pottery, Woodlands, Wake's Arms Inn, Woodside Farm, West Hill, Woodridden Farm, White Horse Plain, Wall-grove Lodge, Woodyer's Farm.

Yardley House.

In the compilation of this volume the author has found great difficulty in determining what best to select from the vast quantity of *data* to hand, which he has culled at various times during the past twenty years from rare MSS. and printed works. The early Deeds, Grants, Court Leet Admittances, Registers and other local documents of interest in the writer's possession are to some extent valuable as materials for history. If these manuscripts, together with the ancient charters, etc., relating to the Abbey Church, Town and Forest of Waltham, now preserved in the British Museum and Public Record Office, could be arranged and published in an entire form with explanatory notes, they would not only tend to show what the public and private buildings in the town were like in past ages, but throw considerable light upon the habits and customs of men once famous in the renowned parish of Waltham Holy Cross. Many interesting chapters of local history have appeared at various times in the *Weekly Telegraph*. This excellent weekly paper was originated in Waltham Abbey, by Mr. Joseph Taberham, of Highbridge Street, and edited by the late W. T. Wakefield, Esq., of Farm Hill, in this town, and published May 30th, 1863, under the annexed title, "Waltham Abbey and Cheshunt Weekly Telegraph, Enfield Lock, Waltham Cross, Woodford, Epping, and Enfield Advertiser." In the following January (1864) this paper became the property of Mr. George Wetton Cowing, who greatly enlarged it, and subsequently altered its title to "The Weekly Telegraph for Waltham Abbey, Cheshunt and Districts, and General Advertiser for West Essex, South Herts, and North Middlesex." Edited by Mr. John Charles Yates. Publishing Office, Highbridge Street, Waltham Abbey.

W. WINTERS.

CHURCHYARD, WALTHAM ABBEY.
January, 1888.

HISTORY OF WALTHAM ABBEY (OR HOLY CROSS.)

"The treasures of antiquity laid up
In old historic rolls, I opened.—*Beaumont.*

HE radical change made in the appearance of the town of Waltham Holy Cross* within the past fifty years is really amazing. Various modern improvements (?) have been made, to the sacrifice of nearly every vestige of antiquity. What the houses of the original settlers were like, of upwards of eight centuries since, is difficult to say: they were probably little more than rude huts, without either chimneys or glazed windows, notwithstanding their builders had the finest sites at command, as also the whole forest to cut timber from; and were free to build in whatever style they chose. In the days of Edward the Confessor there were twenty persons in Waltham occupying houses and paying rent; and in William the Conqueror's time there were thirty-six tenants paying rent. There were also at the same time twelve houses in London belonging to the manor of Waltham Holy Cross, worth twenty shillings.

WALTHAM, in the time of Tovi le Prude, or Tofig the Proud (A.D. 1035—1041-2), was a mere wilderness, overgrown with forest trees, and unmarked by any house or Church. Its derivation is from the Saxon, *Weald-ham, i.e. Weald,* a wood, and *ham* a town; hence a village or dwelling near a wood. The extensive Forest with which this district was covered must have been a favourite resort of the Saxon Kings, as it was after the subversion of their independence, of the Saxon Thanes of this country; hence Tovi chose for himself this spot as the most favourable for hunting, as he possessed also *Cheshunt, Enfield, Edmonton*, and the *Mimms'*, the barony of which afterwards passed into the possession

---

* The Parish is usually called Waltham Abbey. Its proper name, *Waltham Holy Cross*, did not originate, as presumed by some, from the *Eleanor Cross*, a short distance west of the town; but from the early *legend of the Holy Cross.*

of the Mandeville family. The forest of Waltham, which originally extended nearly over the whole county of Essex, was well known for hunting purposes in Saxon and Norman times. By charter, written in rhyme, Edward the Confessor granted to Ralph Peperking the wardenship of the royal forest. Swein, the brother of the Confessor, and founder of Rayleigh Castle, co. Essex, is mentioned in the charter, with bishop Wolston and Howelin the steward—

> "Ich Edward Koning,
> Have geven of my Forest the keping,
> Of the hundred of Chelmer and Dancing,
> To Randolph Peperking and to his kindling."

A similar rhyming charter is mentioned by Weever as having been in the Register Office of Gloucester, and which he had seen in the possession of his friend Aug. Vincent, relating to the conveyance of land by William the Conqueror to Pauline Roydon, and which was similar to one collected by Stowe out of an old Chronicle in Richmond Library—

I, William Kyng, the thurd yere of my reigne, give to the Paulyn Roydon, Hope, and Hopetowne, with all the bounds both up and down, &c.

And then follows the mode of sealing the document—

> I bit the whyt wax with my tooth
> Before Meg, Maud and Margery,
> And my thurd sonne Harry [Henry I.]

William the Conqueror granted the forest privileges which his royal predecessors had instituted to William the Bishop, (probably the Bishop of London) and Godfrey the Portreeve." A great many portions of woodland were given by Harold to his Church at Waltham, as mentioned in his grant of *seventeen lordships.* Stephen transferred the wardenship of Waltham forest to Ralph de Montfitchet; and Henry II. confirmed the same to his heirs. In the reign of Richard I. the office of forester was in the Fitz Aucher family, of Copthall. The Magna Charta of King John, signed June 17, 1215, ameliorated a few clauses in the forest laws, which before were very rigid, and which Henry III., in 1218, introduced into a new charter. Edward I. confirmed certain perambulations of the ancient forest and ratified by letters patent, the Great Forest Charta. The old abbots of Waltham realized many forest privileges, and which they retained until the dissolution of the Abbey. Edward and Eleanor, celebrated in the history of the *Eleanor Cross*, frequently visited the Abbey of Waltham and the forest during the protracted wars of Scotland. On the Easter of 1290, the King and Queen spent several days in Waltham, and as the story goes, the King sought to be quiet after a long hunt in the forest of Waltham, but seven of the Queen's ladies unceremoniously invaded the royal chamber of the King, which was close to the Abbey Church, and seizing hold of their majestic master proceeded to "heave him" (an old custom then called "heaving") in his chair till he was glad to pay a fine of fourteen pounds, two pounds for each lady, to enable him to enjoy "his own peace and to be set at liberty again." On another of these Easter days the King spied the Queen's laundress, named Matilda, of Waltham, among the lookers on, in the courtyard, while the hounds were being coupled and the gallant hunters mounted for Easter Hunt. The King, being in a merry mood, wagered that Matilda could not ride with them on a fleet hunter. She accepted the challenge, mounted the fast steed and rode with such success that the King was fain to redeem his good horse for forty shillings.

On February 23, 1608, John Wright received £71 8s. 4d. for repairs at the lodge in Waltham Forest. August 6, 1610, "a grant was given to Mr. Graham of money found in Waltham Forest, a good quantity of gold is in the hands of Sir Gaven Harvey, and is to be seized for the King who desires further information about it." February 23, 1611, a warrant issued to pay to Edward Lord Denny £23 4s. for the erection of bridges in Waltham Abbey. Also a warrant to pay £40 to Sir Robert Leigh for the repairing of bridges in Waltham Forest, September 26, 1611. Easter Hunt flourished most in the middle ages, when Kings and Lord Mayors shared in the sport and feasted under the "greenwood shade." Strype writes of the Londoners, "Riding on horseback and hunting with my Lord Mayor's hounds when the common hunt goes out.". In 1827, Tom Hood, the poet; George Cruikshank, the artist; James Wright, sen., and James Wright, jun., of

Waltham, met at the house of Thomas Rounding, Esq.,
on the forest side, to celebrate the Easter Hunt; Cruikshank
sketched a portrait of old Squire Rounding, the huntsman,
to which Hood added some humorous lines.

In 1871, a committee was appointed to confer with the
Government, as to how the Corporation of London could
best secure parts of Epping Forest to the liberty of the
public for recreation, &c.   And on May 6, 1882, Her
Majesty came to High Beech and declared the forest open
to the public.*

THE HAMLETS OF WALTHAM HOLY CROSS.

WALTHAM HOLY CROSS, in the Half Hundred
of Waltham, in Edmonton Union, and in the
diocese of St. Albans,† rural deanery of Chigwell
and Archdeaconry of Essex, is bounded on the north by
Harlow Hundred; on the east by the Hundreds of Ongar
and Becontree, and is separated on the west from the
county of Herts by the old river Lea.   The form of the
parish is almost triangular, and is about six and a half
miles in width from north to south.   The parish contains
about 1,000 inhabited houses, an area of 11,870 acres of
land, ratable value £38,897, and a population (1881) of
5,377, being 180 more than in 1871.   Waltham is divided
into four *wards*, viz.:—*Township, Holyfield, Sewardstone,* and
Upshire.   The TOWNSHIP has an area of 741 acres and a
population of 2,998.

HOLYFIELD is situated between the Lea and Cobbingbrook,
and contains an area of 3,146 acres, which extends three

* On Saturday, May 6th, 1882, Queen Victoria paid a royal visit to
High Beech, and a tree was planted in front of the "Royal Oak" Hotel
in honour of the event.

† Previous to 1854, the parish church was *not* under episcopal jurisdiction,
and for years the churchwardens were threatened with ecclesiastical
proceedings. The churchwardens had to appear at Doctors' Commons.

miles northward of the town, and includes Galley Hill, Monkhams Hill, and a portion of the Gunpowder Mills.

Holyfield Hall is a fine domestic building of the 16th century date. The land surrounding it belonged to the Crown at the dissolution of the Abbey.* Thomas Cromwell, Chancellor of the Exchequer, *temp.* Henry VIII., held lands in Holyfield to the annual value of £20. King Henry VIII. granted Holyfield Hall and lands to Sir Anthony Denny; and in 1571, Queen Elizabeth bestowed them to Richard Hill and William James. In 1664 the Holyfield estate belonged to William Collard, in whose family it continued until 1747, when it passed to Alexander Hamilton, through the co-heiress of Adey Collard. Members of the Chapman family have occupied the estate for upwards of a century. During the residence of old Mr. Chapman, a burglary was committed at Holyfield Hall. The burglars were caught and tried at Chelmsford on March 10, 1819, two of the prisoners — Robert Wolfe and Joseph Litchfield — were sentenced to death by Justice Bayley, and hanged at Chelmsford on the 26th of the same month. Henry Wollaston, justice of peace, resided at FISHERS' GREEN, Holyfield, in 1620. Several fisheries, &c., were connected with Holyfield.

MONKHAM'S HILL is in the locality of Holyfield. The Hall, on the crown of the hill, called Monkhams or Monghams, is beautifully situated. In early days it was no doubt the seat of the monks of Waltham, as the name indicates, Monkhams (the residence of a monk). The first occupier of this Hall, on record,† *temp.* Henry VIII., was Richard Camp, of "Monghams Hill;"‡ he was succeeded by John Somner "of Mongames Hill," who was buried August 30,

---

* Much of the property in this hamlet belonged in the middle ages to the Abbey, hence the sacred title of "Holy-field." According to the charter of Richard I., A.D., 1189—1199, the estate belonged to Gilbert de Hallfield or Holyfield, from which place he derived his name. A manor called "Hookes" may have been situated in the hamlet of Holyfield, as "Hooks Marsh" is between the township proper and Holyfield. "Hooks" or "Hokes" is generally spoken of in conjunction, with "Pinnacles."

† Add. MSS. 25,289, British Musuem.

‡ Richard Camp, of Monghams Hill, held his estate under the Abbot of Waltham. 12 Hen. VIII., 1521. See Hunter MSS. 25,289, fol. 92.

1607. The Booth family in later times held this Hall, and it is now possessed by Richard B. Colvin, Esq.

SEWARDSTONE.—This hamlet is situated 2½ miles south of the town, over *Quintin Hill*, and on the main road to Chingford and London. It is supposed to have derived its name from its early possessor *Siwardus*, a person of note in Harold's day. The locality is called in the charter of Hen. II. (A.D. 1177) Siwardstune. Probably a memorial-stone of Siwardus was erected in the neighbourhood at some remote period. Some presume that the manor took its name from a low water mark, *Sea-ward-stone* (similar to High Beech), when the Thames ran up the Lea Valley. The manor does not appear under that name, either in Edward the Confessor's Charter, or in that of Harold. It was given by the Second Henry with other grants to the Abbots of Waltham. On the list of the revenues of the dioceses of London, in 1266, the returns for *De Sywardestune* is £13 0s. 0d. The earls of Oxford possessed the manor at a very remote period, Robert de Vere, earl of Oxford held the manor in 1278, *in captie*.† Sir Ralph Sadler held the manor with that of Woodridden, *temp*. Ed. VI., and afterwards alienated it by licence to Sir Anthony Denny, through whom it passed to James Hay, earl of Carlisle, at whose death, in 1660, it became the property of William, earl of Bedford, who sold it about the same time to William Pocock. In 1673 the manor was again sold, and was purchased by James Sotherby, and by whose descendants it is still retained. ‡ C. W. Sotherby, Esq., is the present lord of this manor, whose manor-house is at High Beech.

THE MANOR OF SEWARDSTONE *from the reign of Henry VI. to that of James I.*, taken from the Harl. MSS. (3361), viz., An abstract of the Rolls of the Right Hon. Edward Lord Denny for harriotts of copyhold lands harriotable § within the manor—

James I. 12 Jac. Isaac Lightfoote admitted to *Shotfields*. 10 acr. 13 Jac. Agnes Field daughter of Isaac Greene adm.

---

† Harl. MSS. 391, fol. 29.

‡ The author is in possession of an inventory of Pentensary House and other MSS. relating to the forest in this manor.

§ *Hariot custom* is the holding of property by paying a hariot or *fee* at the time of death to the lord of the manor.

to a cottage. 6 Jac. Edward Dixon adm. to a message
har. called *Warleys.* 9 Jac. Edward Floyd adm. to all
that Tenement called *Motts* and 1 acre in *Mott Streete.*
1 Jac. John Taylor adm. to a garden lying between
little Warden and the king's highway called *Chawntdore*
gardens. 3 Jac. Roger Bowyer died seized of lands called
Homescroft.

Elizabeth.—11, Eliz. Raheim Abraham held an acre of
land in *Shotfield.* 15 Eliz., 3 acres of land in *Shotfield.*
11 Eliz. Agnes Stephens held a tenement called *Motts.*
12 Eliz. Hen. Johnson surr, a garden, half a rod lying in
hedge croft. 5 Eliz. Rich. Ashe dyed seized of a Tenement
called *Leopards* [Lippets Hill]. 4 Eliz. William Bowyer
surr, a tenement called *Parks* lyeing sevally in a field
called *Seward.* 3 Eliz. Adam Storke surr, a tenement and
17 ac. land called *Repitts* or *Phillip* and 3 Roode in *Padn-
Pool*, abutt. uppon the head of *lorge Dole.* 42 Eliz. Andrew
Lowen adm. Tenante lands and Tenements called *mayne-
goods.* 40 Eliz. Tho. Hale surr. 2 ac. 39 Eliz. Wm.
Peirson dyed seized of a tenement called *Warley.* 33 Eliz.
Joane Purvey surr. *Holdcroft, East lands,* &c. Nicholas
Blinco adm. Tenant of lands called *Hurlebutts.* 15 Eliz.
Adam Storke surr. one acre called *Sextone.* 21 Eliz. John
Cooke surr, a Tenement, 9 acres and a cottage with garden
abutt uppon *Gillwell.* 2 Philip and Mary, Richard Ashe
surr, a croft called *Longe croft.*

H. 8.—33 Hen. 8, John Crow held a tenement called
Wardleyes one acre, in *Sowmead.* 35 et 36 Hen. 8, Robert
Sexton lyeing sicke surr, a Tenement called *Leopes.* [Leo-
pards or Lippets.]

Hen. 7.—15 Hen. 7, John Abraham surr, 3 tenements,
2 called *Pottell.* 19 Hen. 7 Rob. Burmeham held a tenement called *Oldcrost.*

Ed. 4.—2 Ed. 4, John Briggs surr, lands called *haywards.*
14 Ed. 4, Richard Potsman surr, a croft of land 4 ac. called
Megrecden.

Hen. 6.—1 Hen. 6, Ann Hooke surr, land called *Cameles
fields.* 1 Hen. 6, Rich. Rolfe died seized of the third part
of the moyty of one yard land* called *Gillrolfes.*

---

* A yard-land *virgata terra*, a rod or yard to girt; in the north, to
gyrd. Hence a *yard* or *close.*

33 Hen. 8, Joseph Stoner held certain lands and tenements late coppiehold land by Indenture for terme of yeares
to paye atte every death or alienacon 40s. for fine and 20s.
for a herriott. 19 Hen. 7. Presented by the homadge that
Margery Scott suffered her houses to decay, having had
warning to repayre them, and that she did cutt down ten
okes whout lisence and sould hem away contrary to the
custome thereof.

The contributors to the first payment of the Queen's
subsidies in 1587:—Town of Waltham, Henry Standish
xvd, John Tanner xd. Upshire and Holyfield, William
Hodge, vid., Jane Kirbye widowe xiid., William Simons xiid.
Sewardstone, Thomas Lake xd.* Sir Edward Denny,
Justice of the Peace in 1601.

The inhabitants of Sewardstone have a right to cut wood
from the *forest* at a certain time of the year.

A Board School was erected in this hamlet in 1874, for
136 children.

Pentensary estate in the hamlet of Sewardstone, is very
old; the house (near the Pound) in connection with it is
rapidly decaying. These premises were published many
years ago for sale by auction by the late C. Pryor.

Gilwell House, Sewardstone, is a large and picturesque
building, formerly the residence of the Chinnery family,
also of Gilbert Goss, Esq., and now of William Gibbs,
Esq., a poet of high repute and the inventor of the Hay
Drying Machine. Gillwell estate is mentioned in Harl.
MSS. 3361 *temp* Elizabeth.† The Silk Mills in the valley
were once the property of Carr and Dobson, of Cheapside,
and in later years were occupied by W. Connell and Co.,
Dyers and Scourers. These Mills, which were probably
built on the foundations of an ancient Fulling Mill, were
demolished in 1885. Some antiquarians have asserted that
an old church once stood in the hamlet of Sewardstone. I
have not found anything to authenticate such a statement.
An old iron chapel (served by the curates of Waltham) stood
for many years in a field on the left hand side of the road

---

* Lands. MS. 52, fol. 161.
  † Old Gillwell House, in the reign of Hen. VIII., was used as a royal
hunting lodge ; and possessed by Sir Anthony Denny.

opposite the "Luther's" estate, which building, however, has long since disappeared. This hamlet includes High Beech, Lippets Hill, and Sewardstone Green. Sewardstone possesses an area of 3,022 acres.

HIGH BEECH, south-east of the town is 759 feet above the level of the sea (some say only 350 feet). In 1837 it was formed into an ecclesiastical parish out of the hamlets of Sewardstone and Upshire, and is situated on the border of Epping Forest. The church of St. Paul's, now a complete ruin in disuse, is a plain brick building with bell turret, and cost about £900. Holy Innocents Church (on the highest part of the forest) opened in 1873, is a gothic stone building, consisting of chancel, nave, transept, and spire, with a peal of 13 bells which are played by machinery. The register dates from the year 1837. The living is a vicarage, yearly value of £90 in the gift of the Bishop, and held by the Rev. Josiah Norton, M.A., of St. John's Coll., Cambs. The land taken out of the forest near the church has been recently appropriated as a burial ground. A School has been erected by Thomas Charles Baring, Esq., which will hold 100 children. Area 1,500 acres. It is said that Henry VIII. came to High Beech before the execution of his unfortunate Queen Anne Boleyn, in order that he might be at a distance, and still have the satisfaction of hearing the Tower guns fired as a signal of that awful tragedy being ended.

UPSHIRE hamlet,* eastward from the town, contains in area 4107 acres; and extends to the forest, and along the south side of Cobbing Brook, including Warlies Park, Sergeant's Green, Broomstick Hall Common and Honey Lane Common. In the year 1868, the locality of Honey

---

* The customary tenants of Upshire claimed in the wastes of the Forest Common of Pasture all the year for all their commonable cattle, except in the forbidden months, and common of wood cutting by pre-scriptions in the Woods called *Otehawes, Redding-hills, Woodriddens, Harth-hills, Longrunning, Burnet-heath, Leadyng—Queane, High-Beech-green, and Amersbury* (near the road to Epping). The Lord of the Manor of Holyfield claimed to hold a capital messuage and 100 acres in the hamlet of Upshire, and to have free liberty to cut trees *growing upon his own ground* for repairs of *hedge bote and fire bote (vide Morant's Hist. Essex).*

Lane having severely suffered from drought, Sir Fowell
Buxton caused a large tank to be constructed near the four-
want-way, into which water is conveyed by means of a great
length of piping from a spring in the Waltham Forest. A
smaller tank is also provided for the benefit of cattle.
Upshire Manor, together with Holyfield, remained in the
possession of the crown till the reign of Queen Elizabeth.
With this hamlet were included 91 acres of arable land
with a portion of the forest, also two parcels of land in
Queen's Mead, the parsonage in the Churchyard, and many
other tenements. Upshire Hall is a fine old building some
distance east of the town.   WARLIES PARK, occupied by
Sir T. F. Buxton, Bart., is a beautiful country seat,
situated about two miles north-east of the Church, and near
Copthall. This was once the residence of Samuel Foxe, son
of John Foxe, the martyrologist.

COPTHALL.—The estate of Copthall, part of which is in this
parish and part in the parish of Epping, is full of interesting
detail from the time of Richard I. to the present century.
Queen Mary, when Princess, resided for some time at Copthall. Queen Elizabeth and later sovereigns have visited the
old noble hall which then stood within the parish of Waltham
Abbey. The present mansion stands on the borders of
Epping parish. During the residence of the poet, Charles
Sackville, Lord Buckhurst, at Copthall, he was guilty of
notorious riotous acts, as appears by the "State Papers,"
under date March 10, 1662. He was imprisoned in
Newgate with Edward Sackville, Sir Henry Bellasyse, K.B.,
and two others (one of whom being ill with small pox) for
the robbery, with violence, of John Hoppy, at Waltham
Abbey, in February, 1662. Hoppy died in the April following, from injuries received by the robbers. Sir H.
Bellasyse and three other prisoners were tried at the Middlesex Sessions for manslaughter of the said John Hoppy,
tanner. A warrant for their pardon was then issued and
the prisoners were liberated.

HAROLD'S PARK, situated near Nazing, was so named,
after King Harold, who gave it to his church at Waltham,
and which was confirmed with certain grants by King
Henry II., A.D. 1177.

An ancient manor called "Pynnacles" was probably in

the locality of Copthall, as it eventually fell into the possession of the Fitz Aucher family.

OBELISK AT BREACH BARNS FARM NEAR WARLIES
PARK.—The presumptive evidence that this obelisk marks
the spot where the unfortunate Boadicea, Queen of the
Iceni fell, awaits confirmation. Tradition alone points
to Nazing Common as the scene of a celebrated battle in
which 80,000 of the incensed Romans were slain and all
the colonies of ancient Verulum and Camelodonum destroyed by the Britons. Amesbury Banks was evidently the
site of an ancient camp ; a similar one having been discovered near Danbury, and one adjoining the north-eastern
roads at Walden in this county. There were trackways
connected with these camps generally which were known
to the Saxons by the name of streets, the principal of which
were the Icknield Street, Ryknield Street, Ermyn Street,
Ikeman Street, the Saltway, the Fossway, and the Watling
Street, several branches of which seem to have passed
through different parts of this county. The situation of
the Amesbury entrenchments being near the boundaries of
the Cassii, the communication which Cassivelaunus must
have established with his allies will account for their being
well acquainted with its position. The banks are considered by Cæsar to be the last stronghold of Cassivalaunus.
The generality of writers have identified the *oppidum* of
Cassivelaunus with Verulanium, or St. Albans ; but the last
named place was the capital of the Cassii, and the only
cause that led to this supposition appears to be, that no
other answered any better to Cæsar's description. Some
writers imagine that the kingdoms of the East Saxons and
the Mercians were separated in the upper part of the county
of Hertford by the Ermyne Street, and in the lower part in
Cheshunt parish, near a bank which in early days reached
from Middlesex through Theobald's Park, across Goff's
Lane to Thunderfield Grove, over Beaumont Green to Nine
Acres Wood. On the north, the same natural boundaries
were most likely preserved which, under the Romans, had
separated this district from the Cassii. If this memorial
pile really marks the spot where Queen Boadicea died, it
must have been erected very many years after the fatal

occurrence took place.   Near this obelisk is "Dallance" or "Dallings" Farm, now occupied by Mr. Bott, farmer.

DALLANCE FARM, GALLEY HILL.—In the reign of Queen Elizabeth "Dallance" Farm, in Waltham, was owned by Henry Denny, as we find in the following note :—"To all faithful in Christ To whom this present writing indented shall come.   Henry Denny, of Dallance, Essex, Esquire, Greeting in the Lord for ever.   Know ye that I, the aforesaid Henry Denny, in the performance of divers covenants bearing date 12 March, 12 Elizth, made between me, the aforesaid Henry Denny on the one part, And the very noble man Arthur Grey, knt., Lord Grey of Wylton, Walter Mildmay, knt., one of the Privy Council of the said Lady the Queen, Thomas Wroth, of Enfield, Middx., knt., John Brockett, of Brockett Hall, George Horsey, of Dixewell, and Henry Cocke, of Ponnesborne, in the County of Herts, Esq^{res}., of the other part, Have given, granted, and by this writing confirmed to the aforesaid Lord Grey and others All those my mannors, Lands, and tenements of Waltham Holy Cross, Sewardston, otherwise Sywardstone Nasinge, Hallyfield, Woodridden, and Claverhambury in Essex, with their rights, &c.   On the 28th October, 1569, Henry Dennye, of Dallance, Essex, Esq., gave and conceded to William Potter, of Kyngs Hatfield, als Busshops Hatfeilde, in Herts, yeoman, in consideration of good and faithful services, the office or place of keeper of his park of Beddwell, called Bedwell pke in Herts, and of deere and greate game, from the date of the Indenture, for life."   Henry Denny died March 24th, 1574; and at an Inquisition taken at Waltham Cross on the 8th of June in that year, before John Cooke, Esq., "escheator," on the oaths of "William ffordeham and others, who say that the said Henry was seised in his demeasne as of fee of and in the Manors of Meryden and Parke, alias Parkeburge, with appurts and other property in Essex and Herts, being so seised made his will." Henry Denny, Esq., of Dallance, was buried in Waltham Church, April 8, 1574.   The Register gives "Mr. henry denye, esquire, the funerall the 8 daye Aprill, 1574."

INCIDENTS RELATING TO WALTHAM ABBEY IN CONNECTION WITH KINGS OF ENGLAND.

ILLIAM THE CONQUEROR, A.D. 1066—1087.— From the death of Harold to that of the Norman Conqueror, little is known of what occurred either in the Church or in the town of Waltham, except that the lands in the parish bestowed on the deans and canons by the founder were wrested from them by William I., on pretence that they were the private property of Harold, and in no way connected with their church. At the survey they held but half-a hide; the remainder of the town was given by the Conqueror to his favourite bishop Walcher, of Durham* On the death of Walcher the lands reverted to the Crown, and were afterwards appropriated to the queens of Henry I., who in due course returned them to the canons with interest. The following extract from the Domesday Book gives the survey of Waltham, as it appeared in the reigns of Edward the Confessor and William the Conqueror, viz.:—

Domesday Survey, relating to Waltham Holy Cross, A.D. 1080—1086. (Translation.) "The lands of the Bishop of Durham, in Essex. The Half Hundred of Waltham.—Waltham was held by Harold in the time of King Edward for i manor and xl hides. There have always been lxxx. villeins,† and xxiv. bordars.‡ Then vi. serfs,§ now vii. Then vii. teams in the

---

* Walcher afterwards purchased the earldom of Northumberland, where he behaved himself so insolently that he was torn in pieces by the populace, . 4th May, 1080.

† Villians, *Husbandmen* who held their dwellings at the will of their lord as part of the property of the manor.

‡ Bordars possessed houses of their own on the condition of serving the table of their lord, and were called "Bord." The same are now called copyholders.

§ Serfs, domestic slaves which were bought or sold as other property.

demesne, now vi.   Always xxxvii. teams of the homagers.
Wood for M.MCC, swine, lxxx acres of meadow land, ii horses,
xx beasts, lxxx. sheep, xii. goats, xl. swine.   There is pasture of
the value of xviii shillings.   Then i mill, now iii, v fisheries,
and then xx tenants paying rent, now xxxvi.   And i team,
might be re-established in the manor.   To this manor belong ii.
socmen* who held vi hides in time of King Edward, now v.
And the half of the vith hide is held by the HOLY CROSS, and
the other part was taken by William of Warren.   And there are
moreover vi. Soc-men of ii. hides and half a virgate.   And
besides this there belonged to this manor i hide, all but xv acres
which the same William has taken.   And Ralph the brother of
Ilger has taken xxx acres of arable land and vi. of meadow.
All those Soc-men, who now are there, have vii. hides and xv.
acres; and they had in the time of King Edward in their
demesne iv teams, now iv and a half, and always i villein.
Then vi. bordars, now viii.   Then ii serfs, now none.   Wood
for clxxxii swine; xvi and a half acres of meadow, and vi acres
of pasture.   From the whole of this and from the manor,
Harold received in the time of King Edward xxxvi pounds,
and the bishop's homagers value it at lxiii pounds, and v. and
iv pence.   But now according to the testimony of the other
men of the Hundred, the value is c pounds.   In London there
are xii houses belonging to this manor which yield xx shillings
and i gate which the King gave."

Twenty years had elapsed since the death of Harold, when
his great foe and successor to the throne of England finished
his part in the drama of life.   William died early in the
morning of the 9th September, 1087, while his physicians were
regarding the tranquil night he had passed as a sign of his
recovery.

WILLIAM RUFUS, A.D. 1087—1100.—Lambarde remarks that
William the Conquerour toke from this House (the Church)
the Town of Waltham, and gave it to Walter the Byshop of

---

* Socmen, tenants who held lands by *socage*, or inferior service to the
lord of the fee.

† This large estate was what Harold had possessed, and, with the
exception of North Land (Abbey Fields) formed no part of the lands
granted by him to his College of the Holy Cross. See notes on Domesday, as far as relates to Waltham, by C. Marsh.

Durham, to repose himself at, when he should be called to counseil out of the North Countrye. William Rufus, his son, spoyled Waltham of 6666 pounds of money, besides Jewels and Churche Ornamentes, al which he transported to Cane in Normandie. Howbeit afterward in part of amendes, he restored to them the Towne of Waltham, with al the Landes thereto of old Tyme apperttayninge. This was the state of Waltham before the Tyme of Henry II.*

HENRY THE FIRST, A.D. 1100—1135.—Henry I., apart from his two wives is little known in the records of Waltham. Matilda or Maud, Henry's first wife presented the Abbey with a corn mill† on the site of which stands the present mill, occupied by Mr. James Carr. She also bestowed other favours on the Canons of Waltham. Adelicia, of Louvain, the second wife of Henry I., was also a great benefactress to Waltham. Being possessed of Waltham as part of her revenue, says Dr. Fuller, "she gave all the tithes thereof, as well of her demesnes as all tenants therein, to the Canons of Waltham. Meanwhile, how poorly was the priest of the place provided for! Yea, a glutton monastery in former ages makes an hungry ministry in our days. An Abbey, and a parsonage unimpropriate, in the same place, are as inconsistent together as good woods and an iron mill. Had not Waltham Church lately met with a noble founder (Sir Edward Denny, Earl of Norwich) the minister thereof must have kept more fasting-days than ever were put in the Roman Calendar." ‡

KING STEPHEN, A.D. 1135 — 1154. — In a contemporary manuscript, which has been translated and largely quoted by Dr. W. Beattie, occurs a curious account of an affray between the townsmen of Waltham and several Flemish soldiers in the turbulent reign of Stephen. "When every man was at war with his next neighbour, and which is naively characterised in the legends of Waltham as being *seditionis tempore.* The town as part of the dower of Adelicia, Queen of Henry I., belonged to her second husband, William de Albini, Earl of

---

* Lambarde's Hist. Dict. 433.

† Domesday Survey mentions one mill in the parish ; this is probably the same as above. In the middle ages there was a Fulling Mill in Highbridge Street, used for scouring cloth.

‡ Fuller's Hist. Waltham, p. 260.

Arundel, between whom and the outlawed baron, Geoffrey de Mandeville, a deadly feud had arisen.   One day he brought or sent to Waltham a body of his Flemish auxiliaries who set fire to the town, and the flames spreading quickly, communicated with the houses of the Canons.   In the midst of the confusion, the invaders penetrated to the Church, where the town's people had deposited the most valuable part of their effects.   The Canons who appeared to have considered themselves entitled to the special protection of Geoffrey de Mandeville (as Earl of Essex), after vain endeavours to prevail with his men by fair words to desist from their enterprise, had recourse to what was then looked upon as a last and desperate expedient—they dragged from its place above the altar, the Holy Cross, which was supposed to spread its protection over the neighbourhood (?) and threw it upon the floor ; and it was handed down as a tradition of the place, that in the very hour of the throwing down of the cross Geoffrey de Mandeville received his death-wound at the siege of Burwell.   The Canons of Waltham boasted that their Church was rescued from the rage of the plunderers by divine interposition ; and that five Flemings, who had already filled their sacks with precious articles, were thrown miraculously into such a state of mental confusion that they could not find their way out of the Church, but remained wandering among the boxes and packages, with which the interior of the Church was encumbered, until they were taken by the townsmen on their return from the pursuit of their enemies, whom they had driven away.   The Canons now rescued the offenders from the vengeance of the people of Waltham, and after having administered to them the monastic discipline, namely, a severe flogging, they set them at liberty.   One of their leaders named Humphrey de Barrington, who, entering the Church on horseback, had been active in inciting the Flemings to plunder and violence, is said to have been struck with madness (perhaps with paralysis) as he was leaving the town ; he was carried back to the Church and died within three days ; but not till he had repented and made some compensation to the Church of Waltham by giving to it fourteen acres of land in *Luchentuna** (probably) *Loughton.*

---

* Castles and Abbeys of England, p. 279.

KING HENRY THE SECOND, A.D. 1177—1189.—Henry the Second visited Waltham Abbey several times, and granted charters, confirmed others and gave the church a new title, *i.e.*, ST. LAWRENCE; but the greatest change wrought by him in connection with this church was the ousting of the dean and secular canons instituted by the founder, Harold, and supplying their place with those of the Augustine order. This was effected on June 11th, 1177.* As the power of Rome gained strength in England it had constantly brought with it the dissolution of the Anglo Saxon Colleges of secular priests to make way for a more rigid discipline of the regular monks, who were considered literally to be the soldiers of Papal Rome. No doubt, however, the old secular canons of Waltham had fallen into a low state of discipline since their foundation, situated as they were amidst the fatness of the earth. They were accused of luxurious living which seems to have fully justified the king in bringing about a radical change—

" By him the people wider rights acquired
Whereat the proud, licentious clergy fired."

Henry increased the number of canons. There were sixteen regular canons of St. Augustine, six of Cirencester, six of Oseney, and four of Chich.† This the king did because, to use his own words, " it was fit that Christ's spouse should have a new dowry." He not only confirmed the primitive patrimony mentioned in the confessor's charter *cum pecüs terræ* with pieces of land and tenements, which their bene-factors since bestowed upon them, but also confirmed the rich manors of Sewardstone and Epping on this Monastery.‡ The benefactions to Waltham in Henry the Second's charter were meadows adjacent to the monastery then known as Normede, Chelnoseie, and Greater and Lesser Ward; a meadow that

---

* *Anno Domini* MCLXXVI., *a moli sunt canonici sæculares de Waltham et introducti regulares.* Harl. MSS. 4321, fol. 117. Singular to say Matt. Westminster states that the same year [1176] the secular canons were removed from Waltham, &c., but it was towards the end of the year, and the business was not entirely completed this year. Probably June 11th, 1177, was the finishing of the affair.

† The King had the consent of Pope Alexander III. for the suppression of the secular canons.—*Fuller.*

‡ The King gave the canons Waltham Hall in Takeley, ; Stanstead-Thele, or Thule, the tithes of hay of the Lordship of Waltham, and the house of Walter de Geldethorp.

Philip de Swinehey had given them; others given by Geoffrey
the cupbearer of Enfield, Alexander of Enfield, Portehors,
and the wife of Gilbert of Hillifield, the tithe of hay on the
demesne of Waltham and the Mills. In Epping they had
acquired the land of Helynoth and Nazing with the tithe of
Langrich. In the gift of Humphfrey Barrington is mentioned land
at Lamburne and Purlai. He also granted the canons of
Bridlington pannage for hogs in the forest of Scalby. In
Dunton the Chamberlain had given land to Waltham. The
estates of Hitchin and Lambeth have already disappeared from
the rent roll. Besides these lands we know from John of
Salisbury that the Abbots of Waltham had claims in Walthamstow, and we have already referred to their property in London.
It appears that the King vowed as a part of his expiation for
the death of Thomas-a-Becket to found a new institution.
Money was scarce with him, and he did not scruple to evade
the spirit of his vow by fulfilling it at the expense of the
canons of Waltham. On the authority of Roger de Wendove,*
Ralph, canon of Chichester, received the government of the
Abbey from the King, the Pontiff, and the Bishop of London,
to whom as diocesan he bound himself to pay canonical
obedience. Pope Lucius III. by his bull confirmed to the
monastery the exemption from all episcopal jurisdiction, and
Pope Celestian III. indulged the abbot of Waltham with the
right of wearing pontificals, *circa* 1191. At the time of the
induction of the regular canons to the church of Waltham,
King Henry II. gave the church a new title, as before stated—
St. Lawrence, as well as new estates.† The bust of *St. Lawrence*
within a circle is erected above the door of the inner west-end
porch of the Abbey, and which was restored in 1859-60.

In the 19th year of Henry the Second's reign an *assize* or
"tallage" was imposed on the town of Waltham Holy Cross
by Sefred, Archdeacon of Chichester. Wido or Guido, dean of
Waltham, was one of the "Justiciers" and co-operated with
Sefred and others. In 1169 the town of Waltham was assessed
with the consent of the Justiciers, when Ralf le Napier, of
Waltham, paid xxs. and four others their respective sums. Also

---

* *Vide* Flowers of History, Bohn's edition, Vol. II. p. 35.

† Stow says Henry II. rebuilt the church, and proposed to augment its
revenues and make the building capable of supporting eighty or one hundred
canons, but which desire he failed to carry out.

"the Commune of Waltham" paid xl*s.* and the rest of the townsmen iiij*l.* iij*s.* iiij*d.* Tallage appears to have been a rate according to which barons and knights were taxed by the King towards the expenses of the state. When tallage was paid out of the knight's fee it was called *scrutage.** In the 26th Henry II. Maurice de Creon and Gervase Painel (or Pagnell) was fined to the crown in v. marks with a view to gain a plea in the King's Court respecting some land held by the said Gervase in Waltham. In 1182, the King came to Waltham surrounded by the first nobles of the land, namely, the Bishops of Winchester and Norwich, Geoffrey the Chancellor, Walter de Constantüs, Geoffrey de Lucy, Ralph de Glanville, Roger Remfrid, Hugh of Morewic, Ralph son of Stephen the Chamberlain, and William Rufus. Here the King made his *last will and testament,* which is handed down to us in the writings of Giraldus de Barri.† Five years previous to Henry making his will he restored the church, and rendered such service to the canons of Waltham that to grant them anything more was not considered needful by him. His gifts were principally used in assisting the crusades to the Holy Land. Pierre Langtoff writes :

" To Waltham gede the Kyng, his testament to make,
And thus quathe [bequeathed] he this thing, for his soule sake."

KING RICHARD THE FIRST, A.D. 1189—1199.—In 1189 Richard I. granted to the Canons of Waltham the whole manor of Waltham, with the great wood and park called Harold's Park, 300 acres of *essart lands* with the market of the same, the village of Nazing a member of Waltham and 160 acres of *essart lands* in the same with all rights, &c., paying yearly into the exchequer at the feast of St. Michael only £60, for all service with other ample liberties.

Richard also granted a third charter in which he bestowed to Waltham the churches of Windsor, Hertford, Alrichsea, (Arlsey) and Nazing; and confirmed certain lands to Richard Fitz Aucher called Copt Hall (which Henry II. had previously given him) to hold in fee and hereditarily of the Church of

---

* The origin of this assize is attributed to Alfred the Great, and which was reduced into its almost present shape in the time of Edward I. In the 1 Rich. I., the King's demesnes and other lands in Waltham were *tallaged* to which the men of Waltham paid vij*l.* xvj*d.* *Vide* Madox Hist. Exchequer.

† The Will commences thus : " I make known to you that at Waltham in the presenee of * * * I have made my will, &c."

Waltham.   The Abbots of Waltham possessed a fine vineyard
at Windsor *temp* Richard I.   Lambarde says in the "recordes
it appeareth that tythe hathe been payed of wyne pressed out
of grapes that grew in the Little Parke neare to the Abbot of
Waltham, which was parson both of Old and New Wyndsore,"*

KING JOHN, A.D. 1199—1216.—King John, according to
his itinerary, visited Waltham frequently.   He was at Waltham
on Wednesday and Thursday, October 13th and 14th, 1204,
and again on the 18th.   John came from Ongar, where he had
been staying for two days, probably at the Castle there, and
rested at Waltham on his way to Westminster August 11th
and 12th, 1204.   Two years elapsed before he again visited
Waltham.   In 1207 the King came from Westminster, and
rested at Waltham, October 29th and 30th.   A note states,
October 30, 1207, Waltham " Allow on account to Robert de
Leveland what he expended in straw and fine sand for our
house upon our arrival at Westminster, when we slept there,"
&c.   On Oct. 28, 1208, the King visited the town of Waltham,
and not again until Dec. 20th, 1213.   He returned to Waltham
from the Tower on Dec. 23rd, and again on Dec. 29th, 30th,
and 31st.   On the first of January, 1214, the King was at
Waltham,† viz., " Know that on Wednesday, the feast of our
Lord's circumcision we received at Waltham £126," &c.   King
John left the following day for the Tower.   In the Cottonion
MSS. Claud. D. II., is a plate representing King John hunting
(probably in Waltham Forest).   King John, in his 9th year, to
punish the people (who he justly concluded hated him) pro-
hibited the diversions of hunting and hawking, commanding
all the fences to be thrown down near the Royal Forest of
Waltham, that his deer might have access to the corn fields;
but on June 17th, 1215, the barons of England, after many
difficulties, obtained from him the famous charter, in which
are a few favourable clauses with regard to the laws of the
forest.

KING HENRY THE THIRD, A.D. 1216—1272.—Henry III.
was a liberal benefactor to the church of Waltham Holy Cross,
to which sequestered place he often retired during the varied
scenes of his lonely kingly career.   This will be seen by the

---

* See Eccles. Annals Mid. Ages by W. Winters, p. 43.
† See description of Patent Rolls.—Pub. Rec. Off.

number of royal grants signed at this Abbey. He gave the parishioners the privilege of holding an annual *fair* for *seven days*, and a *weekly* market. *

Waltham Fair in 1257.—An agreement of peace made between the Abbot of Waltham and the citizens of London. *Septima pars Hen. iii.* "About the feast of ye Natynyte of our Lady, a concord and a peas was concluded atwene the Londoners and the Abbot of the Holy Crosse of Waltham, the whiche hadde been in suyte many yerys before, for certaye dystressys taken by thabbottis offycers of the Londoners when they came with theyr mercymonyes † unto the fayre of Waltham, where as now it is agreed that all suche dystressys shulde be restoryd, and if any were perysshed or loste for longe kepynge that than the Abbot to content and pay to the partyes the value in money of such dystressys so perisshed or loste, and that ye cytezyns shulde enioye the lybertyes of ye fayre ever after without paying of any tallage or tolle. Anno Dom. MCCLVII. Richarde Hardell, Richarde Ewell, Wyllym Ashewy."

In 1242, says Matthers Paris, Waltham Abbey was solemnly re-dedicated by the Bishop of Norwich, King Henry III., and many of his nobles being present; this was probably in consequence of some alterations or additions. In the 30th of the King's reign, the Abbots had a dispute of some duration with the towns-people respecting the rights of pasturage in Waltham marsh, several of the Abbots' horses were killed, as also their keepers, by the violence of the people in driving them out of the marsh.

---

* In the year 1219, the Abbot of Waltham's Court was amerced at xxx marks for a trespass in putting certain men to the judgment of water. *Vide* Madox Hist. Exchequer. "There were several sorts of ordeals used in England at this period, viz., the ordeal of the cross; the ordeal of the consecrated bread; the ordeal of cold water; the ordeal of hot water, and the ordeal of hot iron. The ordeal of cold water was most in use among the common people. The person about to be tried was placed under the direction of a priest, who caused him to fast for three days and to perform various acts of devotion, after which he was taken to a pool of water and thrown into it ; if he floated he was declared guilty, if he sunk deep enough to draw the rope (which was placed about his waist) under the water he was instantly taken out and declared innocent."—Strutt's Chron. Eng., Vol. ii. 200.

† Fabyan (under date 1258) calls the word "merceamentys." Holinshed says "The King (Hen. iii. 1265) took them to *mercie* upon their fine."

Exchequer subsidies in the reign of Hen. iii. Ville de
Waltham. An assessment of the subsidy of three *grotes* upon
every person *laica* granted 4 Ric. II. within the town of
Waltham.

Calendar of Royal Charters dated from Waltham.—Grant
to the canons of Bridlington of acquittance of pannage for
their hogs in the forest of Scalby. Hen. II. Waltham 1154—
1162, *ex transcripto antiquo*.

"Hen III. Grant to William Longespé of free warren in all
his demesne lands in various counties. Dated Waltham, 1252,
20 December."

"Letters Patent to Pain de Chaworth. Dated Waltham 1270,
15 June."

"Letters Patent, Henry de Percy, to do homage to Edward
the King's son. Dated Waltham 1270, 15 June."

"Letters Patent commanding Henry de Lacy to do Do.
Waltham, 1270, 15 June."

"Letters Patent to Robert de Stockport to do Do. Dated
Waltham, 15 June, 1270."

"Letters Patent to Adam de Holand to do Do. Dated
Waltham, 1270, June 15."

"Letters Patent to John de Vescy to do Do. Waltham, 1270,
16 June."

"Letters Patent to Abbot of Furness to do Do. Dated
Waltham, 1270, June 16."

"Letters Patent to William le Botiller to do Do. Dated
Waltham, 1270, June 16."

"Letters Patent to the tenants of the Manor of Newcastle
to do Do. Dated Waltham, 1270, 16 June."

In 1258 the Parliament having refused King Henry money
he procured a messenger from the Pope, one *Mansuetus*, to
come to England and beg assistance from the Abbots; and the
Abbot of Waltham was "among the first applied to on this
occasion;" this man, partly by threats, and partly by entreaties,
obtained from him a security for 200 marks, which the King
could procure of the merchants. In the early part of the reign
of Henry III., *circa* 1218, a hospital was built within the precincts of the Monastery of Waltham by the Abbot and Convent.

KING EDWARD THE FIRST, A.D. 1272—1307.—Edward I.,
it will be remembered, stands immediately connected with the
history of the Eleanor Cross, Waltham Cross, erected with others

by him, in 1291, to the memory of his beloved consort, Queen Eleanor. In the Public Record Office, under *Ancient Deeds and Charters* (No. 59) is *Inquisione Post Mortem* 20 *Edward I.* an agreement between Regnaldi, formerly Abbot of Waltham, and Roger Levenoth, Prior of Southwerk (Southwark) respecting a tenement there; to this document is appended the name of John de Monastio (John of the Monastery). Dated Feb. 6, 1292. And in the *Chancery Series* (No. 81), 34 Ed. I. occurs the annexed note respecting the Forest of Windsor—*Abbas et Conventus de Waltham Sanct. Crucis. De una acra vasti in foresta de Wyndisore eis concessa.*

Crusades to the Holy Land were very popular events in the reign of Edward I. John de Badburgham, Abbot of Waltham, was appointed by the King collector of the *disme** for the crusade in 1301. This Abbot received a letter bearing date Nov. 15th, 1301, from John Hatton, Bishop of Carlisle, asking for an indulgence to his diocese in the collection of *disme.* The Bishop also describes its miserable state and requests the benefices to be taxed according to the present value.†
The Dean of St. Paul's (probably William de Montford) who represented the suffrages of the clergy, fell dead at the feet of King Edward I., when speaking in their behalf, and which was taken as a divine visitation.

On the death of Edward I., which occurred at Burgh, on Sands, during his onward march to Scotland, July 7, 1307, his remains were solemnly conveyed to the Abbey of Waltham. Before his decease, he enjoined the Earls of Pembroke, Northumberland and other of his nobles to inform his son of his dying command, namely, "that his heart should be carried to the Holy Land, attended by 140 Knights, who should have 32,000lbs. of silver for their maintenance whilst thus employed, and that his corpse should remain unburied, and be carried in the van of the army till Scotland was reduced to obedience."

---

* In the 2nd year of Richard I, Henry de Cornhill accounted for money by him laid out in buying ships for the expedition of the Holy Land, and in *Liveries, Sturmans* and *Mariners* for that voyage, to wit, for MMCCL*l.* which he had received out of the King's treasury by the view of Peter de St. Marie Church, the Chancellor's Clerk, and of John de Waltham, the Treasurer's Clerk, whereof MCCC*l.* were in blank silver and DCCCCL*l.* in money.

† Raine's Hist. Pap. and Letters from Northern Registers, XCVIII. p. 151.

Little regard was paid to these commands; for the council ordered the Bishop of Chester, his treasurer, assisted by the King's household, to convey the royal corpse to Waltham Abbey, where it arrived with great funeral pomp, attended by many of the principal nobility. Peter, cardinal of Spain, went to meet it, and also a number of the English clergy. The body remained at Waltham Abbey fifteen weeks; during this time six religious men were chosen weekly from the neighbouring Monasteries to attend it night and day, and none were permitted to depart without special license till the King's remains were removed to Westminster Abbey, where they were interred in Edward the Confessor's Chapel, October 28th, 1307.*

In the days of Edward I., Copt Hall,† or *Copthall*, in the joint parishes of Waltham and Epping, was the noble seat of the Fitz Aucher Family. Richard I., as has already been stated, gave this manor to Richard Fitz Aucher to hold, of the Abbey of Waltham, and here he built a large mansion and enclosed it with a park. He was succeeded by his son Richard, whose eldest son, Stephen, dying without issue, Copt Hall passed to his son Sir Henry, who had a licence granted, in 1295, to add 15 acres to his park out of the forest of Waltham. He died (in 1304) possessed the estate of Copt Hall, the manor of Shingle Hall, and held the office of forester, which his family possessed many years by grand serjeancy of the forest of Essex. In 1374, the Abbot of Waltham enclosed 120 acres out of the estates of Harold's Park and Copt Hall.

KING EDWARD THE SECOND, A.D. 1307—1327.—In the 9th Edward II. the Abbot of Waltham having appointed before the King two persons to be his attorneys, viz., Peter de Waltham and Lawrence de Bosco to claim his franchise in the Exchequer, the King by his writ commanded the barons to receive them as such.‡ In the 12th of Edward II. Hugh de Waltham and John de Dalling were Sheriffs of London.§ In Riley's Memorials of the City of London occurs, under date

---

* Walsingham's Hist. Eng.

† See Warlies and its surroundings, by W. WINTERS; also Harl. MSS 3736, fol. 427.

‡ Madox Hist. Exchequer vol. II. p. 177.

§ Probably of "Dallence" or "Dallings Farm," near Galley Hill in Waltham.

November 11, 1312, an acknowledgment by John de Lung, butcher, of London, of a debt of £16, to Thomas de Ware, canon and kitchener of Waltham Holy Cross. Hugh of Waltham, common clerk of the City of London, September 18, 1314, was authorised by King Edward the Second to write letters patent in favour of the Black Friars (*i.e.*, preaching Friars) of London. A lease was drawn up, October 12, 1318, between Hugh of Waltham, clerk, and John atte Stouples, fishmonger, respecting a bakehouse situated near the Pillory, at Cornhulle (Cornhill). This was a bakehouse belonging to the Bishop of London, formerly the superior lord of the Soke. This same Hugh of Waltham was instructed by the City Authorities to draw up a deed, under date July 13, 1331, relative to the depositing a box in the safe keeping of Henry de Seccheford, chamberlain, by Richard & William de la Pole, Sir John de Putteney, Mayor. The following sums are recorded by the said Hugh of Waltham : £10 19s. 6d. paid to Simon de Swanland, "late mayor," for expenses incurred at the coronation of Lady Philippa, consort of Edward III. There are many ancient documents relating to *Copt Hall* and the Fitz Auchers, of the date of Edward the Second's reign, preserved among the "Deeds and charters" of the Public Record Office. Henry Fitz Aucher, of Copped Halle, granted 12 acres of arable land, and 2 acres of woodland in Holcroft, in Parochia de Waltham to Henry de Dongaye and Rosiæ, his wife. Dated at Copt Hall, 1309. In 1312 the son of the above Henry granted to the same Henry and Rosa one messuage situate in la Potteryshylle, in Waltham. The same place, in 1314. is called "Pottershill." This may refer to an ancient Pottery near Copt Hall. Edward II., in the course of his itinerations, often visited Waltham Abbey, when certain writs were signed by him, viz., 1308, September 28th, 29th, 30th ; October 1st, 2nd. 1309, May 1st, July 11th. 1310, January 29th, 30th, 31st ; February 1st, 2nd, 3rd. 1316, May 20th. 1317, October 15th. 1320, June 7th. 1326, August 7th.

KING EDWARD THE THIRD, A.D. 1327—1377.—Edward III. was a great benefactor to Waltham, and whose armorial bearings appear on the spring of the great arch of the Abbey gates. In the collection of ancient deeds and charters is a deed between Henry Fitz Aucher and William Pikeman, son of Elene Bleeche, relative to land in Copt Hall, for which the said William gave "five marks sterling." 4 Ed. III., 1331.*

KING RICHARD THE SECOND, A.D. 1377—1399.—Richard II. resided at Waltham during part of the time of Wat Tyler's insurrection in 1381. The tenures belonging to the Abbey, 1 Ric. II., are given as follows:†   John Morice, sen., Galfred de Hunden; Jo. Morrice, Jun., John Matthews, Vicar de Nazing et John King de Chesthunt, qd, ipi xxs. redd exeunt de; mess. 80 ac. terr. 20 ac. pra. 10 ac. pa. et 20 ac. bo. in Waltham sc. crucis dare possint abbis et con. de Waltham pd et sur suis imppm qr tenent de pdc Abbe p sg ixs. P an-et sect cur ipius Abbis de Villa de Waltham.

KING HENRY THE FOURTH, A.D. 1399—1413.—The *Issue Roll* 11. Hen. IV., 1410, contains entries of repayments of divers borrowed sums of money (*inter alias*). To the Abbot of Waltham £336 6s. 8d., with several others. Again to the Abbot of Waltham, in money paid to him in discharge of 100 marks which he lent to the Lord the King at the receipt of the Exchequer, on the 26th day of March last past, as appears in the roll of receipts of the same day, £66 13s. 4d. (44 Ed. III.)

KING HENRY THE SIXTH, A.D. 1422—1461.—Sir William East-field, Lord Mayor, *circa* 8 Henry VI. held lands in Waltham. His daughter married William Cressey, of Waltham, son of Sir John Cressey, Knt.

On May 3rd, 1446, Margaret, daughter of Richard Duke of York, afterwards Duchess of Burgundy, was born in Waltham Abbey.

KING EDWARD THE FOURTH, A.D. 1461—1483.—*Hooks* and *Pynnacles* in this parish were held by Sir John Say under the Abbots of Waltham (*Inquis*, 18 Ed. IV.) The Say family resided at Broxbourne. Salmon says that *Pinnacles* was "possessed by Philip, grandson to Vitalis, which Philip was hanged for a pretended robbery, and this estate given to Fitz Aucher, whose mother had been too free with Philip. I find a memorandum, but without authority, that Hokes and Pinnacles belonged to the Marquis of Exeter, and Gertrude, his wife attainted. John, son of Walter Morewe, passed the

---

* In 1371 William Harding, a messenger, was sent with letters of privy seal directed to the Abbots of Waltham Holy Cross, paid 13s. 4d.

† Lansd MSS., 327, fol. 6.

estate of *Hokes* and *Pinnacles* to John Kirby and Elizabeth his wife."

In 1473 several tenements at "Copped Halle" were sold by Robert Bardesy and Thomas Lyffyn to William Gladwyn, and in 1502 lands at Copt Hall were sold by William Petyte, of Braburn, Co. Kent, and Margery his wife to Thomas Lupsed, which lands were formerly held by William Gladwyne, of Waltham, and for which lands the said Thomas Lupsed paid "£xii. of lawful money."

KING HENRY THE EIGHTH, A.D. 1509—1547.—The Abbey of Waltham, which for centuries had been the resort of kings, was frequently visited by Henry VIII., who is said to have possessed a small house in the *Romeland* where he occasionally sought pleasure and retirement. There is a traditionary anecdote relating to one of Henry's visits. The King was one day hunting in the forest, and wandering from his companions he came to the Abbey about dinner time, in the disguise of one of his own guard. He was immediately invited to the Abbot's table, and a sirloin of beef was placed before him. The King was hungry and ate very heartily, to the great admiration of the Abbot, whose pampered stomach had been spoiled by the good fare of his house. "Well fare thy heart!" he said to his guest, "here is a cup of sack, and remember the grace of thy master. I would willingly give a hundred pounds on condition that I could feed as heartily on beef as thou dost. Alas! my weak stomach will hardly digest the wing of a small rabbit or chicken." The King pledged his host, and then thanking him for his hospitality departed as secretly as he had arrived. Shortly afterwards a pursuivant suddenly made his appearance at Waltham, and to the consternation of the whole fraternity the Abbot was carried to London, and committed a close prisoner to the Tower, where he was kept for some days strictly confined to a diet of bread and water. The severity of his imprisonment was then as suddenly relaxed, and a sirloin of beef was set before him, on which to use the quaint expression of the old narrator of the story, "he fed as heartily as a farmer of his own grange." The King immediately entered from a small lobby where he had been looking on unobserved, and demanded of his prisoner a hundred pounds, the sum promised to him who should restore his lost appetite, which the Abbot paid immediately, and lost no time in returning to enjoy again the good cheer of his own refectory.

In the State Papers (Foreign) under date August 8th, 1529, the King was at Waltham and paid £10 to James Morice for mending bridges between the Abbey and Hunsdon. On September 18, 1530, the King again appeared at Waltham. An entry occurs in the King's accounts, viz.: To Robert Acton's servant for bringing 2 skins to the King at Waltham, 5s. Also paid (Sept. 20, 1530) to Robt. Lee and Robt. Shere, for finding a buck and the hounds in Waltham Forest when they were lost, 9s 4d. The King was at the Abbey on the following day according to the annexed entry. To a woman that gave the king *quene apples* at Waltham, 4s 8d. On Oct. 2, 1531, King Henry was at Waltham, and on the day following his Majesty paid for a cart to carry the hounds from Antyll to Waltham, 5s. Oct. 9th, paid to a Frenchman that my lord of Norfolk brought to the King in the garden at Waltham £7 10s. Oct. 20, to Olyves, one of the keepers of the Forest of Waltham, 6s 8d. Oct. 25, paid to the wife when the King shot a tame buck in the Forest of Waltham, 7s 6d. Oct. 26, to Serjeant Rolte and old Stoner, rangers of Waltham Forest, and to 6 keepers there, 67s. 6d. Dec, 15, to the keeper of the Abbot of Waltham's Park (Copt Hall), 7s 6d. Grants were signed by the King at Waltham, 1531—Sept. 23, Oct. 3rd, 4th, 8th, 11th, 13th, 14th, 16th, 24th and 26th. 1532.—July 4th, to one who brought chickens to the King at Waltham, 7s 6d. July 24th, to Old Stoner of Waltham Forest and 3 keepers, 30s. 1533.—Feb. 18th, a warrant was issued under the King's seal to Cromwell, master of the Jewels, to pay Tho. Roberts £200 for certain lands in Waltham Holy Cross, purchased for the King's use. These lands were at Holyfield. In the same series of entries occurs a letter from Sir Humphrey Brown to Lord Cromwell, viz.: "You spoke to me for my house and land at Waltham. If I may have a little house called Alderbroke, once belonging to Heron, I should be content if it be of the like value" (25 Hen. VIII.) Sir Humphrey Brown resided in High Bridge Street, Waltham Abbey, *temp*. Henry VIII. The Abbot of Waltham to

Cranmer, May 7, 1533.* In this document the Abbot solicits Cranmer to give the office of prior at St. Gregory's, Canterbury, to John Symkyns, *Cellarer* (probably of Waltham). The Abbot recommended Master Cressy to Cranmer for his (Sympkins') qualifications. Dated at Waltham Holy Cross,† 1534, is an agreement made by Tho. Cromwell in the King's behalf with Robt., Abbot of Waltham, relative to an exchange of the manor of "Coppydhall" and the manor of "Netyswell" near Hunsdon for a messuage called *Saxbes* and other lands purchased of Humphrey Brown, serjeant at law, with provision that if the King at his own cost appropriate the monastery of Waltham, the Abbot and Convent shall make sure to the King and his heirs the manor of Epping. On June 12th, 1534, the King slept at Waltham, and then rode on to Hunsdon. In 1534 Cromwell wrote a paper of the "obsequys" of the Lady Regent of France, the King's grandmother, holden at Waltham. Cromwell's lands in Waltham were of the annual value thus : The fee farm of Waltham £50, and of Holyfield £20. Robert, Abbot wrote to Cromwell June 2nd, 1534, thus : " I received your letters desiring me to deliver to Tho. Pykrynge the counterpane ‡ of Nasynge Farm with the bonds until you and I shall be agreed upon the covenants. I now send them by my servant, John Archer." On June 13th in the same year Sir Roger Cholmley wrote from Waltham to Cromwell relative to his fines of Knighthood.

---

* See Harl. MSS. 6, 148, fol. 78.

† At the dissolution of the Monastery, *Temp.* Hen. VIII., Robert the last Abbot, was seized of messuages and lands in Waltham, called *Crabtree-field*, vii acres; *Sprotts*, vi ac.; *Yerdfielde*, ii ac.; *Bedrepfelde*, vii ac.; one Hedgerowe adjoining, vii ac.; *Longcrofte*, vi ac. with a Hedgerowe on the South, iv ac.; *Combertons*, iii ac. and viii half ac.; *Hoberds-Hatche*, xvi ac.; two fields called *Cobefelds* [Cobfields], xlv ac.; two fields belonging to the same, xii ac.; lands by *Cokslane*, held by Thomas Heyne, called *Highfelde*, iii half ac.; *Mageffelde*, iv ac.; a Hedgerowe, i ac.; in the pysshe of *Waltham Holy Cross*. Also *Ptrich-grove*, v ac.; a *Close* adjoining, ii ac.; *Jaks*, ii ac.; *Great Chissels*, xx ac.; *Bushey Hyll*, viii ac.; three ac. adjoining, called *The Hoopes*; a *Grove* adjoining *Brode-lane*, iii ac.; *Stony Hyll*, vii ac.; *Gladwyns-meade*, i ac.; a *Grove*, viii ac., between the said mead and *Coks* in *Upshire*, in the pysshe of Waltham, which, in the whole, amounts to clxxxiii acres ; and whiche sayde pmisses deu adioyne and lye nere to the manᴿ or pke of Coppedhall &c. (See full account in Warlies and its surroundings, by W. Winters.) Hatch a Barr or bolt whence *hatch* as Buttery Hatch, became bolted or *apprehendere tenere;* to hold fast. Harl. MSS. 3739.

‡ *Counterpane* means the corresponding copy of a deed, now called counterpart.—*Nares Glos.*

THE DISSOLUTION OF THE ABBEY.

MARCH 23RD, 1540.

THE Abbey of Waltham was surrendered to the King on March 23rd, 1540, having continued 480 years under several Deans and Abbots. This surrender was made by the last Abbot, Robert Fuller, who had previously exchanged the estate of Copt Hall with King Henry VIII., for the farms called *Canefields* and *Woods*, at *St. Pancras, Kentish Town*, and the Manor of *Dame Elyns*, in *Little Warley*, co. Essex (Harl. MSS. 3739, fol. 427). Its possessions were valued by Dugdale at £900 4s. 3d., and by Speed at £1,079 12s. 1d.

The following is a brief list of the ancient gifts to the Church and the benefactors :—Hugh de Nevil gave the manor of Thorendon; John de Chishull, Bishop of London, the Church of South Welde; Robert de Valvines, All Saints', Hertford; Geoffrey de Scales, that of Badburgham; his daughter, Juliana, Sudecamps, both in Cambridgeshire; John, Bishop of Sarum gave the Churches of Old and New Windsor; Simon le Bret, the Church of Wrangle, and John, son of Alward that of Leverton, both in Lincolnshire; Everard de Geist the Churches of Geist, and Geisthorpe, and the third part of Norton, in Norfolk; Roger de Geist, the Church at Tatersham in Surrey; John Morrice in 1377 gave 40 acres of land; and in 1383, John Morrice, Senior, and others gave messuages and lands in Waltham, Nazing and Roydon; John de Tanny gave the Abbots the Manor of Theydon Bois; the Abbots possessed the Lordship of Waltham with its dependencies, and nearly the whole of the Parish, with the Rectory of Alphamston, the Manor and third presentation of Great Parndon, the Manor of Cullings, with the advowson of St. Nicholas, Standford le Hope; the Manor of Abbots, in Stanway, and Watermans in Matching; the Manors and Rectories of Wormingford, Blackmore, Margaretting; and the Manor of Priors in Broomfield, which the

Abbots of Waltham received from Henry VIII. for Stansted Abbots; also the Rectory of Hormead, and the Manor of Lambeth. An account of the possessions of the Abbey, written by the last Abbot, may be seen in the British Museum.*

It appears by the accounts of the Ministers of the Crown for the County of Essex, 34 Hen. VIII, that the possessions of the Abbey accruing to the Crown at the Dissolution were as follows:—Manor or lordship of Waltham with its appurtenances, £169 0s. 7½d.; site of the late Monastery of Waltham, with the Grange called Waltham Grange, and with the demesne lands to the same Grange belonging, £72 2s. 4d.; Rectory of Waltham £23 10s. 2d.; the Water Mills in Waltham £26 13s. 4.; Manor of Claverhambury £23; Woodridden Farm, Waltham Abbey, £8; lands called Pekenpshire £3 6s. 8d.; rents in Seward-stone £11 3s. 4d.; Manor of Nazingbury £31 18s.; rents at Nazing £33 8s. 3¾d.; Manor of Loughton £46; tenements and rents in Loughton £10 19s. 7d.; Manor of Woodford and Hill-house £30; rents at Woodford £9 9s. 5½d.; Manor of Epping £53 6s. 8d.; rents, &c., at Epping £6 0s. 6½d.; Manor of Shingle Hall £8 10s.; a tenement called Parvills,† in Epping £4 13s. 4d.; Manor of Theydon £18; Manor of Nettswell £30 12s.; Manor of Pasfield, not answered for because granted 34th Hen. VIII. to George Harper, Esq., his heirs and assigns; a tenement called Buckhurst £2 13s. 4d.; farm at Willingehall £3 9s.4 d.; lands in Bromefield £3 6s. 8d.; Manor of Katoynes, in Parndon Magna £4 13s. 4d.; lands at Tillingham £5 6s. 8d.; Manor called Abbots, in Stanway £3 6s. 8d.; Manor of Takeley £8 6s. 9d.; Manor of Wormyngford with the Rectory £13 0s. 3d.; Manor of South Welde or Weald with the Rectory £4 18s. 2d.; Manor of Stanford le Hope £20; rents in Stanford £5 7s. 3½d.; Manor of Blackemore (reserved rent) £2 9s. 4d.; Manor of Gynge Margaret with the Rectory (reserved rent) £1 14s. 10d.; Manor of Alrychesey (Arlsey) co. Beds. £35 6s. 8d.; Manor of Millhoo (reserved rent) £1 1s. 2d.; Manor of Brickendon with Rectory, not answered for, because granted 33 Hen. VIII., to Thomas Knyghton, gent., and Mar-gery his wife and their heirs; Manor of Wormley (reserved rent) £1 13s.; Manor of Cullings £8 4s. 2½d.; Rectory of Horemead

---

* Harl. MSS. 3739; also Eccles. Works of the Middle Ages, by W. Winters, p. 56.

† Parvill's Farm still exists and is known by the same name to-day.

Magna £11; Manor of Newhall £4 13s. 4d.; Manor of Amwell £6; rectory of Geisthorp £3 6s. 8d.; rectory of Skarninge £2; Manor of Wrangley, Lincolnshire £45; Manor of Badburgham £20 1s. 9½d.; rectory of Sudicamps £2; Manor of Caterham, Surrey, £6 16s. 1d.; Manor of Windsor £17 17s.; Manor of Haywood not answered for, because granted 32 Hen. VIII. to Sir John Norres; Canelands and Canewood, St. Pancras, co. Midd., £13; rents in London £13 5s. 4d.

At the dissolution of the Abbey, 24th March, 31st Henry VIII., certains pensions were given to various persons connected with the Abbey (see the list of pensions subsequently given).

In 1547, King Edward VI. made a grant of the conventual estates of Waltham, including the right of advowson, the tithes, the patronage of the vicarage and the site of the Abbey, with the Manor, to Sir Anthony Denny, one of the executors of Henry VIII.* for thirty-one years, Sir Anthony dying soon afterwards, the reversion in fee was purchased by his widow Joan, the daughter of Sir Philip Champernon for £3,000. The church remained a curacy or donative, in the gift of those who held the site of the Abbey, with only the small stipend of £8 per annum, until Sir Edward Denny (grandson of Sir Anthony Denny), Earl of Norwich, and Baron of Waltham settled in 1633, £100 per annum on the curate† and his successors, payable out of the estates of Claverhambury.‡ The ouly daughter and heiress of Sir Edward Denny was Honora, married James Hay, Earl of Carlisle; their only son James, Earl of Carlisle, dying without issue, the gift fell to the descendants of the Denny family, who subsequently sold it to the Trustees of Sir W. Jones, and hence to the Wake family. The presentation to the vicarage was afterwards invested in three families or trustees.§ When the present Vicar, the Rev. F. B. Johnston, M.A., was appointed to the living at Waltham Holy Cross, in 1885, there was some difficulty in obtaining the whereabouts of the trustees. After several meetings of those interested in the matter, new trustees were appointed. The names of these gentlemen are: Sir T. Fowell Buxton, Bart.,

---

* Hen. VIII. granted so Sir Anthony Denny with the demesne of Waltham, Sigmor Downs, and a part of Holyfield Hall; also lands in co. Herts.

† John Guibbon was then curate and one of ¿the Westminster Assembly of Divines.

‡ This will is given by Farmer, p. 170.

§ Ogbourn History of Essex, p. 193.

R. B. Colvin, Esq., J.P., and Mr. T. Chapman, Jun.* John Dudley, Earl of Warwick, received permission, June 25, 1547, to alienate to Sir Anthony Denny, Harold's Park, and in July of the same year he purchased of Sir Ralph Sadler the manors of Woodridden and Sewardstone with the tithes of both. Sir Anthony Denny died possessed of nearly the whole parish of Waltham. His son Henry, born in 1540, succeeded to the estate, whose eldest son Robert dying without issue, the estate fell to his brother Edward, born 1569, and who was knighted in 1589, and summoned to Parliament as Baron Denny of Waltham 27 Oct., 1604, created Earl of Norwich by Charles I., and died 24 Oct., 1637. He married Mary, third daughter of Thomas, Earl of Exeter. This great benefactor to Waltham, Sir Edward Denny, is said by Stow to have met King James on his progress to London "attended on by a goodly company, in number seven score, sutably apparelled in blew livery coates, and white dublets, hattes, and feathers, and well mounted on horses with red saddles ; Sir Edward, after humble duty done, presented his majesty with a gallant horse, a rich saddle, and furniture correspondent, being of great value ; and his highnesse accepted graciously, and caused him to ride on the same before him."

James Hay and his wife Honora were succeeded in their estates by their only son James Hay, Earl of Carlisle, who was a great sufferer for the cause of King Charles I. in the Civil Wars. He married Margaret, third daughter of Francis, Earl of Bedford, and died without issue in 1660. His widow enjoyed part of this estate as her jointure ; she married Robert, Earl of Manchester. At her decease the property reverted to the sisters of Charles Goring, Earl of Norwich, in right of their grandmother Anne, one of the daughters of Henry Denny, who sold it to the trustees of Sir Samuel Jones ; he sold it to Samuel, fifth son of Sir William Wake, who took the name of Jones, and was sheriff of the county in 1699 ; and bequeathed it to his nephew Charles, second son of Sir Baldwin Wake, who died without issue in 1740 ; and was succeeded by Sir Charles Wake Jones, from whom it passed to Sir William Wake, and hence to the present

* For particulars relating to previous trustees of the grant of £100 to the ministers of the Abbey Church. See *Close Rolls*, 8 Geo. III. pt. 14. Mem. 14. Public Record Office.

representative, Sir Herewald Wake, of Courteen Hall, Northampton, J.P., born 19 July, 1852, married 14 April 1874, Catherine, youngest daughter of Sir Edward St. Aubyn, Bart.*

THE ABBEY MANSION.

THE old mans.on ca ed the ABBEY HOUSE, built by Sir Edward Denny in the reign of Queen Elizabeth, and partly re-built by Charles Wake Jones, was demolished in 1770; and the stables were converted into a dwelling house now occupied by Mr Thomas Chapman. The original mansion† was very large, with a wing on each side of the front. Farmer describes it thus (1735)—"It is beautiful to behold, and leads down to a spacious fine garden [now the 'Abbey gardens']; a fine canal encompassing the same with plenty of all kinds of fish. There are the most curious evergreen hedges, walks, groves, and for variety of fruit 'tis scarcely to be equalled by any private gentleman's. There are also fine kitchen gardens, vineyards, a bowling-green, nay in short, everything else that is commendable and praiseworthy. The whole garden contains about 12 acres of land, and is walled in with brick. The Abbey House has a sumptuous Hall, in length it contains 16 yards and a half; in height 9 yards one foot. It is exceeding handsome by reason of the wainscotting‡ and extraordinary paintings. At the entrance out of the *Romeland* you pass over a bridge into a court-yard, which both leads to the Abbey House and to the stabling, and in which are two large rows of tall and stately

* The family descended from Hugh Wac, temp. Hen. I.
† For a plate of this mansion see Farmer's "History of Waltham Abbey" (1735), p 159.
‡ Specimens of this wainscotting may now be seen in the old house in the Green-yard, Waltham Abbey, occupied by Mr. Thompson. See Visitors Handbook of Waltham Abbey, by W. Winters, p. 27 (Edition 1877).

Sycamore trees.* There are also rich and large lordships belonging thereto, namely, the Town, Upshire, Holyfield, and Nazing, which afford plenty of all manner of game, and are endowed with great privileges and profits accruing from the Forest." The old Abbey House was at one time occupied by W. Pigbone (churchwarden in 1706), and was possessed in 1770 by James Barwick, Esq., J.P.

KING JAMES, A.D. 1603—1625.—During the reign of James I. nothing particular occurred in connection with the Abbey, beyond the erection of the Almshouses by Frances Green, and the King's visit to the Abbey during the curacy of Joseph Hall, D.D., who preached at times before his Majesty at Theobalds. In the last year of James' reign he visited Town and Abbey Church.†

KING CHARLES THE FIRST, A.D. 1625—1649.—Several entries occur in the Churchwardens' Accounts of Charles I. coming to Waltham Abbey. Dr. Fuller says, "Anno 1641, King Charles came the last time to Waltham, and went, as he was wont where anything remarkable, to see the church, the Earl of Carlisle attending him. His majesty told him that he divided his cathedral churches, as he did his royal' ships, into three ranks, accounting St. Paul's, in London, York, Lincoln, Winchester, &c., of the first form; Chichester, Lichfield, &c., of the second; the Welsh cathedrals of the third, with which Waltham church may be well compared, especially if the roof was taken lower and leaded." The king granted a "toll of cattle" to be made for the repairing of the church and the paving of the town. But the design was "dashed" by archbishop Laud, because the Earl of Carlisle first consulted the king on the subject instead of his grace.

---

* The Poplar Trees that once adorned the edge of the mill stream from the Abbey Gates to Harold's Bridge have, within the last few years, nearly all fallen down owing to the foundation of old massive stone walls just below the surface of the earth running in that direction. Old foundations of ecclesiastical buildings may be seen to exist (in the summer months) in the Abbey Fields, west of Harold's Bridge.

† Item.—Given to ye ringers at ye King's coming through ye Towne iis. His Majesty probably visited the Abbey House and Copt Hall. See "Our Parish Registers."

An estate was left for the repair of the church, from William Lake and Thomas Stock, of this Parish, in trust to Thomas Fox and others, bearing date 5th December, 1637.

The Pilgrim Fathers of Nazing and Waltham Abbey.— About this period (1637), and earlier, many local worthies were forced for conscience sake to quit the shores of old England for America. Since the publication of "The Pilgrim Fathers of Nazing," &c., in 1882, we have realised great pleasure in collating from parish registers, manuscripts and rare printed works in the British Museum, materials for biography of the Eliots and others who emigrated to the New World during the middle of the seventeenth century, and whose ancestors resided in Waltham Holy Cross, Nazing and other antique towns and villages in England. During the last few years several of the descendants of the Waltham Abbey and Nazing pilgrims have visited the places familiar to their forefathers. The names of some of the Waltham and Nazing friends are well known in the historic Annals of America; such as Curtis, Ruggles, Graves, Heath, Payson, Peacock, Uffett, Gore, Morris, Burr, Bright,* and others, who left England between the years 1630 and 1640.

John Eliot was the son of Bennett Eliot, and one of the first of the Nazing pilgrims who quitted the shores of Old England for the more peaceful lands on the other side of the great Atlantic. We have noticed specially the Eliots of Nazing, Waltham Abbey, Cheshunt, Hunsdon and Stortford, being evidently closely related to the Apostle to the Indians, John Eliot. It is, however, difficult to discover where the ancestors of Bennett Eliot resided. It could not have been Nazing, as the name does not occur in the registers of that church earlier than 1602-3, when the first John Eliot was baptized. See extracts from Registers; also "Memorials of Pilgrim Fathers," 1882, by W. Winters.

KING CHARLES THE SECOND, A.D. 1649—1685.—George Hall, son of Joseph Hall, born in Waltham Abbey, August 24, 1613, bequeathed by his will, dated August 22nd, 1668, £100 *for the use of the poor* of his native parish. Farmer has confused the two names, Joseph and George. Joseph Hall was curate of Waltham many years, and eventually became Bishop of

---

* *Vide.* The Brights of Suffolk, p. 5, pub. Boston, N.E., 1858.

Exeter and Norwich.* His son George Hall was Bishop of
Chester. It is stated that the £100 were spent in decorating
the altar piece of the church by the then churchwardens.
(Shame!) Another deed specifics property left to the church in
trust from Edward Goulding, Nicholas Hodge, and Henry
Williams to Edward Clayton and others, 26 Sept. 1681; and a
counterpart of Mr. Acourt's lease, 20th Dec. 1683. The rent of
the above property in 1735 was, viz., a messuage in the
occupation of Mary Spencer and Ann Bennett, £10. Seven
acres of land in possession, £9. Three acress of land called
Paternoster Hills (Broomstick Hall); and two acres of land called
Hostlage, near Wolmerford-bridge; and other lands called
"Church fields," also one acre of meadow, lying a Wolmerford,
in the possession of Mary Williams, £14. Total, £33 per
annum.† According to Farmer (p. 165) many of the gifts to the
church were not appropriated by the Churchwardens, agreeably
to the wills of the respective donors. If the church had had
no more generous donors than what it has had of late years it
would have been poor indeed.

---

* The Almshouses at High Beech were built by Bishop Hall. On the
chimney of these houses is the following inscription—"A gift of Bishop
Hall. William Shotbolt, churchwarden, 1705." These houses are in a
most dilapidated condition. The three Almshouses at Copthall Green originally belonged to this parish, but subsequently became private property.
They were destroyed a few years ago by fire.

† Fields adjoining Broomstick Hall Common. The slip of land east of
Waltham Abbey Lock, near the River Lea, was called "Church land."
We have an original deed, dated 1467, which states (in Latin) that Richard
Carter, of this parish, confirmed by deed to Edward Briggis and Walter Cok
of the same place, one croft of Land called *Pick-croft*, containing 3 acres,
situate near *Paternoster Hill* (a place where the makers of paternosters or
rosaries resided), and abutting upon a place called *Childwin-downe* and the
King's highway leading to *Pickhill*. Also two acres of Land in one croft
called *Hostelage* (probably an Inn mainly used by the Abbots on their way
to Copt-hall), near Wulnerfordbriggs — (*Wolmerfordbridge*), abutting the
King's highway leading to *Coppidhall* on the north, and a place called *Forst-
sefeld* on the south. Also one acre of wood Land adjoining *Wolmerfordbrigge*,
and abutting upon *Mallend* on the south, and the King's highway towards
Pickhill on the north, and the premises (afterwards called *Church Fields*),
formerly held by John Cowper, Vicar of *Epping*, and Andrew Bright, of
Waltham, and John Archer of *Theydon Gernon*, &c. Witness Johe Hasiai
Thom, Frend, Johe Colynse, Willmo Forth, Nicholaio Forth, Johe Crow, &c.
Dated Waltham, 6 Ed. iv. (Seal gone).

LANDS SEQUESTERED IN WALTHAM IN 1643.*

'¶But on those judges lies a heavy curse,
That measures crimes by the delinquent's purse."
Browne's Satire on tne Rebellion.

SIR Francis Swyft (of Harold's Park) houldelth of James
Earle Carlile,* a delinquent† Lands at per ann. £25.
S. Atkins houldeth of ye said, at per ann. £110. W.
Winspeare for Mistris Sheffield's lease at per ann. £10. Mr.
Grene for *Town Meade* per ann. £3 16. Mr. Genemore for
flood lands per ann. £44. Mr. Vavassor for *Foots* per ann.
£4. Henry Knagg Senier per ann. £141. Items for the
parsonage‡ per ann. £110. Item for a Barne per annum
4d. Item for the Bayliwick houlder of the within named
Henry Knagg of the Earle of Carlile per ann. £20. Sir
Francis Swift for Mr. Nicholls' lease, per ann. £115 8s 4d.
Mr Lyon for the *fulling mill§* per ann. £30. Mr Leverton
for his house per ann. £3 6s 8d. Item for his ground per
ann. £10. Mr. Winspeare per ann. £32 10s. Mr.
Wollaston per ann. £60. Item for *fortye acres* per ann.
£36. Item for other lands per ann. £23 8s. Mr. Geve
(or Jeve) for *Capieshott*‖ per ann. £7 7s. Mr. Church for
Peacock's house per ann. £47. Mr. Wills per ann. £11.
Mr. Chaice per ann. £16 2s 6d. Mr. Greene per annum
£33 6s 8d. Thomas Sawdrie per ann. £50. John Joslin
per ann. £3 6s 8d. John Joslin houldeth more of the said

---

* Add. MSS. 5505.

† " He that practiseth either for his own profit or any other sinister
ends may be well termed a delinquent person."—*State Trials, 1640,
Earl Strafford.* The Earl of Carlisle was an extravagant person. On May
16, of the same year (1643) was issued a draft order for the protection of
James, Earl of Carlisle, against riotous persons who had destroyed certain
ancient *Locks, Mills*, &c, on the *River Lea* in the parish of Waltham and
Cheshunt. *Vide.* Reports of Royal Commissioners on Historical MSS.,
Vol. v., p. 86.

‡ In the Church-yard.

§ In High Bridge Street or at Sewardstone, existing *temp*. Hen. V.

‖ Near the Cemetery, Sewardstone Road.

Earle of Carlile £3 10s. W. Warren houldeth of him per
ann. £103 10s. Nicholas Brewet per ann. £3 16s.
Christopher Harwood per ann. £9 6s. John Fullham per
ann. £8 16s. Thomas Coather per ann. £9 10s. Mr.
Neale per ann. £48. Mr. Wills per ann. £10. Lettice
Francis per ann. £16. Mrs. Chaire per ann. £20. Henry
Knagg per ann. £34 2s. Mr. Bridges per ann. £49 11s 4d.
Item by Mr. Bridges more per ann. £26 9s 2d. John
Bridges and John Hodge* per ann. £32 13s 4d. John
Gowing for *Serrit Hills* per ann. £29 2s. Item more for
Cobhill per ann. £33. Christopher Goulding Junior per
ann. £37 6s 8d. Item for further *Eastfield* per ann. £50.
Item more for Penerley's lease per ann. £13 10s 8d. Item
more for Woodhouse lease per ann. £8 18s 4d. Item more
for Christopher Goulding's Sen. his lease per ann. £5 2s.
William Nashe for the. *Parke Ground* per ann £40. Giles
Carter per annum £14. Sir Edward Fleetwood per ann.
£14 10s. Samuel Nash per ann. £100. John Barnett per
ann. £2. Abraham Hudson the Miller per annum £80
Mr. Bowers' assignees per ann. £24 13s 4d. William Nashe
for the *ffishing* there per ann. £30. Lawrence Biggins
houldeth per ann. 1s. Mr Chaire for the *Park grounds* per
ann. £1 14s. Abraham Hudson of the *Turnpike* per ann.
£123. Abraham Hudson and Josias Richardson houlde of
Mr. Robt. Mell a delinquent per ann. £54. James Clebbone,
Thomas Wakefield and John Hayward houlde of Patrick
Winch delinquent per ann. £24. William Nashe holdeth
of Nicholas Blencoe gent. a delinquent per ann. £30.
John Robinson houldeth of the said Mr Blencoe per ann.
£4. Marmaduke Howe houldeth of the Bishopp of Norwich
(Joseph Hall, formerly of Waltham Abbey) a delinquent per
ann. £3.

SEWARDSTONE.—Thomas Peocock houldeth of Mr. Nicholas
Blincoe a delinquent per ann. £6. Henry Jepson holdeth
of the Bishopp of Norwich a delinquent per annum £23.
John Greene houldeth of him per ann. £28 10s. John
Bridges holdeth of him per ann. £20. John Smith houldeth
of the same Bishopp of Norwich per ann. £1 6s 8d.
Richard Stock Senior holdeth of Mr Nott a delinquent

---

* Tallow Chandler. See Waltham Abbey *Tokens* 17th cent.—*Boyne.*

per ann. £6. W. Nashe houldeth of the said Mr Nott per-
ann. £20. Thomas Wheler houldeth of him per ann. £23
Richard Peirce houldeth of him per annum £25 12s.*

THE ELEANOR MEMORIAL, WALTHAM CROSS,

THE Eleanor Cross, Waltham Cross, is a noble structure
situated on the road side, near the "Falcon Inn" and
opposite "Ye Ould Foure Swannes Hostlerie," [A.D.
1260] a mile from the town of Waltham, and a few minutes'
walk from Waltham Cross Station, G.E.R.†
This Cross was erected by Edward I. to perpetuate the
memory of his beloved consort Eleanor, who died of a fever at
Herdby near Grantham, Nov. 29th, 1291, aged 47 years. Her
body was brought in right royal style to London, and a stone
cross raised to her memory at every place where the funeral
cortége rested, and Waltham Cross is one of the renowned monuments remaining. This cross, which is now (1887) being
restored, has undergone little reparation since 1832. The base
of the Cross, remarks Dr. Stukeley, was originally surrounded by
ten steps, several of which were removed to widen the road, as
the turning near it was rather sharp. The architecture of the
cross is considered richer, and its sculpture more beautiful than
either of the crosses of Northampton or Geddington. This is
no doubt owing to its being near London, as the Eleanor
Crosses in the Metropolis, which were under the constant eye of
the king, were more elegant than those a long distance off.
The ornamental details of this cross owe much of their sharpness
and preservation to the hardness of the stone. The form of

---

* In 1643 portions of Land were sequestered within the parish of *Nazing*.
The act of sequestration took place before Sir Richard Everard, Bart., Isaac
Man, John Attwood, John Sorrell, and Peter Whetcombe. Sir Richard
Lucy Kt, houldeth of the within named James Earl of Carlile a delinqt Lands
there at per ann. £93 3 4. William King houldeth of the said Earle p. ann.
£88. Sir Francis Swift p. ann. £50. Sir Francis Swifte for *Greene Meade*
p. ann. £3. The names of thirty other holders occur on the *Nazing* list.
Add. MSS. 5505. fol. 25.

† The Great Eastern Railway was opened to Broxbourne on the 10th of
September, 1840, being called at the time, "The London and Essex Railway,"
then the North-Eastern Railway, and since then the Eastern Counties'
Railway, and lastly the Great Eastern Railway.

the structure is hexagonal, and separate from the basement, and consists of three stories or compartments, decreasing progressively at each stage. Each division is finished by an embattled frieze, or cornice, and at every angle is a graduated buttress enriched with foliated crockets and finials. Within the panelled tracery of the lower storey are the shields of England, Castile, Leon and Ponthien (or Poicton). These shields are suspended by their guiges or straps, from knots of foliage, and resemble in style, those in the nave of Westminster Abbey, commemorating the benefactors to the building. The second division is even yet more elegant, both from its rich pyramidical assemblage of open pointed arches and sculptured finials, and from the graceful statues of Queen Eleanor which enrich its open divisions. The three elegant figures of the Queen have suffered by the weather. The upper storey is beautified with panelled tracery and pediments in assimilation to the lower parts, and the whole forms even to-day a splendid structure, and one of the finest examples of the science and genuine taste of our ancestors.* Those who are said to have attempted in drawings to restore the effigies of the Queen have erred in altering their attitude and in placing a sceptre and a *mundus* in the hands of the Queen, for the orb, as a mark of soverignty, can only belong to queens regnant.† The figures of the Queen on this cross are identical with those used on the seals of the period. In the left hand of the Queen is generally seen the cordon of the mantle which is drawn over the shoulders, and in her right hand a sceptre. For details of the expenses of the erection of this cross, see Household Expenses (Latin) *temp.* Eleanor (A.D. 1291) *Vetusta Monumenta*, Vol. 3, fol., also "Queen Eleanor Memorial, Waltham Cross" by W. Winters (1885.)

The present (1887) restoration of the Eleanor Cross has been considerably promoted by the munificent gift of Sir Henry B. Meux, Bart., of the land required for the widening of the road near the Falcon side of the Cross.

The Queen has shown her sympathy with the restoration of the Eleanor monument of Waltham, and has sent a donation, through Sir Henry Ponsonby of £25 to Mr J. Tydeman, secretary of the fund.

---

* Brayley's Graphic Illustrator, p. 406.

† Gents. Mag. vol. 102, pt. 2, p. 107.

THE ANCIENT BOUNDARY OF WALTHAM HOLY CROSS.

HE boundary line which divides the parish of Cheshunt from that of Waltham Holy Cross, has been the subject of dispute between the inhabitants of the two parishes from the 33rd Hen. III. (1248), and which was settled in favour of Waltham, and called finalis concordia, wherein it is stated that the Duke of Savoy "*remised and quit claimed from him and his heirs, to the said Abbot and his successors, the right and claim he had to ask in the same meadows and marshes of the said Abbot.*" Dr. T. Fuller states that the matter broke out again "betwixt Robert the last Abbot and the lord of Cheshunt when the Abbey was dissolved." In 1601 the men of Cheshunt took a survey of their boundary, but evidently without being strictly acquainted with the extent of their parish rights, they overstepped the mark, or so the men of Waltham considered, the circumstance of which is noted in our ancient Parish Register, *i.e.*, The curate of Chesthunt and some of the churchwardens of Chesthunt, on the 19th daye, did come in their pambulation to our hye bridge and for so doing and comming out of their own libertye they were for there paynes thrust into a dych called Hooks Dich. On September 8th, 1643, the boundary of Waltham Holy Cross was found to extend from "the hamlet of Roydon to the River Lea ;* from thence to the corner of the marsh called *Ody* Marsh ; and so passing over the River Lea, including within the Forest all that marsh called *Holyfield* Marsh, to the meadow called the *Fryth* or *Frith*, and so passing the *Fryth* at the place called the *Shirelake*, to *Hook's Marsh*, including within the Forest aforesaid *all those Marshes*

---

* The parishes within the Forest boundary are : Waltham Holy Cross, Epping, Nazing, Chingford, Wanstead, Layton, Woodford, Loughton, Chigwell, Lambourn, and Stapleford Abbots. The ancient perambulation usually began at Bow Bridge, where the Lea divides the western boundary.

called *Hook's* Marsh and *Nor Marsh*; and so going by the River Lea, likewise including *Waltham Great Marsh*; and so over the ditch there to the bridge called '*Smally bridge*' (Small Lea Bridge) extending to the side of the same bridge downward by a ditch or a current of water running to the right hand of the king's highway, leading to Waltham Abbey, as far as *Coldhall*, and presently beyond *Coldhall* turning by a ditch that divides the counties of Essex and Hertford, to a river there, including within the Forest aforesaid all that meadow or marsh called *Canwards*." This agrees with MS. preserved in the British Museum, written in the early part of the sixteenth century, and which bears this title, "THE BOWNDYE BYTWEN THE LORDSHYPYE OF WALTHAM AND CHESTHUNT." Theyse ben the boundye septinge hertford-shyre and Essex by a dyche comynge owte of the Kyngs Streme from a Shelpp callid Bodey Shelpp and there septith holyfeld mersh, in Essex and Stachysholme in hertfordshyre and soo playnly shewyth the pting on the sayde shyre and the sayde hokye mshe till it come to the north corner of the north mersh of Walthm seynt crosse in Essex and the mersh callid Chesthunt mersh in herfordshye. And soo septith the sayde mershis till it come to daffyes mede there the myll streme of Chesthunt myll metith with the sayde shyre dych and so septith the sayde mshes of Walthm seynt crosse mershe and mede till it come to Smallay Brygge and so goth undre the Brygge and turnyth.

In early days there were various gates approaching the forest of Waltham of Waltham, such as "Honey Lane Gate," "Reeve Gate," "Clapgate," "Theydon Gate," &c.

AN ACCOUNT OF THE PERAMBULATION OF THE PARISH OF WALTHAM HOLY CROSS, TAKEN IN 1823.*—An interesting account of the perambulation of the parish was published in 1823, and in which the writer says:—"At the day ordered we met at the *King's Arms*, where a nice breakfast was prepared, and after we had taken what we pleased, we prepared to march. The churchwardens' staff was put into my [James Carr] hands as deputy for them, aud as marshwarden, and we proceeded in due order till we came to *Small Lea River Bridge*. Our Psalm singers pitched up with 'All people that on earth do dwell,' &c.]

---

* "Facts Parochial, &c.," by James Carr, of Waltham Abbey.

and a man was ordered to jump into the river, which he did, and swam a little way, and out again; we followed, not through the water mind, but over a bridge prepared for that purpose. We, however, soon came up with the poor fellow, and proceeded till we came to another part of the river, when he was again ordered to go in, and particularly cautioned to go far enough, that not an inch should be lost, and after having been there long enough to satisfy our captain, he came, and we went on till we came to a mead called the *Hundred Acres*, where we met the Cheshunt people, and a parley ensued as to the parish in which it was situate, but it was very soon abandoned by us, and we went on our course leaving *Holyfield Hall* on our right steering our course to *Langridge Farm*,* leaving the house a little on our, left, across some fields into a lane near the little farm occupied by Mrs. Dellar, leaving that on the right, going on till we came into the road that leads from *Holyfield to Nazing Bury*, when we turned short to the right and soon found ourselves at the *Coach and Horses*, where there was a leg of pork in waiting for us; this was a very seasonable supply after our fatiguing march amidst

"Moving accidents in flood and field"

After we had refreshed our weary bodies the word was given to move on, which was instantly obeyed, bending our way along the road leading to *Nazing*, till we come to the *Blacksmith's shop* occupied by Mr. Low, when we turned short to the right up some fields, leaving *Galley Hill* on the right, and went on till we came to *Mr. Smith's*, at *Harold's Park*. Here again the table was spread, not with pork, but with roast beef of old England; but the pork had performed its office so well, that we could not avail ourselves of the hospitality of Mr. Smith. Before we could proceed further it was necessary for our otter, as he was called, to swim through a nasty muddy pond, which after having done we proceeded by *Mr. Sessions' Farm*, leaving the house on the left till we came to *Mr. Conyers' Park*, where we met the Squire, who our people complimented by bumping against one of his own trees. He, however, took it in good part, and we went on through the park, leaving his house on the left, and came into the road about a mile on this

---

* In 1380, John Langrish possessed land in Holyfield and Edmonsey, and whose name may have originated the title to the above farm.

side of the *Windmill at Epping*, round *Woodridden* home to *Waltham Abbey*, where a dinner was provided at the *New Inn.*" The next day the Cheshunt people perambulated their boundary, and it was reported by them that they intended to repeat the old grievance in laying claim to all that part of the town of Waltham west of *Powder Mill Lane*. This created great sensation in the town and the men of Waltham met their antagonists at the Marshgate, where a desperate battle ensued and when heads were fractured and other personal injuries sustained.

Marsh Land in the Parish.—Owing to the disposal of so much of the public property in the parish, the right of common pasturage is not so valuable to-day as it was a few years ago. The Government about 15 years ago purchased the extinction of the commonable rights of the *Hoppit* and portions in *Town Mead* for £2,600. Afterwards some of *Waltham Hall Marsh* and *Edmondsey* were taken by the Government. The parishioners have also lost the right of commonage in *Broomstick Hall Common. Honey Lane Common*, and part of *Town Mead*. All these, with *Edmondsey*, were Lammas Lands open to the public during certain seasons of the year. Every person renting 40s. per annum in the parish has now an unlimited right on the marshes only. These marshes were confirmed by charter of Henry II., 1177, to the Canons of Waltham who kept a portion of them for *hay* for the king. Richd. I., *circa* 1189, added *Edmondsey* to the town by charter.

RULES OF COMMONAGE IN THE MARSHES were fixed by vestry, August 14th, 1781, and printed. As these rules have become rare the publication of them in these pages may be found acceptable.

WALTHAM HOLY CROSS, ESSEX.—*Regulations respecting the Marsh and other Commons in the said Parish.*

1st. That all Cattle turned on to the said Marsh shall be first marked with the usual Mark $\frac{X}{W}$ twice every year, viz., on Old Lady Day, and on the 18th day of July, for which the Owners shall pay 2d. for every head so marked; and that all Cattle found thereon, not being first marked, will be Pounded and each Head pay 3s. 4d. agreeably to an Order made in Vestry the 14th day of August 1781.

2nd. That agreeably to the Presentments of the Court Leet, any Person who shall put any Horse or other Cattle on the Marsh, Town Mead, or Edmondsey, which are not their own Property, will be fined Forty Shillings, and lose the Common Rights for three years after such offence.

3rd.   That any Stone Horse, or unclean or cut Horse commonly called a Rig, or Bull, or Steer found thereon, will be pounded and each Head pay 6s. 8d.; likewise any Mare found thereon from Old Lady-day until after driving-hour on Old Lammas day, will likewise be pounded, and pay the same fine.

4th. That no Cow, nor Heifer be turned on the said Marsh before 4 o'clock in the Morning, nor remain after driving in the Evening, from Old Lady-day until Old Lammas day: if any be found thereon after driving, they will be pounded, and the owner thereof pay 3s. 4d.   And all the above Fines are to be accounted for by the Marshwardens in their Accounts; and that the Marshwardens are to produce their Accounts to the Jury of the Court Leet and swear to the same; that they are bound to call two Rates within the Year for which they serve, or be liable to a Fine of Forty Shillings, and that they are allowed Two Pounds at each Rate-making.

5th. That no Persons but Householders, and who occupy the same, are entitled to the Common Rights of the said Marsh and other Commons; and that it is the duty of the Marshwardens to superintend the management of the Town Mead and Edmondsey equally with the Marsh.

6th.   That the Owners of Cows and Heifers turned on the said Marsh, during the time of driving, are to pay to the Marshard, Sixpence per Head for his trouble, which has been a custom from time immemorial.

The Jury of the Court Leet, whose names are hereunto subscribed, have examined the above Regulations and do recommend the same to be Printed, and signed by the Marshwardens' Clerk, and that a Copy be given to the Marshwardens on their appointment.

JOHN UPTON (Foreman), FRANCIS WIGGS, JOHN PAIN, THOMAS THOMPSON, JAMES DEATH, LANCE TUCK WHITELY, JOHN LIGHT, JAMES BARWICK, JOSEPH NIGHTINGALE, RICHARD GENTRY, WILLIAM PHIPPS, THOMAS DENCH; JAMES ALLSUP, Clerk to the Marshwardens.

A piece of marsh land situated on the east side of the river Lea near to *Cheshunt Lock*, 15 or 16 acres in extent, and which is bounded on the south by the *Government Cut*, has been the subject of dispute. On to that piece of land, both the parish of Cheshunt and that of Waltham had a customary right of turning "head to head," but just prior to 1870 the marsh-wardens of Cheshunt turned that particular piece of land into a "night lay" for cows belonging to Cheshunt *only*, and at the same time a fence was put up to prevent the Waltham people from turning into the same. This was an infringement of the commonable rights of the parish of Waltham. The Waltham marshwardeus for the time being entered the enclosed land and opened it to the Waltham cattle, and the Cheshunt marshwardens were unable to prove their exclusive right to the land as it originally belonged to Waltham parish. A new Pinder House* at the Waltham marsh gate was built in 1872-3, at the small cost of £250. In early times, as before stated, portions of the marsh and town mead were cut for hay. The whole of Waltham Abbey marsh originally contained 400 acres; this included Cheshunt marsh, which was then *not* divided by the river Lea, and was designated Waltham marsh, causing many hot disputes between the two parishes. Waltham Abbey marsh contains 59a. 3r. 4p.; *Hall Marsh*, 28a. 3r. 36p.; *Edmondsey*, purchased by the Government, 32a.; *Town Mead*, 52a.; *Great Hoppit*, 13a. 2r. 12p.; *Little Hoppit*, 2a. 2r. 28p. These Hoppits now belong to the Government. The land occupied by the river Lea and towing path, 6a. 1r. 30p., exclusive of ditch taken at half a rod wide, 3r. 13p., making a total of 7a. 1r. 5p. The Cut opened in 1770 takes its rise from "Ives Ferry," co. Herts, where it is supplied from the old river Lea. In the year 1772 it was proposed to make a canal from Moorfields to Waltham Abbey for £52,495. This canal was to be 60ft. wide 4½ft. deep, and terminating in a bason 400ft. long by 200ft. broad. This project was never effected from the opposition it met with in Parliament consequent on private interest. Ramney Mead Lock and Cut were opened September 10, 1864. John Want was lockkeeper at the time. The incorporations of the river Lea occurred in 1869. Some state that the Lea was made navigable *circa* A.D. 1424, but it was used for small barges long before that period. Freeholders and copyholders of Waltham had not only a right of turning any number of cattle on the forest at a certain part of the year, but a legitimate claim to fishing in the old marsh river and streams. The Government have held an indisputable right of fishing over their own waters since 1787.

THE FISHERIES.—Waltham Abbey and Cheshunt Fisheries were renowned in the Middle Ages when the abbots flourished in their Convents in Waltham and the nuns in Cheshunt.

---

* Mrs. Clark who kept the Pinder House, at Cheshunt Marshgate, Windmill Lane, was cruelly murdered on the riverside, between Broxbourne and her house, in 1886.

But these waters became famous for fishing in the quiet days
of old Izaak Walton, the friend of Dr. T. Fuller, curate
of Waltham. The Governmeut waters are now preferable to
any preserves for . many miles round. These waters are
private and are annually let to different persons. The *Lower
Corn Mill Stream* is a portion of the river between the *Lower
Island* and *Enfield Lock*. The *Upper Fisheries* extend from
King's Weir to *Thorogood Sluce*. These waters abound with
pike, carp, eels, perch, roach, chub, &c. Tom Taylor, the
great angler, is said to have taken as much as 38lbs. of
roach in less than two hours, near Harold's Bridge.

THE ROYAL GUNPOWDER FACTORY.—The Royal Gunpowder
Mills* in this town are the oldest of the kind in existence.
In the reign of Queen Elizabeth (1561), John Tamworth, a
gentleman of substance in Waltham Abbey, was in treaty
with Marco Antonio Erizzo, on behalf of the Queen, for the
purchase of saltpetre, sulphur, and bow staves for barrels.
The saltpetre was offered to him at £3 10s. per cwt., which
he declared to be too dear. Erizzo, however, could not take
less money, nor could he provide any for some time.† This
John Tamworth is mentioned‡ in certain MS.S. preserved
in the British Museum as the executor of lady Joan Denny,
widow of Sir Anthony Denny, Lord Chamberlain to Hen. VIII.
and Ed. VI.§ John Tamworth's name also appears in the
Churchwardens' Accounts for 1563. Item:—Received of Mr.
Tamworth twenty loads of timber, ready hewed, which he gave
to the parish. Dr. T. Fuller (1655) says, "This gentleman,
by his bounty to the public, seems better known to God
than to me, having neither heard nor read of any of his name
in or near to Waltham." The same writer (Dr. Fuller) became
curate of Waltham Abbev in 1648-9, and referring to the
Powder Mills, he says, "The Mills in my parish have been
five times blown up within *seven years*, but blessed be God
without the loss of any man's life."|| Thomas Gutridge and

---

* See History of Royal Gunpowder Works, by W. Winters.

† Cal. Stat. Papers *(Foreign)*, *temp.* Elizabeth.

‡ Lansd. Charters, No. 16.

§ Lady Denny in 1553 let one Tenement, &c , adjoining *le Armytage*,
in Waltham Abbey, at five shillings per annum. (See particulars for
Grants Pub. Rec. Office.)

|| Worthies of England, p. 318.

Edward Simmons, carpenter, are the first recorded as being killed in these works. The first of the two was buried Oct. 4th, 1665, and the second one on the day following. The next person who lost his life by an explsion was Peter Bennet and who was buried Nov. 27, 1720.* The most serious explosions in this Factory have taken place during the present century, and which have probably prevented many persons of affluence from settling down too near the town. However, their absence is perhaps more than equalled by the number of hands constantly employed in the Royal Works, and which may be considered the life of the town. The following are the explosions that have occurred since the Government have possessed the Factory, viz.—(I.) 1801, April 18th, *nine men* killed. (II.) 1811, Nov. 27, *seven men* lost their lives; (III.) Another *seven* were killed in 1843, April 13; and (IV.) in 1870, June 16, *five* men died in consequence of an explosion at the Lower Island. When John Walton was proprietor of the Powder Factory in this parish (1735) it was then considered to be the largest in Great Britain. The Board of Ordnance purchased the mills of John Walton in 1787, and continued the works in operation by several of Mr. Walton's best men. The Powder Mills at Faversham and Ballincollig were at that time in the hands of the Government, and which eventually became incorporated with the Waltham Abbey Factory under Sir W. Congreve, "Comptroller of the Royal Laboratory," who under date December 31st, 1799, gives an account of the progress of the Mills at Waltham Abbey, viz.: "Per contract—balance remaining in favour of these mills on this date after having paid off the original debt incurred, namely, £10,000; new erections, repairs, etc., so as to set at work, £13,449 7s 6d, making together the sum of £23,499 7s. 6d., which debt, with interest of 5 per cent. per annum, was paid off by the profits arising from the manufacture of gnnpowder at Waltham Abbey from 1st March, 1790, and 31st December, 1795." The property of the Board of Ordnance, now War Department, in connection with the Powder Mills, is a narrow slip of land varying in width and running from the *Aqueduct, King's Weir*, through the town of Waltham to the *Lower Island*, towards *Enfield Lock*.†

---

* See "Our Parish Register."

† From the Sewardstone *Manor Rolls* (private) occurs the following note under date July 3rd, 1648.—John Berisford admitted on ye surrender of

A Summary of the Buildings, Lands, etc., in Waltham
Holy Cross Parish, Occupied by the Government in 1887.
—There are 246 acres in Waltham Holy Cross parish belonging
to the Government; 67½ acres are let to various individuals;
108 acres in the exclusive occupation of the War Department or
its officers; 175½ acres belonging to the Royal Gunpowder
Factory; 54½ acres are let to various individuals; 16 acres in
the exclusive occupation of the War Department, or its officers
of the Royal Small Arms Factory—246 grand total. There are
7½ miles of the *River Lea*, besides numerous tributary streams
and several mill heads, the water from which works the water-
wheels for the manufacture of gunpowder. Over 250 War
Department buildings are composed of wood and were in
existence when the property was purchased in 1795* as also
several of the brick buildings, all in good condition. There are
six quarters for officers and 38 cottages for workmen. A large
corn mill with two water-wheels, worked by a mill head. The
land is for the most part marsh, and often flooded in the winter;
and there are several plantations of alder and willow. No rents are
payable by the War Department for property which has come in
the occupation of the department since 1st January, 1861.
" Hall's " and " Hook's " marshes, let to Mr. W. Hudson at £3
per acre—13a. 1r. 35p. Rates and taxes paid by tenant.
Possession resumed 29th September, 1874. Great Hoppitt is
planted with willows—13a. 2r. 21p. Right of cutting grass is
sold to Mr. W. Oram, at £3 per acre. The tenant is not liable
for rates and taxes. 16½ acres in Cheshunt parish, planted with
alders and walnut trees. One acre in Nazing parish planted
with willows. *The Fisheries* let by the War Department are those
of Mr. A. Wheeler for £3 per annum, consisting of the Corn
Mill Stream and a portion of the river between the Lower Island
and Enfield Lock ; and the Upper Fisheries just let to Mr. R. B.

Richd. Stock to 1½ acres of land lying in a place called ye *Upper-fortye-field*,
and to ye field called *Parkes-field* cont. 4a. with ye water-stream and mills,
called ye Powder-Mills, Tenemts, Edifices, Wayes and Appurts belonging
to ye same and to an Island near ye Town Ambrey cont. 6 perches. abutt on
ye River Lea and to one Rood of Land lying in Mill Holme at ye end of
ye sd. Mill. Fine xls. The Powder Mills here mentioned may have
been situated at Sewardstone.

* The *lands* connected with the works were finally purchased in 1795 ; the
buildings were purchased in 1787.

Colvin, extending from King's Weir to Thorogood Sluice, for £20 per annum.*

The land thus possessed by the Government extends from *King's Weir* to *Enfield Lock*, and takes in Edmonsey,† portions of the Marshes, *Abbey Fields, Town Mead*, and the town proper. The premises near the Church known as the *Corn Mill* and the old *Pin Factory* were purchased in 1809 by the Government of John Halfhide for £9,500. This *Flour Mill* was originally bequeathed to the Abbots of Waltham A.D. 1108, by Matilda of Scotland, afterwards Queen of Henry the First. Gun-cotton was first manfactured by the War Department in the Saltpetre Refinery, Waltham Abbey, in June, 1870.

HIGHBRIDGE STREET.—From the Eleanor Cross or from the G.E.R. Station, Waltham Cross, the town of Waltham Abbey is approached by crossing the Old Lea Stream which runs toward the Royal Small Arms Factory, Enfield Lock (a mile and a half south of the Abbey). The next bridge west of the church spans the navigable river Lea which mainly commences the town proper, of Waltham and is called HIGHBRIDGE STREET (originally *West Street*). This street derived its present name from a high bridge erected very early.‡ This bridge was no doubt the one over Powder Mill Lane Stream, as the yard near it is still called "Barge yard," and where was formerly a beerhouse, known as "The Two Barges." The bridge over the navigable Lea is kept up by the trustees of the river, who pay annually six pounds to the marshwardens for land cut through the Marshes. The bridge and road near the Refinery are kept and repaired by the War Department. The "Board of Ordnance" paid £10 for land cut

---

* Obligingly communicated by the late J Ansell, Esq.

† In 1125 Robert Fitz Walter granted the tithes of Edmonsey to the Canons of Waltham (see Add. MSS. 5,937). Hen. II. (1177) gave the whole of the tithes of Edmonsey to the monastery. "Edmonsey" was then called "Gadwynesheye" (*vide* Hunter MSS. 25,269). In 1380 John Langrich possessed six acres of land in "Edwynseye" (Edmonsey), formerly held by John Matthews, vicar of Nazing. The "Chelnosie" mentioned in Henry the Second's Charter, A.D., 1177, appears from its connection with *Normad-Majorem Warden and Minorem* to be EDMONSEY.

‡ A new high bridge was erected in 1587 by order of Queen Elizabeth at a cost of upwards of £20 (Lansd. MSS. 53 fol. 94)—a heavy sum in those days—for the better navigation of her Majesty's royal barge as well as for barges in general. As far back as 1314 this street was called "Hayestrate" [High Street] and "Hie-street" in 1485.

through Edmondsey and for the accommodation of a cartway and footpath. The other bridges in the town of Waltham, except the one near the Romeland and another on the Sewardstone-road, are repaired by the lord of the manor.

The premises called "THE REFINERY" are used for the refining and storage of saltpetre and for the manufacturing of Gun-cotton. The yard and field adjoining the large red brick house opposite the Marsh, formerly occupied by James Barwick, a local magistrate, were used in the last century for calico printing,* a flourishing trade in the town at that time, and the old storehouses belonging to the Government south of the Refinery were once dwelling houses, occupied by the Jessopp family and Mr Torbut, a miller. In the interior of these buildings vestiges of old domestic architecture still remain, and near them once stood "The Goat" public house, kept by W. Pratt, beadle of the parish. This house has long been demolished as also the old "Leather Bottle" beerhouse and the butcher's shop tenanted forty years ago by Mr. Smith. On the same side of the road stands—

THE ALMSHOUSES.—This row or block of houses was erected in 1818, on the site of those given by Mr. Greene in 1626. Singular to say, the parish possesses no original deed of this gift, nor yet the donor's Christian name. This Mr. Greene was "Purveyor to King James I.," and that is all the parish authorities know of him. From early original documents we have discovered that the founder of the original almshouses in Highbridge-street was *Francis Greene*, whose will, bearing date December 15th, 1637, shows that he gave to Joan, his wife, a life interest in all his property in the parish, including the *barn, orchard, and garden* with the *four Almshouses* in Waltham.†

---

* In 1782 Thomas Littler was hanged at Chelmsford for the paltry theft of a piece of lawn from these calico grounds. Mr. Barwick carried on the calico printing trade in connection with Mrs. Farran with great spirit in 1770. Mr. Hammond afterwards held these premises.

† A barn, orchard, and garden attached to the Almshouses were let in 1626 at £4 per annum. This land was again let some years ago at £20 per annum, and which is worth more in the present day. Out of this amount the four (senior) widows under the original grant were to have £5 per annum, paid quarterly, in addition to 2s 6d weekly from the parish ; and the four (junior) widows admitted on the *new arrangement* of 1818 are to be provided for out of Woollard's gift, which amounted many years ago to 2s 2¼d weekly, and 2s 6d weekly from the parish. The widows are also allowed a portion of Wollaston's bread gift. These houses require reparation.

The Court Leet *fine* was then paid. The documents alluded to, which are a portion of the book of *fines* of the Lord's Court Baron of this manor, are much worn with age, and are in the author's possession.* The parts referring to the *Almshouses* are here published in full for the first time:—13 Car. Mr. ffi. Greene's will, by which he gave to Joane, his wyfe, for her lyfe his Copyholld land in Waltham, viz.:—*Hyme Holmes* pc. Exc. the barne, orch. & gards, and *iiij almeshowses* in Waltham. And he did give his dwell. ho.[use] & all his mess., lands, tents, and hered, as well free as Copy in Walth. (*intr alia*) lyinge in *Upsheire* & *Sewardst.* in Walth., wᶜʰ he pᵗchased of Tho. Ellyott & of Edw. Younge, late of *Chingford*, and all his lands in *Nasing*, wᶜʰ he lately pᵗchased of Mr. Jo. Fflud., Exc. that wᶜʰ was given to his wyfe for her lyfe wᶜʰ rem. over as in the Will lately bowght of Jo. Standish.

And he gave the Orch., gardens, barne & *Almeshouses* to them & their heires upon trust and confide & to such uses as in the will is mentioned.† This document is dated December 7th, 1638. Mr. Greene in 1630, in the "time of scearcitie and dearth of corne," gave to the poor of Waltham £i. i. iiii. for bread. Francis Greene may have twice married, as the register gives the burial of his first wife "Buried, Mrstris Elizabeth Greene, wyfe to Mr. Ffrancis Greene, in the church the 24 day Sept., 1607." His second wife was probably *Joane*, who survived him. Francis Greene was buried 19th November, 1638 (which date agrees with his will, and Edward Greene, his son, was buried August 12th, 1639.

The original ALMSHOUSES, erected for *four* persons, were destroyed and rebuilt in 1818, during the curacy of Thomas Pickthall, with room enough for double the number of inmates.‡ This undertaking was effected by the funds realised from the interest of Robert Mason's gift. These Almshouses were repaired out of the church rates, which rate has long been abolished.

---

* 15th December, 1637, intr. Mris. Joane Greene adm. for her lyfe to some Cop. Land in Waltham ; ffines xxxiiii£ adm. tent, intr. fee far cop. vs.

† Mr. Edw. Green, Ch. Goldinge (son of Chr.), Jo. Searle, Andr. Searle, Adm. tents of the Almeshowse. *intr.* & ffines iiii£ Cop. vs.

‡ The widows (mostly from the Township) are chosen and appointed by the Churchwardens.

On the front of the Almshouses within a recess appear a dozen lines of poetry, probably written by the good donor himself :—

> " Birth is a pain : life, labour, care, toil, thrall :
> In old age strength fails ; lastly, death ends all.
> Whilst strong life lasts, let virtuous deeds be shown ;
> Fruits of such trees are hardly thereby seen or known.
> To have reward with lasting joys for ay,
> When vicious actions fall to ends decay.
> Of wealth o'erplus, land, money, stock, or store,
> In life that will relieve aged, needy poor.
> Good deeds defer not till the funeral rites be past ;
> In lifetime what's done is made more firm, sure and fast ;
> So ever after it shall be known and seen
> That leaf and fruit shall ever spring fresh and GREENE.—1626."

THE COUNTY COURT.—*County Court*, a substantial building erected in 1849, and in which monthly sittings of the court are held.   John Thomas Abdy, LL.D. judge ; W. J. Bruty, registrar ; H. J. Jenour, high bailiff.   This court stands on the site of the old silk printing factory carried on by the Littler family.*   In a line with this court are the Government " BANK HOUSES," occupied by persons engaged in the Royal Powder Mills ; and in front of which Mr. Hales, fifty years ago, carried on his work as " Fellmonger and Wooldealer."   These premises are now occupied by Mr. J. Carr, miller.   A SILK FACTORY, sixty years ago, stood in the centre of Highbridge Street, on the site of Mr. Marshall's house, near " COX'S PASSAGE."

SUN STREET was originally called "*East Street*," and is the main way to Nazing, Epping, Loughton, Woodford, Chingford and London.   At the top of the street near the *Market Place* is " The old corner shop," in front of which are two wood carvings of grotesque characters representatives of Bacchus, the god of wine.   In this street once lived and were known to the writer :— Messrs. Pain, Want, Sadd and Death.   The "*Sun Inn*," in the centre of this street, flourished in 1633.   Lower down is the POLICE STATION, erected in 1874.   A lofty flour mill, erected in 1883-4, stands opposite "*Bland's Yard*," or "*Chetwood's Yard*." The earliest known document relating to *Sun Street* is in the author's possession, and dates 25 Hen. VI., 1447.   In this MS.

---

* In the house next to the County Court a great number of soldiers (Royal Artillery) from Woolwich, were billited during the Chartist riots in 1848.

the street is called *Eststret.* Another of the same date relates to the same parties, *i.e.*, the Abbot of Waltham, William Orgor and Alice his wife ; John Love, butcher ; Thomas Lok, plumber, and others. In a document dated 1516 is mentioned *Trykkeryslane* or *Cryketteslane Estrete.* Later on this lane is called *Crekette*-lane and in 1578 *Crecks-lane.* It may refer to " CROOKMILE," leading to Holyfield and Nazing. At the east end of Sun-street is an old house recently restored adjoining Mr. H. Lee, the brewer's house, which tradition says was once occupied by John Foxe, the martyrologist. In 1871 a Gothic chimney-piece was discovered consisting of Reigate stone, carved with various floral devices and coloured with vermilion, green and gold. Near the spring of the arch on the left shield were characters I.V., and on the surface of the arch above the initial letters F. and F.S.

SEWARDSTONE STREET.*—This street runs south from the Market-place and ends at " Frank Harvey's field." It is certain that the Government have now (1887) purchased Quinton Hill Farm (to which they anticipate removing the Gun-cotton works from High Bridge Street). Sewardstone Street will be extended to the brook near the present farm ; and a road will be made from Enfield Lock to meet the said street. At the lower end of Sewardstone-street was an ancient Ford, now arched over near the public pump. This street formerly reached to the farm at "DYER'S HILL," on the way to Sewardstone. In the middle ages persons held property in this part of the town named Fross and Foot. In 1326 this street was called *Eldworthstrate*, in which was a place called *Frosshenlane* (Frosslane) also *Fotyslane* (Foots Lane). Probably " Quaker Lane." Before the street received its present title it was known as *Eldford Street* (or Old Ford Street), then *Sheepcot Street* (1333), and in 1633 *South Street*, and lastly *Sewardstone Street.* The houses in Woollard Street were built on *Woollards Garden.* The right hand *through path* leading to the TOWN MEAD near the pump by *Frank Harvey's Field* is of recent date. QUAKER LANE in Sewardstone Street derived its present title from a Quaker's meeting house on the left, which was pulled down in 1844, and on the site of which stands the

---

* Samuel Howell was master of an Academy held in the large red brick house in Sewardstone Street early in the present century. In 1816 he published " Village Rambles and other poems."

Boys' School Room.* George Fox, the founder of the Quakers, came to Waltham Abbey in 1654 and here he held services. He says " I went to Waltham Abbey and had a meeting there ; the people were very rude, gathered about the house and broke the windows." It appears that he went out with his Bible in his hand and appeased the people. The BOARD SCHOOLS are in this lane as also the *Wesleyan Chapel. Woollard Street* and *Green-field Street* are situated at the end of Sewardstone-street.

SILVER STREET, in early documents, is called *School Street* (or Skolestrate, 1342) and *Carbuncle Dunghill*, and which leads from the Market Place to FOUNTAIN PLACE, formerly called the " Bumbey," a place of refuse. The " Black ditch," then open, ran on to *Town Mead*. In 1427 there were several fords in the town which were afterwards bridged over ; there was a street called *Clowsebrige Street* (or *Clowesbruggestrete*), a bridge by a close of land. In 1633 *Catebriggdownhill* was in South Street. *Silver Street* was at one time called *Kilhog's Lane* from the property there held by Nathaniel Kilhog. The Bassano family, celebrated for their musical talents, had property in *School Street*. In 1708 a place called *Goddards* was situated in the same street.

ROMELAND (situate north-west of the Church) is synonymous with " Romescot " or " Peter's Pence," which shows the name to be of early date. This open space has been used for centuries as a cattle and corn market and for the holding of fairs—one on May 14th and the other on September 24th and 25th. The latter is called the " Statty " (*i.e.*, Statute Fair), which used to last seven days, and was principally for the hiring of servants. In August, 1877, an artesian well was finished by Mr. Green, of Plaistow.† The following is a table of the different strata passed through in sinking this well :—Surface deposit, 5ft. ; river sand, mud, small stones, and fresh water shells, 9ft. ; rounded flint stones ("Lee Ballast "), 7ft.; London, or blue clay, 32ft. ; clay sand, full of water, 8ft. ; London clay, 16ft. ; grey iron stone, 3ft. ; chalk, rubble, sand, and flints, 10ft. ; various coloured

---

* The premises on the right hand side of the top of Quaker Lane, now occupied by the Church Sunday School, were occupied as Silk Mills many years ago

† The East London Water Works Company have sunk a well near *Canward*. On February 16th, 1886, the ratepayers met and strongly pro-tested against it. The Company, however, carried out their plans, to the great annoyance and injury of the townsfolk.

sands, 6ft.; Thanet sand, grey and green, 41ft.; hard chalk, 28ft. 9in.; layer of flints, from which the water supply is derived —total depth, 165ft. 9in. A granite cross was erected over this well. In the summer of 1533 a private conference was held at the house of Mr. Cressy, in the *Romeland* near the Abbey, to debate the subject of the divorce of King Henry VIII. from Queen Katherine of Arragon. Cranmer, says Fuller, retired hither (in the time of a plague at Cambridge) to teach his pupils [the young Cressy's]. Thus did Waltham give Rome the first deadly blow in England." Cranmer, who was related to the Cressy family,* had the care of two of Mr. Cressy's sons at Cambridge. Singular to say that a place called *Romeland* was connected with the Abbot of Waltham's London house. This house was a massive stone building situated in the parish of St. *Mary-at-Hill*, London, between that church and the said *Romeland* (an open space at the wharf of *Billingsgate*). Several ancient charters of the Abbey show that its possession of the property was as early as Henry II. One of the documents mention "the stone house which Walter first Abbot of Waltham built there.† The early churchwardens' accounts of St. Mary-at-Hill speak of "the Abbots Inn" as existing in the year 1500, 1502 and 1503. In 1501 the south aisle of the church of St. *Mary-at-Hill* is recorded to have been erected on the site of the Abbot's kitchen. In 25 Hen. VIII. the "Abbot's Inn" was demised by the Abbey to Roger Chaloner.

THE CORNMILL.—This cornmill was given to the Abbots of Waltham, as before stated, by Maud, the wife of King Henry I., A.D. 1108, in exchange for the site of Holy Trinity, Aldgate.‡ This mill was then valued at thirty shillings. The purport of the ancient deed runs thus :—"I Henry King of England, to Richard bishop of London, and Hugh de Roch, &c., and to all his lieges throughout all England, greeting. Know ye that I have granted to Queen Maud my wife that she place canons regular in the church of the Holy Trinity in London. Know ye also that this same church is free and discharged from subjection to the church of Waltham and for which surrender Waltham receives the mill. Maud also restored Northland

---

* See Add. MSS. 5524, fol. 184, also Harl. MSS., 1504, fol. 53b.
† Walter de Gaunt was Abbot of Waltham from 1177 to 1201.
‡ *De Inventione S. C. Waltham*, Cott. MSS. Tib *c.* ix.

(Abbey Fields) which Bp. Walcher had occupied; and established two fairs in Waltham.* In 1790 Mr. Halfhide rented the cornmill and which is now used by Mr. J. Carr. The premises adjoining the cornmill were for many years known as " the Pin Factory," and early in the present century Mr. Francis, of Gracechurch-street, and father of the late Vicar, Rev. James Francis, was the proprietor. In the year 1792 the Waltham Abbey Pin Makers flourished, and they celebrated the birthday of George III. in a manner peculiar to that day. A writer in the *Times* gives a description of the occasion, viz.:—"Waltham Abbey. On Monday last, a gentleman who employs some hundred hands in the pin manufactory at this town, to show his loyalty, illuminated his house and ordered a holiday to be given to all his hands, with a handsome sum to drink his Majesty's health and confusion to all levellers; and a cart load of fuel to burn Tom Paine's effigy. In consequence of which the whole town followed the example, and assembled in the Market Place at six o'clock in the evening with a figure dressed in a suit of mourning, a French natural cockade in his hat, and in his hand 'Rights of Man.' They paraded every street in the town, preceded by two men on horseback with drawn swords in their hand, and a third on horseback rode near to the culprit, who at stated places read his 'last dying speech and confession.' When he arrived at the place of execution he was raised upon a gibbet twenty feet high, and, to the general satisfaction of the inhabitants, burnt to ashes. The magistrate, clergyman, and all the principal inhabitants attended the execution, and during the process, joined by a band of music, 'God save the King' was sung." Small shoe nails were then made with the letters " T.P." upon them, to signify that those who wore them intended to stamp Tom Paine under their feet. Of pin making at the above period Charles Dibdin wrote in his humorous style thus :—

> "The ladies, Heaven bless them all !
>   As sure as I've a nose on,
> In former times had only thorns
>   And skewers to stick their clothes on.
> No damsel then was worth a pin,
>   Whate'er it might have cost her,
> Till gentle Johnny Tilsby
>   Invented pins in Gloucester."

---

* Adelicia, second wife of Hen. I., restored or dedicated the tithes to the canons of Waltham, and addressed a quaint letter to the parishioners.— *Stubbs.*

THE ABBEY GATES are situated north of the church, and consist of two ancient pointed arches, a larger and a smaller one. On each spring of the larger is a shield, surmounted by an angel bearing the arms of Henry III., or Edward III., which are now nearly obliterated. Many years ago the room over this gateway was in use. This was one of the entrances to the Abbot's house, the south wall of which is still standing. The bricks are remarkably large, some of them measuring fifteen inches by three and a half. The stone-pointed doorway (now bricked up) led to the south tower, which is hollow and has loopholes. There were originally two octagonal stone towers, but the foundation of one has long since been demolished. The bridge leading to the gate is of brick, with three arches. The original bridge was of stone, with one broad span, similar in form, according to the bondstone, to the old "Stoney Bridge."

SUBTERRANEOUS PASSAGE.—Not far distant from these *gates* there is a subterraneous passage which tradition states leads to *Cheshunt Nunnery*. A short time ago workmen were engaged on sewage operations in the Abbey Gardens, a few yards north of Mr. G. King's house. About three feet below the surface of the ground the workmen came upon a very hard stony substance, which appeared to be the massive foundation, probably of a chapel or northern wing of the ancient monastery. Near this foundation was discovered a very small coin, which on examination turned out to be Roman, *temp.* Constantine. On the reverse is a wolf suckling two twins, *Romulus* and *Remus*. The impression of this coin is very similar to the silver coin of Ethilberght II. (A.D. 725—760). It presents the king's head to the left; the inscription is almost obliterated. Attached to this foundation is the wall of the mysterious passage, which it was found necessary to break into once more, the hole being made in the arch sufficiently large to admit of entrance. Messrs. W. J. Bates, Stacy Bates, F. King, and the author, carrying candles, etc., thoroughly investigated these underground passages for the purpose of testing an old tradition that the principal passage led to a subterranean building at some remote distance from the Abbey, which contained images, objects of sculpture, etc., forming also a connection between the Abbey of Waltham and the Nunnery of Cheshunt. The monks of the former house, according to this tradition, are accused of having sought the company of the gentle occupants of the latter house by means of this subterranean passage. It is evident, however, that the monks sought no such hidden road by which to pay their visits to the Nunnery; but no doubt, according to the rumour current in Dr. Fuller's time, there must have been some ground for this scandal, The subjoined story has found a place in the "Church History." "One Sir Henry Colt, of Nether Hall in Essex, much in favour of King Henry VIII. for 'his merry conceits,' came to Waltham late at night, being informed by spies that the monks were on a visit at Cheshunt Nunnery. In order to intercept them on their return, he pitched a buck stall (which was used to take deer in the forest) in the narrowest place in the marsh, where he knew the monks must pass, and placed some of his confederates to watch it. The monks, as was expected, ran all into the net, where they were secured till the next morning. When Sir Henry Colt brought the King to show him his game, the merry monarch is said to have burst into a loud fit of laughter and to have declared that 'although he had often seen *sweeter*, he had never seen *fatter* venison.'" Later historians are not certain that there was a *Sir Henry Colt* existing at this period. The Colt family were residents of Waltham at an early period, and many of the members lie interred within the precincts of the Abbey. Of course, as was expected, the search for such a building and medium of intercommunication was altogether fruitless. On entering the opening we found a clear running stream from four to six inches deep. The tunnel has perpen dicular sides, measuring in places from two to six feet in width— the angles being sharp and narrow. The height is from three to seven feet, consisting chiefly of brick and stone. Turning in a north-eastward direction we passed under the "cress shed," where, at the back, there is a small outlet; then on to the "bowling green," where is another outlet, sealed. This "green" formerly belonged to the Earl of Carlisle, who had it ornamented with a "leaden fountain," near to which the remains of Harold's Tomb were discovered some time in the early part of the seventeenth century. Turning out of the main course to the right, the passage, which is higher than the other, was dry, and on reaching the extremity found that it was blocked up; a stone there recorded the names of three previous travellers. ("W. Cohen, G. Cleverly, T. Dunn, April 14, 1865.") A short distance onward to the left is another dry passage, leading apparently westward to the Abbey gates. On quitting this part we found the water divided into two courses, running almost in a parallel direction; this the author explored alone. About the centre of this branch the arch heightened considerably, forming separate compartments, chiefly of brick. Here many portions of the arch, built apparently at different times, are of stone, well squared, and interspersed with large flat red bricks almost square. Passing on a little distance westward we crossed a hollow place. It is very probable that a similar passage, yet undiscovered, runs beneath towards the cornmill stream. Before we arrived at the sluice-gate near Mr. Thomas Chapman's stackyard, we found both the arch and the floor of the passage to be of solid stone for a long distance. The stream appeared to come from the "Mile Ditch" mainly; but here was another passage bearing more southward, the arch of which was lower than the rest. The water close to the back of the church became gradually deeper, till it emptied itself into the cornmill stream. The stone used in these arches appears to be principally fragments from the Abbey. Contiguous to this passage stood the stately mansion occupied by Sir James Hay and Lord Edward Denny, as well as other domestic and conventual buildings associated with the ancient Abbey Church. The above nobleman had a very large canal in the garden, stored "with great plenty of all kinds of fish," and probably these passages were originally made for the purpose of carrying off all the surplus water. There is no presumptive evidence whatever left to substantiate the tradition respecting the underground route from Waltham to Cheshunt, the channel being so extremely low that a person can only just manage to crawl on "all fours" through it; and, moreover, as such a passage would have to pass under the bed of several streams, it would be impossible to prevent such an irregularly built arch from speedily filling with water. This channel was previously tested by Mr. James Death, of Cheshunt. The late Mr. E. Littler also explored these passages. These letters appear on the wall of the main passage —"J. D." and "J. Upton, 1859." No relics of any great antiquity have ever yet been discovered in these passages. Many years ago a small but curiously-made lamp was found and also an old metal tankard.

Some few years ago, while the workmen were making drains for the sewage across the Market Place they came across the basement of two massive stone and flint walls, running parallel towards the south-east end of the Churchyard. It might be at once seen by the materials that it was contemporary with the old monastery; and according to the cruciform style of the original structure, these walls came in direct conjunction with the eastern transept, and formed a subterranean passage from the Abbey into the centre of the town southward to Sewardstone-street, or what was anciently called *Shepescotestrete*. Each of these newly-discovered walls (one foot below the surface) measured in depth four feet from the top to the first narrow set off, and twenty-two inches to the second or broader set off, from which to the extreme base they measured exactly six feet. The first of these projections was about six inches thick; the second about sixteen inches. The walls are about four feet wide at the top, but increase in substance and strength towards the bottom. As the earth was opened they appeared to lie in an angular position. The distance from each angle was precisely eleven feet six inches. The inner surface was quite flat and faced three feet from the bottom with plain red tiles, having a lump on the reverse side of each to help secure it when placed in the mortar against the wall. These tiles were not exactly of the ordinary kind, and measured eight inches by ten, though not one whole one could be seen among them. The earth between these walls to the depth of about ten feet consisted of ashes, tiles, bones, etc.; and although the workmen dug to the depth of thirteen feet six, yet no kind of flooring or pavement could be discovered. At the bottom of this made-up earth, ten feet below the surface, a small vase was dug up and thrown out. This vase when found was perfectly empty, It is of common earthenware of a light brown colour, and was originally glazed outside, the upper part of it being of a greenish hue. Its shape is somewhat globular, with two slight projections at the base of the neck, and a small hole through each by which it was doubtless supported. It measures twelve inches round the centre and two inches in diameter at base. The neck is two inches long, by one and a quarter broad across the mouth; the height is five inches. Bottles of this kind were used by the ancient shepherds, and especially by the pilgrims who trudged their way

" To Wynsore, to Waltam,
  To Ely, to Caultam,
  Bare footed and bare legged apace,"

STONEY, OR HAROLD'S BRIDGE.—This bridge is situated a short distance from the Abbey Gateway, in the *Abbey Fields*

(Northlands), and spans the Cornmill Stream, which is of contemporary date with the Church. Its arch is eighteen feet wide and contains now only three ribs. These ribs are broad and chamfered, the joggles being bound together with lead. The parapet and face of the bridge are quite gone, and in a few years the whole of this relic of the past will probably disappear. In the summer season the brown grass shows the ancient roadways from this bridge leading to the Abbey Farm, where once stood the ancient *Tithe Barn*. There are still remaining a few fragments of stonework in the outhouses north of the Abbey House.

THE WHIPPING POST, 1598.—This instrument of torture, which stands opposite the Church (west) is not now exhibited *in terrorem* but *in memoriam* of the old-fashioned mode of punishment in this town. This *post* or stocks stand five feet nine inches high, made of oak neatly carved with iron clasps for hands and feet, the seat for the culprit was beside an oak pillar of the old *Market House*, which was destroyed in 1852. The old pillory, newly erected by the side of the ancient whipping post, is not to be used as originally intended, for the punishment of petty offenders, who were not only subject to have their heads, arms, and legs fixed, while their goods and chattels were burnt before their eyes, but to have their ears cut off and noses slit. Lady offenders, *i.e.*, "scolds," were more tenderly dealt with. They were placed on the high step or stand of the pillory, bound hand and foot, and with a *brank* (or gag, *parughe*) over their jaws. Only part of the pillory now exists, and which for many years was preserved in the upper room of the Old Market House. The pillory consists of an upright oak post fourteen feet high, with its fixed lower crossbar measuring five feet six inches, and hollowed out for the heads and hands of two individuals. The platform or stand for the unfortunate offenders is now gone. The Old White Horse Inn, Sun-street, and the row of five houses opposite the Harp Inn in the Market Square were destroyed—two in May, 1864, and the other three in 1865. These houses were purchased by the parish with the interest of money received from the sale of the property in Edmonsey to the Government.

In the OLD MARKET HOUSE were preserved for many years the *fire-hooks* attached to long poles which were used to pull thatch off the roofs of houses when on fire, also portions of the old *tulip tree.*

THE BAKER'S ENTRY.—In 1846 the *Baker's Entry* was destroyed. This ancient building stood near the Milltail Stream, S.W. of the Church, on the way to PARADISE ROW and the GREEN-YARD.* The upper storey of this house projected over a broad public footpath, which was arcaded on the side next to the road and a few feet from the river, with wide open pointed arches of oak arranged in three pairs, standing on a breast-high wall; the pairs were divided by larger piers with corbels supporting three high projecting gables; the southernmost gable with its pair of arches, returned at a slight angle from the face line towards the building. Within the house there was a great deal of wood-carving, and when the place was pulled down there was dis-covered under the plaster a small oak-frame window of good work; and the oaken lintel of a pointed arch doorway with 𝔍𝔫 𝔇𝔬𝔪𝔦𝔫𝔬 + 𝔠𝔬𝔫𝔣𝔦𝔡𝔬 carved in relief within the spandrels, the letters diminishing in length towards the centre.† The Bakery was built in character with the rest of the house, having carved wood-work around, and on the wall were the following lines painted :—

> " Remember man that thou art made of dust ;
> And in this life thou hast not long to trust ;
> Then lead thy life while Health to thee is given,
> That being dead, thy Soul may go to Heaven."

The ancient oven was used until the place was destroyed. Originally the upper rooms rose to the roof; they were afterwards ceiled throughout. When the ceiling was broken through there was found on the walls a portion of a painting representing a naval engagement, also an ancient wheel for drawing up flour from below, which determines the place to have been a Bakery, no doubt belonging to the Abbey. A small tile was also found on which was a seal of Flemish order, of the 14th century. This Bakery was near Bethel Chapel, in Church Street.

---

* The old Workhouse and Garden were situated up the "Backway." This house was first used for the poor of the parish in 1734. It has since been destroyed.

† This old lintel appears, at the present day, above the doorway attached to Paradise Chapel Manse.

PARADISE ROW is south of the Bakers' Entry. The principal thing of note there is the Baptist Chapel, erected in 1836, on the site of the original chapel, built in 1729, for John Arthur, its first pastor.

South-east of the chapel is FOUNTAIN SQUARE (or PLACE). In December, 1870, a pump was inserted in the centre of this square, where the old fountain so long flowed, and near to which is another chapel called "Ebenezer," and of which the author is the pastor. The chapel was built in 1868 and enlarged in 1879. Contiguous to this Chapel is MEAD LANE, anciently called "BLACK BOY ALLEY," from the sign of the "Black Boy" beerhouse in the lane. This lane leads to the sewage works in Town Mead. In Paradise Row was once a passage* leading to the GREEN YARD, through which was a right of way to *Enfield Lock*, but which has long since been cut off. At the entrance of this yard was THE OLD CAGE, well-known, in the days of the *Charlies* and Bow Street Runners. This ancient order of watchmen was instituted about the middle of the thirteenth century, and carried on its functions, growing yearly more feeble and inefficient, until, in 1829. The "Charlies," as they were termed, found themselves superseded by the police, organised by Sir Robert Peel. The only qualifications necessary for the post of those midnight guardians would appear to have been extreme old age and general incapacity. They suffered many things at the hands of the young "bucks" of the town. A watchman found dozing in his box in the intervals of going his round to utter his monotonous cry, was apt to be overturned, box and, all, and left to kick and struggle helplessly until assistance arrived. Or he would be kindly offered a dram to keep him awake, and this dram being drugged, quickly sank him into deeper sleep than before, in which state "Charley" and his box, being transferred to a truck, were forthwith trundled into another quarter of the town, and he left to awake at leisure.

GREEN YARD.—In the house of Mr. Thompson, there is a splendid specimen of ancient carved work in that style called "Francis First," executed in the early part of the sixteenth century. There are upwards of one hundred panels

---

* The body of a person having been brought for interment through this passage in flood time, determined it to be a free right of way from the Green Yard to Paradise Row.

no two of which are alike. They consist of grotesque animals supporting coats of arms, and in the centre heads of busts ine very variety of costume, which are well worthy of notice. In the reign of Henry VIII. and Queen Elizabeth this style of carved wainscoting was much in vogue in the mansions of the wealthy of our land. Sir Anthony Denny's Mansion, at the Abbey, from which this curious piece of antiquity came, was one of them. Similar ornamental work may be found in a house on the left hand side of the "Ordnance Arms" yard, in High Bridge Street. This house, many years ago, was used for the sale of beer. From certain documents we find an old *outhouse* called " THE CAGE," to be situated in the "Green Dragon" Gateway, Church Street, Waltham Abbey, approximating the rear of the "Three Tuns Inn," and adjoining the premises of Mr. J. Upton, bootmaker, Market Place. This cage belongs to the Lord of the Manor, and was no doubt used by him in days long past as a petty *lock up* for trespassers on his domains.

THE ABBEY CHURCH.

MANY persons who visit the Abbey Church, are moved with feelings of disappointment, when they first glance at the exterior of the building ; but they entertain a better opinion of its antiquity and architectural grandeur, the closer their examinations are. That the existing Church of Waltham contains fragments of Harold's foundation is a fact beyond doubt. The nave is unquestionably his. The north side of the nave and the "herring-bone" work angularly laid in the outer wall of the south east transept indicate great antiquity. According to Freeman the Church was not originally intended for parochial use ; there being no mention made in the charter respecting any congregation ever being present as in the general services of to-day. Congregational worship was then altogether secondary and subordinate, almost accidental. At the dissolution part of the

Church which belonged to the Abbey was pulled down, but the parochial part remained untouched, and the central tower was allowed to remain till 1552.

THE ABBEY CHURCH BELLS.—There were bells in the original tower long before the Reformation. This tower stood in the centre of what was then a cross-shaped building; and just above the "Rose" window. At the east end of the exterior of the Church are the remains of the spring of one of the main arches upon which rested the ancient tower. This tower was struck by lightning in the year 1444 and much damaged.* The old tower fell in 1552. Strype says "February 9th, 1552, between the hours of seven and eight of the clock in the evening the great steeple of Waltham Abbey, in Essex, fell down to the ground and all the great bells; and the choir and much of that stately church demolished with it."† The bells from the fallen steeple were placed in the churchyard between two yew trees during the time the present steeple was in course of erection, which was finished in 1556, or as some writers affirm, in 1558, and which stands 86 feet high from the ground to the parapet. The whole cost of the erection of this tower in 1558 was £169 17s. 8d., and in 1798 the tower was restored at a cost of nearly £2,000, one-half of which was raised by a general rate of 1s. in the £. An original tablet, about a foot square and bearing date 1558, appears over the western doorway, but the inscription is now obliterated. The tower contains a peal of eight bells, which were cast at Hertford, by John Brian, in 1806, and whose name, with the date of casting, appears in relief on each bell. In 1656 a treble bell was purchased by the voluntary contributions of the "maids and bachelors" of the parish of Waltham, and which amounted to £13 12s. 8d. On the 27th February of the same year (1656) a rate was made in order to purchase a "great bell," and by June 14th, 1656, the churchwardens had collected for that purpose £36 4s. In 1735 there were six bells in the tower, and which chimed every four hours—at four, eight, and twelve. These chimes were given by the Earl of Carlisle, and cost

* Ingulph's Chronicles, p. 402.

† E. A. Freeman thinks that the Norman Church was originally designed to have three towers, but that the two western ones were never finished. This he considers to be apparent from the appearance of the present building.

£42 10s. 6d. In 1735 the great bell rang, from Michaelmas to
Lady-day, at four o'clock in the morning to call the apprentices
up to their work, and again in the evening at eight for them to
leave work.   There are several boards in the belfry containing
bell news.   The first peal on the present set was rung on Sunday,
July 20th, 1806.   The boards are arranged thus :—

No. I. BOARD.—Waltham Abbey, Sunday, July 20th, 1806, the
Society of Cumberland Youths rang in this steeple a complete
peal of Treble Bob, 8 in, consisting of 5,056 changes, in 3
hours and 16 minutes, containing 15 courses, with the 6th 12
times wrong and 12 times right, being the first peal on those bells
performed by the following persons :—Geo. Cross, 1st ; Joh.
Hints, 2nd ; James Nash, 3rd ; Malachi Channon, 4th ; Tho.
Freeth, 5th ; Jas. Stichbury, 6th ; Will. Shipway, 7th ; James
Marlton, 8th.   Composed and called by Mr. G. Cross.—John
Pain, John Smith, and Rich. Banks, churchwardens.

No. II. BOARD.—Waltham Abbey Youths, Monday, June 15th,
1819, rang in this steeple Mr. Shipway's 5th part peal of Bob
Major, etc.

No. III. BOARD.—Waltham Abbey Youths, Monday, September
27th, 1819, rang in this steeple a true and complete peal of
Grandsire Triples, etc.

No. IV. BOARD.—Tuesday, 23rd day of October, 1860,
members of the Cumberland Society rang a true peal of Triples
on Steadman's principle, etc.

No. V. BOARD.—On Saturday, October 29th, 1864, eight
members of the Ancient Society of College Youths rang in this
steeple a complete peal of Kent Treble Bob Major, etc.

No. VI. BOARD.—January 7th, 1865, eight men of the above
society rang upon these bells Mr. John Holt's one-part peal of
Grandsire Triples, etc.

No. VII. BOARD.—*Ancient Society of College Youths.*—On
Tuesday, October 19th, 1875, was rung in this steeple, Mr Holt's
ten part peal of Grandsire Triples, etc.

No. VIII. BOARD.—*Waltham Abbey Society of Change
Ringers.*—November 10th, 1877, eight of the above Society rang
Mr. Thomas Day's 6th part peal of Grandsire Triples, etc.

No. IX. BOARD.—August 17th, 1878, eight of the above Society rang Mr. E. Taylor's 6th part peal of Grandsire Triples, e:c.

No. X. BOARD.—*Waltham Abbey Society of Change Ringers.* —On Monday, February 3rd, 1879, eight of the above Society rang Brooks's variation of Mr Thurstan's peal of Stedman's Triples in three hours.

BENEFACTIONS TO THE PARISH OF WALTHAM HOLY CROSS, A.D. 1830.—(From the boards in the porch of the Abbey Church corrected by original documents.)—The ecclesiastical benefice of this Church is a perpetual curacy, being a donative in the gift of Trustees under the will of the Earl of Norwich, who gave a Messuage (*for the Habitation*) ten loads of firewood (*for fuelling*) and a rent charge of £100 a year payable out of the Manor or Farm of Claveringbury "*for the Perpetual Supportation and Maintenance* of such Minister and Preacher as should officiate the cure, celebrate Divine Service, administer the Sacraments, and preach the Word of God sincerely within the Parish Church of Waltham Holy Cross."*

PAROCHIAL FEES.—The duties or fees payable in respect of the soil and building of this Church and the soil of the Church-yard are payable to the Churchwardens in trust for the parish.

CHURCH ESTATES.—The estates particularized below are vested in trustees "for repairing and maintaining the Church" and (conformably to ancient usuage) the rents and profits are received by the Churchwardens and applied accordingly, and an account thereof is laid annually before the parishioners in vestry assembled.

A.D. 1579.—Margary Gidney of London widow, gave 20s a year (payable at Christmas) to poor inhabitants of the parish or of the Hamlet of Sewardstone, and also gave 20s a year (payable at Whitsuntide) for repairing the highways principally decayed in Sewardstone.—Charged on premises at Sewardstone, in the occupation of Mr. Jn. Josh. Buttress, the property of R. C. Bazett, Esq.

---

* In 1868 the church rate was abolished, and the offertory after each church service was commenced on the 11th October, 1868. The first day's collection realised £7 13s 2½d.

A.D. 1585.—Robert Rampston of Chingford Essex gentleman gave 40s a year payable in November to the poor of this parish.—Charged on lands at Dunnmow, the property of Lord Vist. Maynard.

A.D. 1587.—Robert Browne formerly of this parish, one of the Servants of Queen Elizabeth, gave 30s a year (payable at Lady Day) to the poor people of the town of Waltham to be laid out in bread.—Charged on a messuage, etc., now the Cock Inn, in this town, the property of Messrs. Christie and Cathrow.

A.D. 1597.—Robert Catrow formerly of this parish gave to the poor 20s. a year for ever to be laid out in bread.—Charged on three houses in High Bridge Street, the property of the trustees of Mrs. Soane and Mr. H. Mason.

A.D. 1597.—Robert Dane gave 10s a year (payable at Lady Day) to the poor of this parish to be laid out in bread.—Charged on a house in Sewardstone Street, belonging to the trustees of the Wesleyan Chapel.

A.D. 1616. -Henry Wollaston of St Martin Orgars London draper, gave 52s. a year (payable at Lady Day) to the poor of this parish, 12d. to be laid out every Sunday in bread.—Charged on lands called Fishers, alias Salmons, situate at Holyfield, in the occupation of Mr. Green, the property of the trustees of Fuller's Charity (in London).

A.D. 1626.— Green purveyor to King James the First gave four alms houses in West Street for the residence of four widows. Also the rents and profits of the barn and orchard at the back of the alms houses towards their maintenande.—This barn and orchard are let to Mr. Wm. Clark at £20 pr annum, payable quarterly.

A.D. 1691.—George Waylett Junr of London fishmonger gave 40s. a year for ever (payable at Lady Day) to the poor of this parish to be disposed of half-yearly by the Minister and Churchwardens among the most necessitous and poorest persons as their discretion shall direct.—Charged on lands at Yardley, in Hertfordshire, in the occupation of Josh Young, the property of Robert Pryor, Esq., of Baldock.

A.D. 1807.—Robert Mason formerly of this parish gave £800 Stock in the then 5 Pr Cent Navy Annuities by means whereof the above four alms houses were re-built and four additional rooms for four more widows added thereto.—These four widows receive a weekly payment, also from the next bequest of Mr. M. Woollard.

A.D. 1708.—Robert Grubb formerly of Holyfield, gave 40s a year for ever (payable at Lady Day) to the poor of this parish, to be laid out in bread to be given in the Church.—Charged on lands in Holyfield in the occupation of Mr Dyson, the property of Newell Connop, Esq.

A.D. 1708.—John Edmonson Esqre * formerly of this parish gave to the Churchwardens and Overseers of the Poor the rents etc. of a granary and garden opposite the Cock Inn in this town for the purpose of teaching four poor children to read.—This property is now in the occupation of Samuel Kennerly, Widow Oakley, and the Exec$^{rs.}$ of Mr. George Fawbert, at rents amounting to £18 per annum.

A.D. 1814.—John Halfhide Esqr late of this parish gave £200 Stock in the then Navy 5 Pr Cent Annuities, the dividends to be applied as follows, viz., one moiety for the benefit of the Sunday School at Waltham Abbey and one moiety to be distributed among the poor widows receiving pensions from this parish on the 19th day of January in every year.—This Stock stands in the name of the Churchwardens and Vestry Clerk.

A.D. 1825.—Miss Jane Dobson late of Mary Street St Pancras Midd^x gave £500 Stock in the South Sea Annuities for the benefit of the poor of this parish who actually reside at Waltham Abbey the dividends whereof are directed to be paid and dis׳ tributed by the Clergyman and Churchwardens on or about the 29th October yearly.—This Stock stands in the name of the Rev. Morgan Whalley, perpetual curate of this parish.

A.D. 1826.—Mowbray Woollard late of this town, gardener, gave the sum of £1350 and directed the annual interest thereof to be applied as follows, namely 2s 6d weekly to each of the four widows occupying the four upper rooms which were added to Green's Alms Houses and 1s. apiece weekly to five poor men and five poor women inhabitants of the Workhouse for providing

---

* Arabella Jones, of this parish, gave messuages and lands bearing date March, 1756. This charity is not given on the boards in the Church porch. It is called in the Charity Commissoners' reports " The Charity of Jones and Edmonson."

themselves with any little comfort not allowed in the Workhouse. —This legacy is invested in the New 4 Pr Cent. Annuities in the names of the surviving trustees named in Mr. M. Woollard's will.

A.D. 1839.—Mary Woollard late of this town, widow of Mowbray Woollard gave £800 new three-and-a-half Pr Cent. Annuties to four Trustees and directed that the annual interest thereof should be applied as follows viz. : £20 pr annum to be expended in bread and distributed amongst such poor inhabitants of this parish (being settled parishioners) as such trustees shall think deserving.   The residue of the said interest (after paying contingencies) to be distributed annually in money clothing or otherwise among such poor and deserving inhabitants of this town (being settled parishioners) as such trustees shall think fit. —This Stock is invested in the names of the four Trustees named in the will of the said Mary Woollard.

Certain lands lying at *Copthall Green* called *Sherris* and other lands at *Woolmonsey Bridge* with two tenements in Elford Street [Sewardstone Street] all let formerly at £29 10s. od. a year now at 30 pounds vested in trustees for the sole repair of the Church. *Margery Gidney* of *London* widow 4th *May* 1579 gave to the poor of this parish 20 shillings a year for ever payable at *Christmas* and 20 shillings for repairing yᵉ highways in the Hamlet of *Sewardstone* payable at *Whitsuntide* both out of a house and land situate in the said hamlet.   *Robert Rampston* of *Chingford* gent by his will *anno* 1585 gave to the poor of this parish 40 shillings a year for ever payable in *November* out of lands of his lying at Dunmow in this county.   *Robert Brown* formerly of this parish and servant to Queen *Elizabeth* of happy memory by his will *anno* 1587 gave to the poor 30 shillings a year for ever payahle out of the Cock Inn in this town.   *Robert Catrow* formerly of· this parish by his will 23 April 1597 gave to the poor 20 shillings a year for ever to be laid out in bread payable out of three houses in West Street in this town.   *Robert Dane* gave 10 shillings a year for ever to the poor of this parish to be laid out in bread payable out of a house in Elford Street. *Henry Wollaston* gent of *St Martin Orgars, London* draper by his will in November 1616 gave to the poor of this parish £2 12s. od. a year for ever to be laid out in bread 12d. every Sunday payable out of his lands called *Fishers*, alias *Salmons*,

lying at *Holyfield.* . . . . *Green*, purveyor to King *James*
the first gave *anno* 1626 four almshouses for four widows with
an orchard and barn adjoining, situate in *West Street* [High
Bridge Street] let at four pounds a year and payable to the said
four widows. *George Waylett* jun^r citizen and fishmonger of
London by his will the 23rd of May 1691 gave 40s. a year for
ever to the poor of this parish payable out of several lands and
tenements situate near *Yardley* in *Hertfordshire* which he
purchased of *John Adkins.* *Robert Grub* of *Holyfield* yeoman
by his will in May 1708 gave 40 shillings a year for ever to the
poor to be laid out in bread.—*Thomas Winspeare*, *William
Goar, jun^r., William Pigbone, jun^r., Churchwardens*, 1744.

THE "LEVERTON" BENEFACTIONS, A.D. 1819.— Thomas
Leverton Esq. of Bedford Square, London, in his lifetime
presented the organ to this parish and erected the same at his
sole expense.

A.D. 1823.—The said Thomas Leverton by his will gave
£6,000 stock in the three per cent. consolidated annuities upon
trust to apply the dividends after the decease of his widow as
follows, viz. :—£80 per annum for educating and clothing twenty
boys and twenty girls ; £10 per annum for books and stationery
to the schools ; £30 per annum to the master for teaching reading writing and arithmetic ; £20 per annum to the mistress for
teaching reading and needlework ; £10 per annum (viz. £5 to
each) to two boys or girls for apprentice fees ; £5 per annum
(viz. £1 to each) to five children as a reward for good behaviour
in their first servitude ; £12 per annum (viz. £1 to each) for a
cloak and gown for six poor women and for a coat for six poor
men ; £5 per annum to be expended in bread every Christmas
Day and given to the poor ; £3 per annum for keeping his
monuments in repair ; £5 per annum for contingencies—£180
per annum.

A.D. 1824 and 1827.—Mrs. Rebecca Leverton widow of
Thomas Leverton Esq. in her life time of her own free bounty commenced the establishment of these schools upon the plan
intended by her deceased husband (but with a limited number)
and fifteen poor boys and ten poor girls are now educated and
clothed at her sole charge at the School House called the
"Leverton School."

A.D. 1824.—The executors of Mr. George Fawbert, formerly of this parish under a bequest of the residue of his estate to them to distribute in such charities as they might think proper, "applied a part thereof in the purchase of a messuage etc. at the corner of High Bridge Street opposite to the West entrance of the church which they pulled down and erected on the scite thereof a School House for the children to be educated by means of the Leverton Donations and the same is now called the 'Leverton School'" By order of the Vestry, 1830. *

The rents, according to the last account of the churchwardens, are as follows, viz.:—Mr Joseph Harding for three closes of

* THE LEVERTON CHARITY.—The following is an extract from the will of the late Thomas Leverton, Esq. The will is dated 21st February, 1823, and in it are the following words :—" I do hereby give and bequeath to the Reverend William Whalley, the incumbent of the Parish Church of Waltham Abbey, Holy Cross, Essex, and to the Reverend Thomas Pickthall, his curate, and to William Sotheby, William Banbury, Edward Burgess and Robert Chalmers, Esquires, Thomas Augustus Jessopp, Joseph Jessopp and Henry Jessopp, Esquires, and also the occupier of my freehold house at Sewardstone for the time being, and their successors, trustees for the time being, to be appointed as hereafter mentioned, the sum of six thousand three per cent. consolidated bank annuities, to be vested for ever upon the trust, to lay out and pay the interest dividends thereof from time to time in the following manner:—First, I direct that there shall be twenty boys and twenty girls elected from the poor of the said parish, to be educated and clothed at two pounds per annum each child, which is six shillings each beyond what is expended on the charity children of St. Giles's-in-the-Fields ; that there shall be allowed for books and stationery in the schools the sum of ten pounds per annum ; that the master shall be allowed for teaching reading, writing, and common arithmetic thirty pounds per annum ; that the mistress shall teach reading, plain needle and useful house work, and have twenty pounds per annum ; that there shall be apprentice fees given to two boys or girls in each year of five pounds each ; that there shall be given to five of the children one pound each who shall have behaved well in their first servitude ; these two last sums need not be paid for six or seven years after forming the schools, and may, if the trustees think fit, accumulate, and the interest arising therefrom add something to the cloathing or benefit of the schools. I direct that some able housekeeper of the parish, the curate (in preference) if he chooses, shall undertake the teaching of the boys in his own house, or such other place as the trustees may approve, and that a competent female house-keeper in the parish shall, in her own house or such other place as the trustees may approve, instruct the girls ; ten of the elder of these are to be taught writing in succession. The said master or mistress are not to take any other scholar or scholars. The children are to be dressed in one uniform and colour, say dark green, and are always to appear at church and school neat and clean, or to be expelled, and they are to attend Divine service with their

meadow land situate at Copthall Green containing 11a. or. 11p. pays £33 2s. ; Mr. Thos. Ricketts for a close of meadow land situate at Paternoster Hill contg 6a. 2r. 24p. pays £25 ; Mr. Joseph Luck for a close of meadow land adjoining Brick Hill Comn Field cont 2a. 3r. 20p. pays £10 10s. ; Mr. John Martin for a piece of arable land in Brick Hill Comn Field contg 2a. 2r. 32p. pays £5 5s.—23a. 1r. 7p. Mr. Daniel Paul for a dwelling house situate in Sewardstone Street in this town, £9 9s.; Mr John Watts for a dwelling house situate do. do., £8 8s ; the total amount of the present annual rents being £91 14s.—By order of Vestry, Iohn Pain, Iohn Gray, Willm Kent Thomas, Churchwardens.*

---

master and mistress whenever it is performed in the parish church. I also direct that the trustees shall expend every Christmas twelve pounds in a cloak and gown, to be given to six poor women, and a coat and underdress, to six poor men, of the same colour as the children of one pound each. I also desire that five pounds may be expended in bread every Christmas Day and given to the poor, and I desire that three pounds per annum may be expended, or reserved, to keep my monument in the church or churchyard in neat and good order, and the surplus of five pounds per annum, which will remain after answering the purposes aforesaid, to be kept by the trustees for contingencies ; the master and mistress to be chosen and re-elected by the trustees every year ; and then I will and direct that in the case of the number of trustees shall by death or removal be reduced to six, then those six shall elect other persons to fill the place of those removed, and shall transfer the stock into their names with their own, or into so many of their names as the rules of the bank will admit. I desire that an annual meeting of the trustees shall be held in the vestry-room of the said parish to audit the accounts of whoever may be appointed treasurer, at which meeting I will and direct that so much of my will as relates to the parish of Waltham Abbey *shall be read over publickly that the extent of the donations may be known.*"

* CHARITY COMMISSIONERS—SALE OF LAND AT WALTHAM ABBEY.— In the matter of the charity called William Berman's Trust, for the benefit of poor ministers and for other charitable purposes, in direction of the Board of Charity Commissioners for England and Wales : Notice is hereby given, that the following property of the above-mentioned charity, viz., several pieces of arable and pasture land, containing together 43 acres or thereabouts, situated in the tithings of Sewardstone and Upshire, in the parish of Waltham Abbey, now leased to Mr. Peter Mills for a term of 21 years from Michaelmas, 1873, is proposed to be sold by the trustees thereof, with the sanction of the said Board, for the sum of £3,000 sterling, to the said Mr. Mills, he paying the expenses of and incidental to the sale, unless some sufficient objection to the sale, whether having reference to the sufficiency of the price or to any other reasons, shall be made known to the said Commissioners within 21 days from the first publication of this notice.—Dated 15th day of June, 1874.

THE LEGEND OF THE HOLY CROSS.

HE legend of the Holy Cross states that several of the little band of husbandmen (sixty-six in number) which formed the nucleus of what now constitutes the populous parish of Waltham Holy Cross had been healed of various bodily diseases by the wonder-working cross, (?) the subject of the war song on the field of *Senlac* when Harold lost his life.* This cross gave the title of "Holy Cross" to the parish, and not the "Eleanor Cross." Relative to this miraculous crucifix, which, as the legend goes, had been found at Lutegarsbury, a place owned by Tovi, Leland says:—"I redde in the boke of the antiquities of Glessenbyri that this town was caullid in the Saxon tyme Logaresburch,"† now known as Montacute, in Somersetshire. With regard to ascertaining the date of the discovery of the cross there is some little difficulty. The writer of the *De Inventione Sanctæ Crucis* considers it to have taken place before the death of Cnut, in 1041-2. However, there may have been an elapse of time between the discovery and the translation, or between the translation and the decoration of the cross by Gÿitha. She "presented a splendid golden and jewelled crown, besides the circlet which she wore in common with all noble women, which was fixed round the thigh of the image, while her bracelets and other jewels were fashioned into a subpedaneum, into which was inserted a wondrous stone, which was to emit rays during the night, and thus afford light to travellers." Tovi, her husband, enriched the church with various gifts of gold and silver. The cross was adorned with the figure of our Saviour upon it, which, after it was transferred to Waltham, gave a name to the place. The legend of the cross ‡ was written in the twelfth century, and is preserved among the Waltham MSS. It was first Englished by Lambarde, a trustworthy writer of the sixteenth century, who gives it thus :—"It might have sufficed to

---

* Harold did not journey from his *Park* at Waltham to Hastings, as tradition states, but from the church here.—See Bayoux Tapestry.

† *Vide* Itinerary, vol. ii., p. 52.

‡ William Burges, Esq., architect, published the "Legend of Waltham Abbey" in 1860, and Bishop Stubbs gave a transcript of it, with introduction and notes, in 1861.

derive the Foundation of Waltham in Essex from Kinge Harold, as Polyd. (followinge Mat of Westminster) and others have before done. But for as much as not only thabbay, but the towne also toke bothe their Beginninge and Increase by a holy Crosse that was muche renowned theare, the hole Discourse of the findinge whereof I have penned by a Canon of Waltham sone after the Tyme of the Conquest, I feared I should do Waltham wronge, and defraude the Reader, if I should not begin at the Roate."

THE LEGEND.—In the Tyme that Kinge Canut reigned in Ingland, theare lyved at a Place called Comonly Lutegaresbyry, in French Mountague,* a simple man by occupation a Carpenter† and by Office Sexton of his parishe‡ to whom on a Night appeared a Vision of Christe Crucified Commaundinge him that as sone as Day brake he should goe to the Parishe Priest, and will him, accompanied by his parishioners in solemne Procession, to go up to the Toppe of the Hyll adjoyninge, and to digge, wheare (if they would beforehand make theimselves by Confession, Fastinge, and Praier, worthy of suche a Revelacion) they should finde a Crosse, the very Signe of Christes Passion. This Plaine Man, Supposinge it a fantastical Dreame, toke at first no great Head therof, save that he imparted it with his Wife, who also thoughte it but an Illusion. Wherfore the Image appeared againe, and so griped him by the Hande that the Dynt of the Nayles remayned in his Hand to be sene the Daye followinge. Beinge thus pricked forwarde on he goeth to the Priest and discloseth the hole matter : He arrayeth his Parishe, displayeth his Banners, putteth on Copes and Surplas, and setteth the Carpenter foremost, as his Captaine,§ they digge awhile ‖ and anone they find a great Marble,¶ havinge in it of black Flynt ** the Image of the Crucifixe so artificially

---

* The top of the peaked hill from which the place in later times derived the name of Montacute.

† W. Burges in his account of the legend states that the man was a "smith."

‡ He had committed to his care "the water, fire, and lighting of the church."

§ "Signing litanies." ‖ To the depth of forty cubits.

¶ It had a great fissure through the middle of it.

** In the south buttress of the tower of Waltham Church will be seen a flint cross inserted *temp* Philip and Mary.

wrought, as if God himselfe (sayth myne Author) had framed it.
Under the right Arme of this Crucifixe thear was a small Image
of the same Forme, a litle Belle * also, and a blacke Booke †
conteyninge the Text of the four Evangelists. All this they
signified to Tovi le Prude then Lorde of the Soyle, Standard
Bearer to the Kinge and his Chief Councelor ; who came to the
place in great Hast, and by thadvice of his Gents,‡ lefte the
smalle cross in the Churche theare determyninge to bestow the
greater in suche Place as God should appointe. Forthwithe
therefore he caused to be yoked 12 red Oxen and so many white
Kyne,§ and layeth the Stone in a Wayne, ‖ myning (if God so
wille) to cary it to Canterbyrye ; but the Cattle could not by any
Force be compelled to draw thytherwarde. When he saw that,
he chaunged his Mynde and bad theim dryve toward his House
at Readinge whearin he had great Delighte ; but still the Wayne
stode immoveable, notwithstandinge that the Oxen did their best.
At the Lengthe he remembred a smalle House that he had
begone to buyld at Waltham for his Disporte, and comaunded
theim to make thytherward. Which Words he had no soner
spoken, but the Wayne of itselfe moved. Now in the way many
weare healed of many Infirmities ; amongste the which threscore
sixe Parsons ¶ vowed their labour towarde the Conveiance of
this Crosse and weare the first Founders of Waltham Towne
wheare was nothinge before but only a simple House for this
Tovi to repose himself at when he came thyther to hunte, notwithstandinge that he had thereby divers Landes, as *Enfield,
Edelmetun, Cetrehunt, Myms*, and the hole Baronie that Goffrey
of Maundville, the first of that Name had. Now when the
Crosse was broughte thyther, Tovi commaunded it to be set up,
and whiles one by Chaunce Perced it with a Nayle,** the Blood
issued out of the Flinte in great Abundance. Wherat Tovi
beinge greatly amazed, fel downe and worshipped it, promiseth
before it to manumitte †† his Bondmen, to bestow possession on

---

* Under the left arm a bell was found, not unlike those seen round the
necks of cattle. A small bell of this kind was discovered in a small vase in
a Gallo-Roman cemetery not long since. See *Gent. Mag.* Dec. 1859.

† This book may have been the Saxon Gospels.

‡ " Church dignitaries both episcopal and abbatical."

§ Cows.   ‖ A waggon.

¶ Persons.

** For the purpose of fastening on the jewelled ornaments given by Tovi.

†† To make free : *manumittere.*

such as should serve it." * The MSS. which contain this legend
will be found in the Harleian 3776, and Jul. D. VI. Cottonian
Library, British Museum. The Crucifix † eventually became the
war-cry of the English ; on the field of *Senlac ;* Harold's war-cry
was " Holy Rood." The Holy Rood of Waltham became an
object of popular worship and pilgrimage. In a " Booke
intituled the fantasie of Idolatrie," occurs about fifty verses of six
lines each on idolatrous pilgrimage and Waltham is named as a
place of resort for pilgrims who walked—

> " Bare foted and bare legged apace."

KING EDWARD THE CONFESSOR'S GIFT TO HAROLD.—The
original endowment of Waltham appears somewhat insignificant
when compared with the Confessor's rich foundation at Westminster.‡ Yet, had this monarch's life been prolonged, he would
have doubtless carried out his good intentions respecting
Waltham, and have bestowed even greater gifts upon the Abbey
than he had already done. Mr Poole in his history of
Ecclesiastical Architecture supposes that King Edward the Confessor granted his lands at Waltham to Harold on " condition of
his building a monastery on the spot." This Mr Freeman justly
disputes, and considers " the foundation of the *College* of
Waltham to have been the spontaneous act of the Earl's own
piety and munificence." The charter of Edward the Confessor
states that the King " found the church of the *Vill* to have been
endowed from old time ; and after the foundation of the
monastery, he caused it to be dedicated according to the King
and his wife Editha,§ and his father and mother and all

---

* With reference to the Legend of the Cross one is reminded of the words
of Cotgrave on " Superstition," that it is " excess of scruple or ceremony in
matters of religion ; idle worship, vain reverence, a superfluous, needless, or
ill-governed devotion," See Holland's " Pliny," b. xxvi. c. 4.

† " In 1192 the cross was covered with silver, but the ornaments on the figure
itself were left untouched, probably in consequence of what had happened a
few years before, when, the crucifix being under repair, Robert, the goldsmith
of St. Albans, took off the circle round the thigh, and all those present were
struck blind for some considerable time !"

‡ Earl Harold's College at Waltham stands in distinct opposition—almost
in distinct rivalry—to King Edward's Abbey at Westminster. *Vide* " Norman
Conquest," vol. ii. p. 442.

§ The restoration of the Saxon line was chiefly owing to Godwine, whose
daughter the Confessor married. The chastity of Editha, and the cruelty of
her father, gave rise to the proverb, " Sicut spina rosam, genuit Godwinus

relations, and enriched the same with many relics of saints, apostles, martyrs, confessors and virgins, and not only with lands whose names are afterwards recited, but also with gospel books, vestments, and divers kind of ornaments ; and, moreover, he found there an assembly of brethren living according to the canonical rule of the fathers, whose office it was by day and by night to sing to the praise of God and his saints."* In Kemble's "Codex Diplom. Ævi Saxonici" (Tom. IV. p. 203) will be found a grant of Edward the Confessor respecting land in Waltham in Saxon characters..

The lordship of Waltham stands prominent among Tovi's great possessions, which, in course of time, came into the hands of his son Æthelstan,† but the excellent qualifications of the father, as is frequently the case, were not inherited by the son : "Æthelstan degenerated from his father's virtues, and lost á great part of his wealth, including Waltham." But whatever he lost the Crown by some means gained, as we find by Edward's gift to Harold, the great temporal lord of Waltham, and ecclesiastical benefactor. The great convent seal, preserved in the British Museum, contains on the reverse two heads looking at each other, crowned with this circumscription : HOC CARTE FEDUS CUM TOVI FIRMAT HAROLD. This is no doubt a figure of the two great contemporary earls,

---

Editham." " King Edward was absolutely father-in-law-ridden," says Fuller. " This Godwin, like those sands in Kent which bear his name, never spared what he could spoil, but swallowed all which came within his compass to devour.

* Among other rich gifts Harold bestowed on his new college of Waltham were seven little caskets or boxes (*scrinia*) for precious things—three of gold and four of silver gilded, enriched with gems and full of relics ; four great *thuribles* (censers) of gold and silver ; six great candlesticks, and four of silver ; three large vessels or pitchers of Greek workmanship, silver and richly gilded ; four crosses of gold and silver, studded with gems ; another cross of silver, weighing fifty marks ; five suits of the priests, ornamented with gold and precious gems ; five other vestments, ornamented with gold and gems, one extremely rich and weighty ; two copes, covered with gold and gems ; five chalices, two of gold and three of silver ; four altars, with relics, one of gold and three of silver gilded ; a silver horn, and various other articles. The relics were even more valuable and numerous, and, according to the monkish legends, miracles were wrought by them. (See Harl. MSS. 3776.)

† He was a son of Tovi by former marriage (Stubbs). In my History of Waltham, with MSS. notes by Sir H. Ellis, it is stated that " Elicha the wife Tovy was likewise a benefactress there." (Winters.)

Tovi and Harold. On the obverse is, HOC . . . . GILL ECCLESIE . SANCTE . CRVCIS DE WALTHAM. It appears that Tovi was on one occasion sent to attend a *sciryemot* at Hertford, held by Bishop Æthelstan and Earl Ranig, the account of which, though not illustrating the life or character of Tovi, gives us one of the most glowing pictures of old English jurisprudence. Tovi or Tofig's surname was needed to distinguish him from his two namesakes, Tovi Hwita and Tovi Reda, who signed documents in 1024.*

Tovi the *thane* is said to have been inseparably connected with the memory of the old Danish king Hardicanute. A circumstance in conjunction with this monarch is worthy of a niche here. On the seventh day of the Ides of June (8th), 1042, the marriage of the Danish Thegn Tovi, or Tofig the Proud, with Gytha,† the daughter of Osgod Clapa the outlaw,‡ took place (probably at Lambeth). Gytha, or Githa, was Tovi's second wife. At this time he was an elderly man, and seems not to have long survived his marriage,§ so that he very probably erected his little college at Waltham as early as 1042. In 1061 he was sheriff of Somersetshire. Mr. Freeman thinks that the Tofig who signs under Edward, in 1054, and was sheriff of Somersetshire in 1061, must, if Waltham narrative be correct, be a different man. He was a great landowner in several counties in England, as appears from Domesday, and nearly all the charters of King Cnut, from 1018 to 1035, bear his name.

THE BURIAL OF HAROLD.

THE place of sepulture of the last of the Saxon Kings— Harold, is a subject much controverted in the present day, and there are many who appear to be entirely opposed to the most authentic version of the story. The writer has lived many years on the very verge of where history

---

* Hist. Norman Conquest, vol. i. p. 769.

† The De Invent. calls her "Glith, daughter of Osegodi Scalp," but she is called more properly "Githa, daughter of Osgod Clapa." See Florence of Worcester, and De Invent. (Stubbs.)

‡ Outlaw in 1046 and died in 1053.

§ Both Ethelstan the son, and Esegar the grandson of Tovi were at his death useful men in public affairs.

and tradition point as the burial-place of the last of the Saxon kings, and he has long laboured to confirm, from documentary and other sources, the truth of what he firmly maintains—*that Harold was buried at Waltham.* However, some persons have entirely rejected the authority of Malmesbury, Wendover, Matthew of Westminster, Wace, Higden, and a host of other later authors, for the fabulous story which was current in the twelfth century, *i.e.*, that Harold escaped from the field of Senlac, "pierced with many wounds, and with the loss of his left eye; and that he ended his days piously and virtuously as anchorite at Chester."*

William of Malmesbury, says Mr. Freeman, "does not write in the interest of Waltham or of England. He is a thoroughly independent witness; so, I may add, are Wace and his brother minstrels.† The most probable solution seems to be that Harold was first, by William's order, buried under a cairn, on the shore of Sussex, and was afterwards more solemnly interred in the minster at Waltham." Osegod and Ailric,‡ two of the canons of Waltham watched the battle, at Hastings, and searched for the body of Harold, but their efforts were without effect. "The find" was in reserve for Eadgyth Swanneshals (Edith-with-the-swan's-neck), Harold's wife, who readily distinguished the mutilated corpse among the loathsome heaps of the unburied, from certain marks upon it, well known to her. This body, as being that of Harold's, was brought to Waltham, and there entombed at the east end of the choir, with great honour and solemnity, many Norman nobles assisting in the requiem.

Although little dependence as a rule can be placed on the unlimited licence which all poets exercise as regard style and colour of character, yet from the more sober and less

---

* *Giraldus Cambrensis.* (This Mr Freeman calls "a wretched fable.")

† In 1160 Wace having gleaned sufficient from the Bayeux Tapestry finished his masterly chronicle of the Norman Conquest. This is an invaluable record regarding the history of the times and the burial of Harold. He appears to have gathered much information respecting the Conquest from old men, who are said to have seen the comet of 1066.—

> " I have seen and conversed with old men in my time,
> Who beheld the said star ; men in their prime."

‡ Ailric was a childmaister or schoolmaster of the abbey, appointed by Harold.

sentimental accounts already given on the burial of England's great king, there is really good ground for the belief that his remains were interred within the precincts of the church of Waltham, "which he let himself rear." It is possible that during the several alterations which took place in the Abbey Church from the Norman conquest to the accession of King Henry the Second, the body may have been removed from its original position. The writer in the "De Inventione," specifies that the tomb of Harold was near the *high altar*, and "at the translation of whose body for the *third time*, according as the state of the building of the church was such as to admit it, or the devotion of the brethren showing reverence to the body demanded it, I can just remember to have been present myself."*

> "This Kyng Herolde at Waltham, which he found
> Of foure score chanons, full fayer was buryed
> At [the] hye aulter, and as a kyng was crownde,
> All yf he were intrusor notifyed,
> And in batayl slayne and victoryed
> Of gentylnessse and Conquerour had so,
> All yf he were afore his mortal fo."

Historians of the seventeenth and eighteenth centuries have come to the conclusion—on the statement made by Dr. Fuller—that Harold "was buried where now (1655) the Earl of Carlisle's† leaden fountain in his garden, then probably the end of the choir, or rather some eastern chapel beyond it ; his tomb of plain but rich grey marble, with what seemeth a *cross-florée* (but much descanted on with art) upon the same, supported with pillarets, one pedestal whereof I have in my house."‡ There is still preserved in the north aisle of the church a coffin-shaped stone of very early date ; on the centre is a cross in relief, nearly the full length and width of slab. This stone measures six feet nine inches in length, thirteen inches wide at the feet, and much wider at the head; it is not early enough for Harold, although some might suppose it to have been the one described by Fuller. The stone which Fuller says was in "my house," and purporting to to be a portion of Harold's tomb, was lately in the possession of Mr.

---

* "De Inventione Sanctæ Crucis," p. 31 (Stubbs).

† James Hay, who attended James I. from Scotland on his accession to the throne.

‡ "History of Waltham" (Fuller), p. 259.

W. R. Clark, of Waltham Abbey.* Some persons have thought that the fragment of ironstone or Purbeck marble in question is not from Harold's tomb, but simply a part of the Earl's fountain; no doubt it formed an ornamental part of the fountain, but Fuller knew its history too well to suppose that it was carved on purpose for his worthy patron's garden fountain. Mr. Farmer, nearly one hundred years later, says, this fragment "I have now (1735) in my house." It is a "curious face or bust of grey marble which by tradition always was, and is to this day, esteemed to be part of King Harold's tomb. This old townsman (author of "History of Waltham Abbey, etc.), says respecting Harold, "It is without dispute that he was buried in the garden under a leaden fountain, where now there is a bowling-green, which formerly belonged to the Earl of Carlisle.†

Both history and tradition determine the sacred burial place as being about one hundred and twenty feet from the east end of the present church, the place of sepulture of ecclesiastics and men of high repute in the Middle Ages. If in a direct line from the great centre aisle of the church it would suggest the probability of the tomb being near the grave of Mr. Jessop or that of Col. S. C. Edenborough, J.P. All that part of the churchyard on which stood the ancient choir of Harold's church, and now called "the new ground," was evidently used as a garden by the Earl of Carlisle and Sir Edward Denny, *temp.* James I. and Charles I.

THE DISCOVERY OF EARLY MONUMENTAL REMAINS IN THE ABBEY.—According to the account given by Thomas Smith (an old inhabitant of Waltham, who died 16th June, 1604), a stone coffin of considerable antiquity was discovered near the foundations of the Abbey Church late in the sixteenth century. Fuller gives the account as follows :—"The ensuing relation written by the pen of Master Thomas Smith, of Sewardstone, in the parish of Waltham Abbey, a discreet person not long since deceased : 'It so fell out that I served Sir Edward Denny (towards the latter end of the reign of Queen Elizabeth of blessed memory), who lived in the abbey of Waltham Cross, in the county of Essex, which at that time lay in ruinous heaps ; and then Sir Edward began slowly now and then to make even and re-edify some of

---

* This fragment is now in the Robing Room of the Abbey (1887).

† "History of Waltham " (Farmer, 1735, 8vo).

that chaos. In doing whereof Tomkins, his gardener, came to discover (among other things) a fair marble stone, the cover of a tomb hewed out in hard stone. This cover with some help he removed from off the tomb, which having done, there appeared to the view of the gardener and Master Baker,* minister of the town (who died long since), and to myself, and Master Henry Knagg† (Sir Edward's bailiff) the anatomy of a man lying in the tomb abovesaid, only the bones remaining, bone to his bone, not one bone dislocated. In observation whereof we wondered to see the bones stiil remaining in such due order, and no dust or other filth besides them to be seen in the tomb.'"

Farmer considers this coffin to have been that of Harold's, but Gough has done his best to overturn all that has been written respecting the remains of the great Saxon king being discovered at Waltham. A coffin with a cross rather *betoné* was found, 1787, in the north wall of the choir, with a leaden coffin within it.‡

The same writer, speaking of the fragment of stone carving, remarks that " from the particulars of the *cross flueri* one might refer the coffin to an abbot."

In 1786 a coffin of Purbeck marble was discovered in the foundation of the north pillars of the choir. As soon as the lead was opened the corpse, which before was perfectly whole, fell to pieces. The lid of the stone coffin was six inches thick, carved with a cross botoné. The distance at which this coffin lay from the present east wall of the church (the north pillar of the centre tower) is about 260 feet, so that allowing the tower to have been thirty feet square, the length of the choir will have measured 230 feet.

For a century or more after the dissolution of the monastery this ancient piece of stone, said to be King Harold's tomb, served as an ornament in the abbey gardens belonging to the Denny family. Dr. Thomas Fuller possessed it in 1655, and possibly he may have left it in the parsonage-house when he removed from the town. Dr. Uvedale, master of the grammar school at Enfield (in 1670), saw it at "Waltham Mill" (Corn mill) adjoining the Abbey. John Farmer possessed it in 1735,

---

* Curate of Waltham. Died April 24, 1604.
† Buried 21st April, 1646.
‡ Gough's "Funeral Monuments," vol. ii., part i. p. 105.

it was then fixed in the wall of his house on the "Bank," in Highbridge Street.* In 1768 it found its way to the great hall of the old Abbey House. In 1780 Gough tells us that he received it by favour of Sir William Wake, baronet. The fragment, however, more than half a century since found its way back to Waltham Abbey, and was in the possession of Mr. W. R. Clark for upwards of forty years. It has the appearance of dark ironstone, extremely hard, and has suffered from very rough usage at some early period.

Mr. Gough, the antiquary, had another interesting relic belonging to this Abbey, namely, the monumental brass from the tomb of one of the Waltham abbots, but what became of it afterwards is not known.

Within the communion rails is the tomb of an abbot of some antiquity. It was adorned with a fine monumental brass, which has long been missing; probably that possessed by the antiquary Gough is the identical one. Round the verge of this incised slab is an inscription in Lombardic characters, but so worn and disfigured that no one can decipher its meaning. Another stone adjoining it, and partly hid by the rails, bears the following inscription :—" Hic Haroldi in Cœnobio Carnis Resurrectionem. Expectat Jacobus Raphael Gallus Demum Scotus, demum Anglus, Denique nihil. Anno ætat, 70, Obit Mar. 30 Anno 1686." "Here lyeth Mr. Swynefield." The epitaph has been Englished thus—" Here in Harold's tomb, James Raphael ; a Frenchman, claimed both by Scotland and England, but now nothing, awaits the resurrection of body. Died March 30, 1686, in the 70th year of his age."†

There are but few representations of Harold besides those on the Bayeux tapestry and his coins. A portrait of the monarch may be seen in an illuminated MS. Prayer Book, written in England about the eleventh century. It is given in Mountfaucon's " Antiquities," and Ogbourn's Hisotry of Essex. Harold is sitting on his throne, holding in his right hand a military banner, and in his left a sceptre surmounted by a dove. On each side of the throne is a stand, on which lies a book open,

---

* Years ago the Houses in Highbridge Street called the " Bank," stood much higher than the road, and a ditch ran along in front of them.

† The parish register records the burial of James Raphael, April 1st, 1686.

and near each stand or lectern an angel or saint, with his hand elevated, is bestowing the benediction. Dr. Fuller states that a "picture of King Harold in glass was lately to be seen in the north window of the church, till ten years since some barbarous hand beat it down, under the notion of superstition. However, there is still a place called Harold's Park in our parish (of Waltham) by him so denominated." It appears that in 1642 the churchwardens' account-book suffered much by "the soldiers;" a note to the effect is written on the margin. Several leaves are torn out. Probably about this time Harold's picture was destroyed.*

The manuscript volume containing the life of Harold is preserved in the Harleian collection of manuscripts, British Museum, and of which (as far as it relates to the burial of Harold) Bishop Stubbs says "is a curious but entirely untrustworthy legend, written apparently to prove that the great King Harold was not buried at Waltham." The volume also contains *De Inventione S.C.*, etc. Mr. Hardy affirms that Bishop Stubbs has gathered all that can be gleaned about the author of the above MS.†

THE CONSECRATION OF THE CHURCH, A.D. 1060.

THE consecration of the church occurred on May 3rd, 1060, although some have thought it to be *two years later* ; but Bishop Stubbs has fixed that date beyond doubt, it being the feast of the Invention of the Holy Cross.‡ The new church had by this time reached such a state of completion as to be fit for divine service. The chief prelate present was Kinsige, Archbishop

---

* Harl. MSS. 3776. This MSS. has recently been published by Walter de Gray Birch, Esq. See Select Passages in the Life of Harold by W. Winters, 1876.

† Chron. Gt. Brit. and Ireland, Vol. II., p. 413.

‡ This festival was formerly kept in England on May 3rd, commemorative of the supposed finding of the *Cross* on that day, by the Empress Helena, the mother of Constantine the Great, between A.D. 305 and 326.

of York, whose name is handed down to us as that of the consecrator. He had been chaplain to Edward the Confessor, and seems to have been looked on as the principal ecclesiastic in England (as Stigand was generally under a cloud). There were present also most of the bishops and earls of the land, with King Edward and his Queen, the sister of Harold. We are informed that "the day was celebrated with great rejoicings : among the festivities great tubs of [Canary or Spanish] wine and mead were tapped in the lanes and streets, and all might drink who would."* Such indulgences were customary in those days, as we find when William, Bishop of Hereford, dedicated the Chapel of St. Thomas at Waltham, he granted forty days' indulgence to all the true disciples of the Pope in Waltham Abbey (*temp.* Hen. II.) King Edward the Confessor rested at Waltham until after the octave, when he left for Winchester, to keep Pentecost the following Sunday.

The proem of the Royal Charter states that King Harold had granted a certain piece of land, called of old by the in- habitants, Waltham, to one of his earls named Harold, who had constructed, to the praise of our Lord Jesus Christ and of the Holy Cross, a Monastery; granting to it first the land called Northlande,† with which he formed the Church of the *ville* to have been endowed from old time; and after the foundation of the monastery he caused it to be dedicated according to the rule of the holy church of God, to the memory of the King and his wife Editha, and his father and mother, and all relations, and enriched the same with many

---

* A similar thing was done in London at the birth of Edward III.

† As to Northland, says the Translator of Domesday Survey, it appears originally to have consisted of three hides, divided into twelve portions, one for each Canon. We are told in the Register of the Bishop of Durham's land that half a hide is still in the possession of the Holy Cross. The remaining two and a half hides appear to have been taken from them by Walcher, the previous Bishop, when he took possession of Harold's property in Waltham, and they are no doubt included in the lands registered as belonging to the present Bishop; for we find that Maud, first wife of Henry I., restored them to the Canons between 1108 and 1118. (Domesday Surv. Trans. 1864, 4to. : page xxxi. : C. Marsh.) Simon of Durham states that the firmness of Walcher not only did not permit any damage to occur in regard to the possessions of the Church, but, further, he augmented them by obtaining from the King that valuable property called Waltham Sanctæ Crucis, "along with its noble church, celebrated for its body of Canons."

relics of saints, apostles, martyrs, confessors, and virgins, and not only with the lands, whose names are afterwards recited, but also with gospel books, vestments, and divers kinds of ornaments. And, moreover, he formed there an assembly of brethren, living according to the canonical rules of the fathers, whose office it was, by day and by night, to sing the praises of God and his saints. These are the names of the lands belonging to the aforesaid monastery : *Passefelda, Walde, Upminster, Walkfare, Tippedene, Alwartune, Wodeforda, Lambethithe, Nesingan, Brikendune, Melno, Alrichescia, Wrmeleia, Nethleswelle, Hicche, Lukintone,* and *Westwaltham ;* all of which the king grants to the Church of the Holy Cross and the brethren there, with sac and soc and other customs. (For an interpretation of these places, see a subsequent part of this work.)

These are the land boundaries to Passefelde : That is, first from the old hatch at Freotherne felde to Presta hlype ; to the brook at Staundune ; to Scealdeforda, and from Scealdeforda to Coleboge Well, from the Well again to the old hatch, and so again to Freothene field.

These are the land boundaries to Welde : First from Dellennorth to the mouth, east to Hafegeæte, east to the Wolf Pit ; from the Pit south to the Purk, from the Purk south to Freobearne's leap, and so to Manne's land and thence again to Dellen.

These are the land boundaries to Upingstre : First at Tigelhyrste south to boundary ditch ; from the ditch west to Ingceburne, and from the bourne north to Beccengare ; and from Beccengare north along the road-weald to Stangare ; from Stangare north into Manne's land again to Tigelhyrste.

These are the land boundaries to Walhfare : First from the Ash to the Old Leap ; from the Leap to the Old Wood hatch ; from the hatch to the old road ; and from the road to Sandæcere ; and from the acre to Beadewan River ; from the river to Winebrook ; from the brook north again to the Ash.

These are the land boundaries to Tippedene : First to Tippaburne ; from the bourne up to the heath ; from the heath to Thetden's boundary opposite Ælfa's hatch, and so to the river ; along the river then again to Tippeburne.

These are the land boundaries to Ælwartone : First at Werdhæcce ; from Werdhæcce to Eacroft ; from Eacroft to Beolle Pool ; from the Pool to Leofsige's meadow ; from Leofsige's meadow to Omermad ; from Omermad to Ætheric's leap ; from the leap to the Wulf leap ; from Wulf leap to Thesfalde ; from Thesfalde to Stanway hatch ; from Stanway hatch to Saters byrig.

These are the land boundaries to Wudeforde: First to Angric's bourne to Alderman's hatch ; to the King's hatch from the King's hatch again to Angric's bourne.

These are the land boundaries to Lambehythe : First at Brixges stane and so on through the grove to the boundary dyke, and so to the Bulke tree ; and from the Bulke tree to Hyse ; and from Hyse to Ælsyge's hatch ; and so east to the road ; and so along the road again to Brixes stan.

These are the land boundaries to Nassingan : that is from Cerlen hatch, along the mark to Scelden boundary ; and from Scelden boundary to the brook ; and from the brook to Butterwyelle; and from Butterwyelle to Thuroldes boundary ; and from Thuroldes boundary again along the mark to Cerlen hatch ; and the meadow thereto belonging lies out by the Lea.

A.D. 1062.—Fifteenth indiction, seventh epact, first concurrent. Subscribed by Edward the King, Eadgytha the Queen ; Stigand, Archbishop of Canterbury ; Ealdred, Archbishop of York ; Ælfwold, the Bishop ; Hereman, the Bishop ; Leofric, the Bishop ; William, the Bishop ; Ailmar, the Bishop ; Leofwin, the Bishop ; Wefwin, the Bishop ; Ælwin, the Bishop ; Ælric, the Bishop ; Walter, the Bishop ; Gyso, the Bishop ; Ægelnoth, the Abbot ; Ælwin, the Abbot ; Wlfric, the Abbot ; Leofric, the Abbot ; Leofstan, the Abbot ; Ælwig, the Abbot ; Hondric, the Abbot ; Ægelsin, the Abbot; Leofstan, the Abbot ; Eadmund, the Abbot ; Sichtric, the Abbot ; Harold, the Earl ; Ælfgar, the Earl ; Tostin, the Earl ; Leofwin, the Earl ; Syrth, the Earl; Esgar, the "Procurator" of the Royal Palace ; Rodbert, the King's Kinsman ; Ralph, one of the King's Courtiers ; Bundin, "regis pal atimus;" Hesbern, the King's Kinsman ; Regenbald, the King's Chancellor ; Peter, the King's Chaplain ; Baldwin, the King's Chaplain ; Brintric, the Prince ; Ælfstan, the Prince ; Wigod, the King's Butler ; Herding, the Queen's Butler ; Adzur, the King's Sewer ; Yfing, the King's Sewer ; Godwin, the Queen's Sewer ; Doddo, the Prince ; Ælfgar, the Prince ; Brixin, the Prince ; Ægelnoth, the Prince ; Esbern, the Prince ; Edwig, the Prince ; Eadric, the Prince ; Ægelmund, the Prince ; Siward, the Prince ; Alwold, the Prince ; Ælpling, the Prince ; Swidar. *Vide* Cartæ Antiquee Roll, M. No. I.

Thus it is evident, as Mr. Freeman says, "that Waltham was a church, in its own age and country, of unparalleled magnificence. It is rather what we should naturally look for under the circumstances. Its founder was the first man in the kingdom, and his private wealth was enormous. Waltham must therefore have made a deep impression on the national mind. Its local worship became the worship of the English people."

ARCHITECTURAL CHANGES IN THE ABBEY CHURCH.

HE architectural changes in the church since the days of the last Anglo-Saxon monarch have been many. Mr Freeman observes that "barbarous mutilations, and hardly less barbarous additions, have entirely destroyed its character as seen from without. And even within, both mediæval alterations of the strangest kind, and the accumulated enormities of more recent days, have gone far to ruin the general effect of the original building. Still a large portion of the original interior remains untouched; an interior deserving attentive study as one of the noblest specimens of northern Romanesque;* and invested with a yet higher interest if we may regard it as called into being by the taste and bounty of the last of our native kings." Hence the ancient charter is correct: "*Ego Haroldus Comes operando consolido.*"† The early author of "*Vita Haroldi*" mentions in one place of the church being completed prior to the date of consecration (1059-60); and in another part, of works going on apparently in the choir as late as 1125 or 1126. The great question of the day is whether any portion of the church is of the pre-Norman period, or whether it does not belong to the time of Henry I. or Stephen. The church of Harold's foundation was undoubtedly of much importance, having a leaded roof, and decorations to the capitals of the columns of gilt brass-work, and no doubt work of considerable importance was going on in the reign of Henry I. or Stephen, which rendered necessary the removal of the body of Harold. Mr. Burges, late architect, thought that the repairs or rebuilding in Henry the First's time, and the removal of the body of Harold, were perfectly consistent with the fact of the present building—that is, the ancient nave—being of Harold's time.‡

* The style of architecture called "Romansque" is a debased kind of work in imitation of Roman architecture. It prevailed in Europe from the destruction of the Roman Empire until the Gothic order was introduced.

† The church of Waltham is built, as a great church of the year 1060 would be built, in the English variety of the Norman style, which was introduced by Edward the Confessor, and which was still in use in the days of William of Malmesbury." (*Gent.'s Magazine*, vol. viii. p. 65.)

‡ *The Builder*, vol. xviii. 71.

There is every reason to suppose that Harold would build in the very best style of which he had accessible patterns, and that strenuous in all things, he would make an end of what he began. Whatever part was finished was splendidly adorned, in a fashion that reminds one more of Eastern than of Western art, as if Harold might have wandered to Constantinople in his earlier days. Brazen plates of gilt were spread over the walls; the capitals and bases of the pillars were curiously carved, and the elaborate ornaments of the altar, reliques, vestments, books and furniture of the sanctuary, are described in terms of regret and indignation proportioned to their intrinsic value.*

T. Wright, an able antiquary, is inclined to recognise the work of Harold in the present existing building on the ground of a plate in the Cottonian MSS.,† which shows the two rows of columns in the nave, of which the shafts are ornamented in the same style as those still remaining in the Abbey Church of Waltham. The MS. referred to is of Anglo-Saxon date, written (*circa* 1050) ‡ probably when the work of the first foundation was in progress. Mr Wright states: "We have then in the MS. under consideration, a series of architectural drawings which are pure Saxon, and of the date of which there can be no doubt. They present a number of characteristics which are sufficient to distinguish a peculiar style, which probably was the general style of Anglo-Saxon buildings. It is certain that the old artists produced nothing on parchment which was not modelled on what really existed before their eyes. It remains for further examination to show how far we ought to refer every example of this style to the same age. The dates of early buildings appear to have been often fixed too arbitrarily. I would merely cite, as an instance, the church of Waltham. This is considered as early Norman, and ascribed to the date of about 1120, because Henry I. and his two wives are recorded as special benefactors to the monastery.§ In the two most authentic accounts of the early history of Waltham, both written late in the reign of Henry II., the ' *Vita Haroldi* ' and the tract ' *De Inventione Sanctæ Crucis Walthamensis* ' (the latter of which brings the history up to the

---

* De Invent. (Stubbs), xv. See Vita Haroldi, MSS. Harl. 3776.
† Cott. MSS. Tit D. xvi. fol. 336. (This MSS. the author has examined.)
‡ Wyatt on Illuminated MSS. p. 11.
§ Mainly in the gift of the Cornmill and Northfields to the Canons.

time at which it was written), we have a particular and curious account of Harold's Church, which was very spacious and massive, and which agrees perfectly with what now remains ; and these same documents give us every reason to believe that no remarkable alterations had been made in the building up to the time at which these histories were written, that is, up to the period of transition. This is very easily accounted for, because the acknowledged character of Harold's building would preserve it from dilapidation, and the jealousy with which it was looked upon by the Normans (as we are informed in the documents) caused it to be treated with neglect. It may be observed also that Harold's Church was most probably built by architects brought over from Normandy, and would therefore have a decidedly Norman character. I will merely add that a copy of ' Prudentius ' in the British Museum, written apparently about the middle of the eleventh century (or very soon after, MS. Cotton. Titus D. XVI.), contains one or two rows of columns, of which the shafts are ornamented in precisely the same style as those which still remain in Waltham Abbey."* In the original MS. the illustration is coloured pale green, blue and red.

A controversy relative to the correct date of the consecration of Harold's Church has been ably fought in the pages of the *Gentleman's Magazine*, through the long period of eight months or more during the progress of the restoration of the Abbey Church (1859-60), and the whole affair seems clearly to have terminated in favour of Mr. E. A. Freeman, Bishop Stubbs, Mr. W. Burges and others, who maintain that much of the present church is of King Harold's work.

Lanfranc, a contemporary with Harold, built a church at Canterbury, consisting of a nave, transepts and an apsidal† chancel similar to Waltham, and which was afterwards taken down and substituted by a long choir. Thus it is presumed that Harold's church ended with an apse directly eastward of the present church, and which was probably taken down early in the 12th century, and a long choir with aisles, chapels and

---

* The *Arch. Journal*, vol. i. page 35.

† Apse, is the semi-circular or octagonal part of the east end of the choir of the church which reached far eastward on the *New Ground*, where the body of Harold was buried. For this part of the original church see Mr. Burges' plan with an imaginary idea in thin lines of the new choir.

transepts added or enlarged.   Mr. Freeman says, speaking
of the documentary evidence alone relating to the age of the
church, "in a somewhat minute account of the fortunes of the
foundation, we find not a word implying, hardly a word allowing
the possibility that the church raised by Harold was other
than the church which the writers had before their eyes.   They
detail the wrongs inflicted on the society of the two Norman
Kings ; no one can attribute the rebuilding to their times.
One author writes under the patronage of the Queen of
Henry I. ; she was herself a benefactress to the College, but
not a word do we find of her rebuilding, enlarging, or com-
pleting the work of Harold.   The other writer extols Henry
II. almost to a level with Harold himself ; he praises his
reforms, he mentions his addition of domestic buildings ; but
nothing is said as to the fabric of the church.   The biographer
of Harold, in describing Harold's church does not directly say
that it was standing in 1205 ; but the reason clearly is, that
he takes it so certainly for granted that he does not think it
necessary to make any direct assertion about it.   In the
face of all this it would require some very strong architectural
evidence indeed to establish the fact of a rebuilding at any
date between 1066 and 1205.   Such evidence, I confess, I do
not find.   I see at Waltham an early Norman church, which
one would doubtless at first sight place after the Conquest,
but which I see no improbability, backed as we are by
such strong historical arguments, in placing a few years before.
Certainly most of the early Norman buildings which remain
are much less ornamented than this of Waltham ; but the
ornament at Waltham, though of a very effective kind, is still
simple and almost rude ; everywhere, except a few details in
the transepts, it is quite of the early Norman school ; there is
something totally different from the elaboration of ornament,
the almost elegance of detail, which might be expected in a
building bearing the date of 1177.   Taking architectural
evidence alone, it is, I certainly think, a lesser difficulty to
attribute it to Harold than to attribute it to Henry II."*
Portions of the nave of Durham Cathedral, built by Bishop de
Carilepho, *circa* 1093, are similar to the nave of Waltham
Church ; also Lindisfarn Church is in assimilation to parts of

---

* Essex Archæological Trans., Vol. ii., 20.

Waltham Church, of which former place Scott sang in his
Marmion :—

> " In Saxon strength that Abbey frown'd,
> With massive arches broad and round,
> That rose alternate row and row,
> On ponderous columns, short and low,
> Built ere the art was known."

The ruins of Lindisfarn are of great antiquity; the arches are
strictly Saxon, and the pillars which support them are short and
strong. One of these pillars, showing the zig-zag grooves,
correspond exactly with those of Harold's work in his church at
Waltham. Pillars with wreathed and indented mouldings were
much in vogue in Saxon times. These mouldings in Harold's
church were, it is thought, ornamented with " fillets of brass ;"
and the writer in the *De Iyventione* mentions the pillars and
arches being adorned with plates of gilt brass. No traces,
however, of brass now remains, nor even the nails by which the
plates were supposed to be fastened, which may have been taken
out and the holes filled up. The ornaments and mouldings of
the arches have some very peculiar attractions about them, which
may excite the attention of the curious.* In the uppermost
arches the indented moulding forms the extreme edge of the
arch, and is turned underneath on the inside or under part of the
arch. In the nethermost great arches also there is a return of
indented workmanship, and the indentations of the outermost
mouldings are much slighter and in less relief than those of the
innermost. Some of the early windows in the Abbey Church
were originally unglazed, glass at that period being very scarce in
this country. These windows have much internal splay, but
externally their glazing is set almost flush with the wall face.
There appears to have been no provision made originally for
fixing panels of glass. A shutter was no doubt designed to close
upon the rebate. " None of the Norman windows show any
preparation for glass, the splay jamb going right up to the
external chamber. In all probability wooden frames were made
to fit in tightly, and secured by interior hold-fasts ; of course one
edge of these wooden frames would have to be chamfered to fit
into the sloping jambs, and upon the inside surface would be
fixed the necessary iron-work for the glass, as at Salisbury,

---

* Some portions of the mouldings of the piers were probably worked out
with the axe.

Canterbury and other places."* Traces of distemper painting have been found in the church, as well as in the lady chapel, at various times, and especially in 1847. Mr. E. Littler discovered in the chevron moulding of the Norman windows and of the arch of the south entrance traces of colour. He observed also a portion of coloured masonry on the soffit of this arch, on the splay of the south window, and on the inner face or the south wall; as also some bold writing in old English characters, surrounded by coloured lines.† This appeared after the white-wash and plaster had been stripped off. In Henry the Second's day the church was enlarged and the order re-modelled. Several conventual buildings were erected at this period, and the only one remaining is the vaulted building in Mr. King's garden, north-east of the church, called the "*Potato cellar,*" which has evidently formed the ground floor of some important apartment. The date would be referable either to the end of the reign of Henry II. or to the beginning of that of his son, Richard I.‡ The simple intersecting of the ribs which support the groining of the vault agree in character with the arched ceiling in the east end of Canterbury Cathedral, built by William of Sens, in 1175.§ No architectural changes appear to have taken place in the Abbey Church during the reigns of Richard I. and John, although the latter king frequently visited Waltham. The very elegant pointed arch at the western front of the church, now forming the entrance from the tower to the interior of the building, appears to date back to the latter part of the reign of the third Henry, or the early part of that of Edward the First. Much, however, of the detail of the sculpture work of this beautiful inner porch has been mutilated by ruthless hands in the erection of the great western tower. On the authority of Matthew Paris, "The church of the canons of Waltham was solemnly dedicated in 1242." This statement has been the subject of considerable discussion, and the validity of it is held as questionable by many archæologists. Mr. Burges considers that the long Norman choir was consequently not destined to last long, and that the dedication

---

* Gents' Mag., Vol. viii., 3rd Series, p. 77.

† Archæological Trans., Essex, Vol. ii., 42.

‡ W. Burges' Tract, p. 5.

§ Will de Ver (or Vere) and Walter de Gaunt were actively engaged in making alterations in the church, 23rd Hen. ii., Madox Hist. Ex.

mentioned by Paris was simply the result of the erection of some important part of the church, not the nave, for, says the late architect, "We know that it remains nearly in the same state as it was left in the 11th or 12th century; it must therefore have been the choir which had been reconstructed or so altered that a new consecration had become necessary." The entire building was rendered dangerous by the cutting away of the aisle arch in the reign of Edward I. (not Edward II., as stated by Mr. Burges), which necessitated a strong-framed strutt to be erected and which still remains as a memorial of a perverted taste. These architectural alterations are expressed in a notarial instrument (in Latin) which is preserved in the Public Record Office, under date September 6th, 1286. This instrument relates to certain repairs authorised to be made in the church, with instructions from the dean of the Abbey as to how the parishioners should help in carrying out the work. On Sunday, the 8th September, 1286, the feast of the Nativity of the Virgin, this document was read publicly in Latin by the dean of the church, and interpreted in English by one of the clergy present. The dean then exhorted the parishioners to set about the work speedily. This exhortation was repeated on the 22nd of September; and on the 29th of the same month, the dean executed his formal and official answer to the precept of the abbot certifying what he had done, and what he expected the parishioners would do in answer to the request. The abbot at this period was Reginald de Maidenhith, who received the temporalities of the church Jan. 29th, 1273-4, and resigned them A.D. 1288. This notarial instrument fixes the precise date of the great alterations that were made in the building in the thirteenth century, when it was found that in consequence of the bad foundations and other causes, the vaulting of the aisles had pushed out the aisle walls and had become very dangerous. The new architect, therefore, took down the vaulting and threw the aisle and triforium into one height; he next tried to remodel the great arcade by throwing the nave arch and the triforium arch into one; however, this was found to be a most dangerous proceeding, so it was given up after the westernmost bays had thus been treated. Then a west front was added, and a very beautiful composition it was, so far as can be judged by what remains. The tracery of the windows is also very peculiar, and has an undulating look. When the present tower was built in the reign of Philip and Mary, the great western window was destroyed and the tower built upon the cill; so there is no means of judging as to what it was like. During the restoration in 1859-60, the top of the old western doors came to light; they were of the same date as the rest of the work, and have been reproduced in the new doors. It was impossible to re-use them as they had become warped. It must be confessed that, in 1286, the parishioners of Waltham Abbey managed to secure the services of an excellent architect, although he did great injury to the building in removing much of the older portions of the masonry. It is not improbable that the architect was the same as erected the "Eleanor Cross" and the Lady Chapel. A portion of the ancient oak wood screen still exists in the north aisle, and dates probably to the 14th century. Another work of the 14th century is a large flowing decorated window in the north aisle. Stone being scarce at this period the architect stripped the whole of the interior and portions of the exterior of all the ashlar he could possibly extract. He also destroyed the filling in of the triforium, and not satisfied with that actually removed the slabs of stone which formed the string at lower part, making good the places with plaster ornament in the Norman style. The bays at the west end had lurched towards the west, probably in consequence of want of care in the foundations, or perhaps from the incomplete state of the western end. The whole edifice would have fallen to the ground long ere this had it not been supported by the western tower. A small three-light window is the only trace of perpendicular work in the building as it remains at present. At the Reformation the east end, as reverting to the crown, and is now held by the lord of the manor, was destroyed, but the nave belonging to the parishioners was preserved intact. Several alterations and repairs were made in the church at the Reformation, as also in the reigns of the Charles', when the second pillar from the east to the south side was refaced. A coin of Charles II. was discovered at the restoration of the church in the foundation near the said pillar. This was the time doubtless when the church became very dilapidated and when a petition was presented by the townsfolk to King Charles II., August 7th, 1668, for permission to make a brief for a public collection to help restore the church. This petition was granted, and in acknowledgment, the thanks of the parish in vestry were sent to the King, February 15th, 1669. On March 21st, 1669, £100 were borrowed and expended "towards procuring the duplicates, printing the briefs, &c." This sum was repaid with interest, January 3rd, 1672, and in the year 1674, £46 4s. 10d. were laid out in repairs of the Church. In 1679 the " School House " (Lady Chapel) was repaired at a cost of £64 13s. 5½d. The before named royal brief only realised £17 5s. 0d. The remainder was obtained from the funds belonging to the parish and from voluntary contributions. Other repairs were made in the Church, in 1673, when on the 23rd of November of that year, a general rate of 2d. in the £ was made for payment of the said repairs. And by another order, dated 22nd July, 1680, reciting that the Church was out of repair and would cost about £100 to defray the expenses. For this purpose it was thought advisable to borrow the £100 then recently given by Bishop Hall for the benefit of the poor. A ceiling was then made to the church, according to Farmer, who states that the church " formerly seemed by the manner of building, with a high roof, more like a barn than the House of God.* But (continues the historian) it is now a vast addition and ornament to the church, and a great advantage both to the preacher and the congregation in hearing the Word of God." The greatest possible barbarities were made by way of architectural changes in the last century. In 1778 the "upper hall" of the tower was taken down, and, as a writer in the *Gentleman's Magazine* says, "a paltry substitute of four stone walls with oblong holes set up by way of a belfry." This writer also vehemently exclaims against the inhabitants of Waltham for allowing the church to be mangled by unskilful builders. This tower was restored, as it now appears, by a rate of 1s. in the £, and completed in 1798, and an inscription to that effect placed over the west doorway. A writer of the period thought that

---

* On June 20, 1663, a letter from Canterbury was written by W. Kingsley to Secty. Bennet respecting the Nonconformists of Waltham Abbey, viz. : There are daily great conventicles in Waltham Parish. On Whit Tuesday, 300 persons met at Hobday's house in Waltham ; others heard preaching in an orchard, and on leaving, they had with them 50 or 60 good horses, several portmanteaus and some bundles supposed to be arms.(?) The liberty taken by fanatics (?) frighten the country. *Vide* State Papers, Domestic Charles III. See also Neal, Hist. Puritans and Bess' Hist. of the Quakers.

the Churchwardens needed not to have placed a memorial stone on the church of the event, the parish would long remember the expense without any stone reminder of it. In 1807 the roof was lowered and a plaster ceiling put underneath it.* This old ceiling remained about forty or fifty years. Some repairs were made in the Abbey in 1818, when Mr. W. Wolesholme, of the New Inn, Sun Street, erected the wooden cross, &c., on the top of the tower. A comparatively modern, ugly, slated porch stood on the south side of the church, and which was destroyed in 1873. Near this porch, and close to the entrance into the Crypt, are the remains of some beautiful diaper work. A few fragments of similar masonry appear in the wall of the inner porch under the belfry, all of which were hidden until late years by plaster and whitewash. The robing room, built by Mr. John Bentley in 1874, for £340, is on the north side of the Church. This room is called a "vestry," but it is invariably found to be too small to hold public meetings in. Most of the old prints of the Abbey Church show a small house at the east end of the church, probably an old Chantry in which were sung, before the Reformation, masses for the dead. This Chantry was dissolved by Statute 1st, Edward VI., 1547, and was entirely demolished about sixty years ago. The Church now consists of the nave of the original " Romansque " building, and side aisles, north and south. The aisles are of the height of the two lower stages, corresponding with those in Oxford Cathedral. The three tiers of semi-circular arches, with zigzag mouldings, are supported by massive cylindrical pillars ; two of them are ornamented with zigzag indentings. The two chancel pillars have a deep spiral groove running round them, and must have looked very grand if filled with brass.† The pillar opposite the south doorway, in the south aisle, retains the marks of the chain to which was fastened Cranmer's "Great Bible," also the "Paraphrase of Erasmus," by the seventh injunction of good King Edward the Sixth; together with Bishop Jewel's "Apology of the Church of England," and John

---

* Several portions of the windows in the north aisle were at this period destroyed !

† On the pillar near the chancel (north aisle) are various initials of persons, names and dates, viz.: E.H. 1651 ; R.H. 1661 ; G.B. 1661 ; S.D. 1702, &c.

Foxe's "Book of Martyrs," edited by his son, Samuel Foxe, of Warlies, in this parish.*

The nave of the Church is about 120 feet in length, its width from the centre of the pillars is about 30 feet, the entire width is 54 feet, and the height is nearly 60 feet. The church will now seat about 800 persons. For a great number of years the inside—where the seats now stand—was filled up with high oak pews, and a massive gallery extended along the south aisle of the nave, while two others were fixed at the west end, one of which supported the organ. These galleries had seriously injured the pillars near them. This western gallery was built by Mr. Burrell, of Norwich, especially for the old organ. The floor of the church was reduced in 1859-60 to its original level, and one of the south western pillars, which had at some period or other sunk four inches, and had been cut away for the reception of the pulpit, has been substantially restored. The floor, which for centuries had been open to receive the dead, may have probably affected the stability of the pillar in question. The graves, or rather vaults, have been filled up with concrete and paved with stone. The subject of the "Rose" window is taken up by the new ceiling, and though a magnificent work of art, it can hardly be said to be in strict keeping with the sacred nature of the building. The ornamental outlines, which were painted by Messrs. Harland and Fisher, were filled up by Edward Poynter, Esq., with a series of paintings exhibiting the labours of the year and the twelve signs of the Zodiac, after the style of Peterborough Cathedral. The oak seats were constructed and fitted up by Mr. Burrell, of Norwich. Prior to the gas being introduced into the church the building was lighted up by candles. A large brass chandelier was suspended from the ceiling in the middle of the church, which held thirty-six candles, and which fifty years ago was lit up every Good Friday evening, as also on other very special occasions. The cost of the restoration of the Church in 1859-60 was discharged by voluntary contributions, aided by a donation from the War Department,† and a grant from the Society for Building and

---

* Besides the books above named there were preserved, in the Abbey, several "Gospels in the Saxon tongue," and other early works in manuscript.

† The War Office contribute £50 annually to the clergy of Waltham for their labour in connection with the spiritual good of the men employed in the Gunpowder Factory.

Repairing Churches. The chancel belonging to the Lord ot the Manor was restored at his expense.* The entire sum expended in the restoration amounted to about £5,000. The re-opening services of the Abbey Church took place on the 3rd of May, 1860, being the 800th anniversary of its foundation. Besides the early communion there were three services, morning, afternoon, and evening. At the first two the musical portions of the service were rendered by members of the St. Paul's, Westminster Abbey, Temple, Church and Chapel Royal choir, under the direction of Mr. Cummings, the re-constructed organ being re-used for the first time. The preachers of the day were the Rev. H. Brown, Norrisian Professor of Divinity at Cambridge and Canon of Exeter; the Rev. Dr. Jelf, principal of King's College and Canon of Oxford; and the Rev. J. M. Hussey, of Brixton. Collections during the day amounted to about £90. A few minor alterations and repairs have taken place since the restoration of the Church, such as the filling in of the east end with an illuminated reredos, a new lectern, an enlargement of the organ, and the restoration of the Lady Chapel; also a screen in the same chapel, and a stained glass window in the tower to the memory of the late Vicar, the Rev. J. Francis, M.A.

THE REREDOS.—Prominent among the most recent gifts to the Church is the reredos, a costly work of art, but which showy imagery, like the "Rose" window above it, is entirely out of character with the general massiveness of the building, and though beautiful in itself, it adds but little to the stately grandeur of the noble edifice, which

> . . . . " For loveliness
> Needs not the foreign aid of ornament.
> But is, when unadorned, adorned the most."

The reredos contains five subjects—(i.) The annunciation of the Virgin; (ii.) the angels appearing to the shepherds and pro- claiming "Peace on earth; goodwill to men;" (iii.) the nativity of Christ; (iv.) the homage of the Wise Men of the East; and (v.) the flight into Egypt. These figures are beautifully sculptured in bold relief and ornamented with gilt and various

---

* The old communion cloth of the Church was purchased of Mr. Chinnery, a banker, of Gilwell House, Sewardstone, for upwards of £40, He purchased it especially with the view of entertaining the father of the present Duke of Cambridge.

colours. Beneath is the following inscription :—" In humble faith this Reredos is erected to the loving memory of Samuel Bolton Edenborough, who died October 23rd, 1873, by his wife Margaret."* Below the inscription the wall is faced with highly polished Devonshire marble down to the floor, which is covered with ornamental tiles. The handsome new communion table of carved walnut-wood is also the gift of Mrs. Edenborough.

THE PULPIT AND LECTERN.—The pulpit is not the least part of the furniture of the Church worthy of consideration—

> "The pulpit therefore (and I name it filled
> With solemn awe, that bids me well beware
> With what intent I touch that holy thing),
> The pulpit."

In addition to the reredos, Mrs. Edenborough gave the newly erected marble pulpit, which is very massive in appearance. Its form is hexagonal, and the body is composed of Dove marble. In each division, after the *High Church order*, is inlaid a St. Andrew's Cross, made alternately of Irish and Roman marble, the latter material having been obtained from an old quarry discovered at Rome. The new pulpit is further adorned with two brass sconces and a small brass lectern. The LARGE·BRASS LECTERN is the gift, through the late Vicar, of an unknown contributor, as a "thank-offering," and bears the following inscription — "A THANK OFFERING FOR THE ABBEY CHURCH, WALTHAM HOLY CROSS, 8 AUGUST, 1872." Its value is estimated at £100. The Church was closed for some weeks during the progress of the work, and was re-opened October 1st, 1876. In the Lady Chapel is an ancient pulpit which once stood in the Church, and in which many of the old divines of the past have preached.

"THE FRANCIS MEMORIAL."—The carved oak screen in south-east end of the Church, between the Lady Chapel and the Church, was raised by public subscription as a Memorial to the late Vicar, the Rev. James Francis, M.A. The committee at first decided to have a window inserted in the west front of the Lady Chapel, but a screen was afterwards decided upon as being most appropriate. This screen is the work of Mr. J. Forsyth, of Finchley-road, Hampstead, and consists of five divisions, the

---

* Mrs Margaret Edenborough is interred near the remains of her husband in the north-east corner of the Churchyard.

openings of which are joined by double tracery arches, and spandrils, with crockets and other carved enrichments. These arches have for their abutments buttresses with intricate penetrating work, which are perhaps the most interesting section of the screen. They are distinguished by great subtlety of treatment, parts disappearing and re-appearing in the most puzzling manner. The cornice is also richly carved, and is crowned with an equally richly carved cresting. Over the central arch there are the figures of two angels with outspread wings supporting a carved cross. The pedestals on which they stand are also richly carved. These figures bear a resemblance to the arms of Waltham Holy Cross. At the basement of the woodwork the following inscription is engraved in old English letters, and extends from left to right of the screen :—" To the glory of God and in memory of James Francis, for thirty-eight years Vicar of this parish. He died March 3rd, 1885." The design of this screen was made by Mr. J. Reeve, architect, of 30, St. James' Street, Bedford Row ; the sculpture work was executed by Mr. Forsyth, as already referred to, and the erection of the screen was superintended by Mr. James Meadows. This ornament cost between five and six hundred pounds, and was unveiled before a large audience of persons on Lord's day evening, November 28th, 1886, by Dr. Claughton, Bishop of St. Albans, who preached two sermons in celebration of the event.

THE ORGAN.—The original organ, the gift of Thomas Leverton, Esq., of Bedford-square, London, in 1819, stood many years in the west gallery. On the front of this organ a small brass plate gave its history in brief—" FLIGHT AND ROBSON, ORGAN BUILDERS TO H.R. HIGHNESS PRINCE REGENT. ENLARGED AND RE-CONSTRUCTED BY J. W. WALKER, 1860." This old instrument was removed in 1879, when the present splendid organ was entirely re-constructed by Messrs. Walker and Son, of Francis-street, Tottenham Court-road, and placed at the east end of the north aisle of the church at a cost of £700. This organ contains three manuals and great swell, with a separate pedal organ prepared for three stops ; one stop—the open diapason of wood—being at present inserted ; also draw stops. The pipes of the other stops only are required. The great organ is prepared for eight stops, seven of which are given. The only stop remaining to complete this portion of the organ is the *posaune* (or reed stop). The swell organ, which is really very fine, contains thirteen stops, and only twelve pipes of the double trumpet are wanted to complete this portion of the instrument. 'The choir organ is prepared for six stops, two of which—the clarionet and flute—are Inserted. The couplers are five in number, and the composition pedals six. Joseph Chalk, Esq., is the organist, which office he has sustained since 1859-60.

ANCIENT MUSIC USED IN THE ABBEY CHURCH.

One of the most curious and interesting manuscripts that once adorned the library of the ancient Monastery of Waltham is now in the Lansdown Collection, 763, and bears the following title in rubric:—" 𝔍𝔲𝔫𝔠 𝔩𝔦𝔟𝔯𝔲𝔪 𝔟𝔬𝔠𝔦𝔱𝔞𝔱𝔲𝔪 𝔐𝔲𝔰𝔦𝔠𝔞𝔪 𝔊𝔲𝔦𝔡𝔬𝔫𝔦𝔰, 𝔰𝔠𝔯𝔦𝔭𝔰𝔦𝔱 𝔡𝔬𝔪𝔦𝔫𝔲𝔰 𝔍𝔬𝔥𝔞𝔫𝔫𝔢𝔰 𝔚𝔶𝔩𝔡𝔢, 𝔮𝔲𝔬𝔫𝔡𝔞𝔪 𝔢𝔵𝔢𝔪𝔭𝔱𝔦 𝔐𝔬𝔫𝔞𝔰𝔱𝔢𝔯𝔦𝔦 𝔖𝔞𝔫𝔠𝔱𝔞 𝔠𝔯𝔲𝔠𝔦𝔰 𝔡𝔢 𝔚𝔞𝔩𝔱𝔥𝔞𝔪 𝔓𝔯𝔢𝔠𝔢𝔫𝔱𝔬𝔯." Annexed to this is the usual anathema which may be met with in most early MSS. belonging to religious houses. It is written by a later hand in black ink, and imports no less than a curse on any who should steal or injure the book:—" *Quem quidem librum, aut hunc titulum, qui malitiosé abstulerit aut deleverit, anathema sit.*" Notwithstanding the admonition here given, the book appears to have fallen into rough hands, probably after the dissolution of the Monastery. The volume is beautifully written on vellum, and contains 131 folios, including an original letter from Dr. John Wallis respecting a Greek MS. found at Buda; also a letter from Humphrey Wanley; a note from Mr. West to Mr. Raper, with reply; and a letter from Daines Barrington. All on musical subjects.

On the first folio of this MS. volume we find the name of the author or transcriber—-John Wylde, Precentor of Waltham Holy Cross. His name occurs also on folio 51 b., and his initials, J. W., after the words *Explicitint Regulæ Magistri Johannis Torkesey de 6 Speciebus natarum*, folio 94 b.

The contents of the volume appear on the fly sheet, *i.e.*, I. Musica Guidonis Monachi. II. De Origine et Effectu Musicæ. III. Speculum Cantatium sive Psalterium. IV. Metrologus Liber. V. Regulæ-Magistri Johan Torksey. VI. Tractatus Magistri Johannes de Muris de distantia et Mensura vocum.

VII. Regulæ Magistri Thomæ Walsingham. VIII. Lionel Power of the Cordis of Musicke. IX. Treatise of Musical Proportions, and of their Naturis and Denominations. First in English and then in Latyne. A fragment of this MS. is said to be in the Bodleian Library, Oxford. The date of the volume is unknown, but from a Palæographical point of view we should suggest that it was written either late in the 14th, or early in the 15th century. The MS. *Quatnor Principalia Musices*, Add. MSS, 8866, is written in a similar hand, and a note at the commencement states that "this treatise upon music called *Quatnor Principalia* is attributed by some to Thomas or John of Tewkesbury, and by others to John Hambois of the name of Tewkesbury. No musical author occurs, and the name is only to be seen on the outside of the leaf of the Oxford MS., to the minor friars of which place in the year 1388 John de Tewkesbury presented a copy of this book." This MS., however, appears to have been written *circa* 1351, and is cited by John Wylde as an authority in support of his arguments, which proves his book to have been written after that date.

John Wylde was no doubt an excellent practical musician of the time, as indeed his office of Precentor of so large a choir as that of Waltham required he should be. His name is now unknown in the musical world, except as the author of this curious MS., which few writers appear to have consulted, except Sir John Hawkins and Dr. Burney. The first of these celebrated writers conjecture that John Wylde flourished about the year A.D. 1400, at which time the Church of Waltham was probably in a very prosperous condition. A Precentor or Chanter like Wylde had the chief care of the choir service, and not only presided over the choristers and organists, but provided books for them, paid them their salaries, and repaired the organs. He had also the custody of the seal of the Abbey, and kept the *Liber Diurnalis*, or chapter book, and provided parchment and ink for the writers, and colours for the limners of books for the library. William Harleston was the Abbot of Waltham in Wylde's time ; he had been associated with the Church for many years, as appears from an early deed* dated 1387. The Chronicles of Johannus de Trokelowe† informs us that this Abbot died of a most pestilential fever and was buried

---

* Deeds and Charters, Augmentation Office, K. 42.   Pub. Rec. Off.
† Chronica Monasterri S. Albani (Riley) p. 334.

near the foundations of the choir of the Abbey Church. His coffin is said to have been disturbed in 1786. It is not known whether Wylde was a married man or not; possibly he was, and unlike his successor, Tallis, he may have had a family to perpetuate his name, as we find several entries of the same in the Parish Registers of Waltham Holy Cross. The name is also mentioned in a private MS. in the writer's possession, relating to the proceedings of the Lord Court Baron of Waltham, *temp.* Elizabeth, *i.e.*, A.D. 1586—A verdict was passed from Edw. Smyth & Eliz. his wyfe to the use of Gilbert Wylde and Joane his wyfe, of a cottage in the Corne Markett, and a garden neere to Catebrigg donghill in Scole streete.

May 28, 8 James I. Joane Willd widow was found to be sesed to her & her heires of a Cot: lyinge in the Corne Mkett late Thos. Turnor's. And that Agnes Somner, the wyfe of Jo: Somner, Glover was the dawt & heire of Joane & adm: tent.

The old Parish Registers record the name in several places.

Wylde informs us that he composed the first part of the MS. abroad, and the latter in England. In the reign of Henry VIII. this book fell into the hands of the celebrated musician, Thomas Tallis, whose autograph is fairly written on the last sheet. From him it is supposed to have paseed into the possession of Thomas Morley, gentleman of Queen Elizabeth's Chapel, who made use of it in writing his " Introduction to Music." It afterwards became respectively the property of Mr. Powle, Speaker of the House of Commons and Master of the Rolls, *temp.* William III. ; Lord Chancellor Somers ; and Sir Joseph Jekyll. At the sale of the latter gentleman's Library, it was purchased by a country organist, whose name is now unknown ; this musician presented it to Mr. West, the antiquary. Dr. Pepusch is said to have taken a transcript of the book. Mr West, it appears, possessed one or two of the Waltham MSS. " Mr. West to Mr. Raper,—Mr. West presents his compliments to Mr. Raper, and sends him the old MS. musick, he mentioned yesterday. The book is very old, and belonged to Tallys the celebrated master of musick to Henry VIIIths Chappel. Mr. West will be very glad to have Mr. Raper's Judgment of it, and to know where the Greek MS. is mentioned by Dr. Wallis in the letter herewith Inclosed.—Covent Garden, Dec. 4, 1767."

After the decease of Mr. West, the doctor states that he was a considerable time ignorant to whom this curious and valuable M.S. belonged ; but at length found that it had fallen into the hands of the Earl of Shelburne. Dr. Burney had it in his possession some time, and published long extracts from it. It is not generally known that Thomas Tallis was organist of Waltham Church *temp.* Henry VIII., probably before he became organist of the Chapel Royal. A short time since the writer discovered the name of " Thomas Talys " on the list of Waltham pensioners preserved in the Public Record Office, dated Anno 31 Henry VIII. This celebrated musician received xxs for wages (which was more than the other gifted men connected with the Abbey received except the priest), with a "reward " of equal amount. John Boston, the old Waltham organist, received at the same time iiis for wages and iiis for reward. This occurred at the dissolution of the Abbey. Tallis appears to have been employed at Waltham up to that time, and that is how he became ·possessed of Wylde's Manuscript Music. William Lyllye was "chaunter " at the same time with Thomas Tallis, and received v£ xiiis iiii., pension. Many of the chanters served as priests, and this accounts for Lyllye's pension being larger than that of the organist. The chanter received for reward at the same time iii£.* Robert Fuller was then Abbot of Waltham, the value of his pension amounted to £200 per annum. When Tallis was at Waltham there were no less than three organs belonging to the church. "A greate large payre of Organs above, one in the northe Quyre and a lesser payre beneth," these were no doubt played at intervals by Tallis, and the " lytell payre of organes " which stood in the Lady Chapel,† and valued at the dissolution of the Abbey "at xxs " were played by John Boston. In 1546 he received "twenty pence for mending the organs." John Boston was a Waltham man, and died sometime before 1564. As we find his wife died a "wedow," and was buried Jan. 30th 1564. Several entries occur in the Parish Registers of Waltham, of this family.

The history of Thomas Tallis is little known, except what may

---

* In the " Liber Niger Dominus Regis," *temp.* Edw. IV., the " Chaplene and Clerkes of the Chappelle " were required to be " Shewinge in descant, clear voyced, well relished and pronouncynge, eloquent in readinge and suffytyente in organes playing."

† See History Lady Chapel (W. Winters), 1875.

be gathered from his own works.* He was one of the greatest musicians of whom England can be proud ; born early in the sixteenth century and received his musical training in St. Paul's School, under Thomas Mulliner, John Redford's predecessor. Tallis devoted himself chiefly to Church music, and studied with Heywood, Newman, Blitheman, Shelbye and Allwood. It is not known whether Waltham was the first place in which he laboured in his profession ; however, he appears to have served in this church in 1540. A few years after he composed and published, in Archbishop Parker's Psalter, eight tunes annexed to "the whole Psalter translated into English Metre."

He served as organist in the Chapel Royal under King Henry VIII., Edward VI., Queen Mary, and Elizabeth, and died November 23rd, 1585. His remains were buried in Greenwich Parish Church. Strype, in his continuation of Stow's Surrey, published in 1720, states that he found a brass plate in the chancel before the rails, with the annexed inscription thereon engraved. The old church was pulled down soon after 1720 and rebuilt, when the memorial brass was lost, but the inscription is preserved :—

> " Enterred here doth ly a worthy wyght,
>   Who for long tyme in musick bore the bell :
> His name to shew, was Thomas Tallys hyght,
>   In honest vertuous lyff he dyd excell.
>
> He serv'd long tyme in chappel with grete prayse,
>   Fower sovereygnes reygnes (a thing not often seene),
> I mean kyng Henry and prynce Edward's dayes
>   Quene Mary, and Elizabeth our quene.
>
> He maryed was, though children he had none,
>   And lyv'd in love ful thre and thirty yeres
> Wyth loyal spowse, whos name yclypt was Jone
>   Who here entomb'd him company now bears.
>
> As he dyd lyve, so also did he dy,
>   In myld and quyet sort, O happy man !
> To God ful oft for mercy did he cry,
>   Wherefore he lyves, let deth do what he can."

---

* In Mr. Arber's "Transcript of the Stationers' Register" (Vol. I., p. 144), occurs the interesting note—" Master Birde and Master Tallis of the Maiesties Chappell."

We are told that in this old church there were inscriptions to the memory of Richard Bower, and Clement Adams, gentlemen of the Chapel Royal.* The autograph of Thomas Tallys, is on the last leaf of Wylde's MS., appended to which is the name re-written in large Roman shaped characters with the following note—

> "xxi gilt bookes in qto and octavo.
> x bookes in folio.
> iii fayre sets gilt bookes."

On folio 124 occurs, in a later hand, " Liber Sanctæ Crucis de Waltham.

This valuable manuscript of John Wylde's is entitled " MONACORDUM" (fol. 3), and divided into two parts; the first is called "*Musica Manulis*," which extends to fol. 18, and the second " *Tonale*," begins at fol. 19.; (fol. 27 is a double sheet). The preface or "*prologus*" commences — " *Quia juxta sapientissimum Salomonem dura est, ut inferius emulatio.*" Wylde observes that the Gamut is adapted to the hands of boys, as they can carry the scale about with them, and adds that the left hand is to be rather used than the right, because nearest the heart. No mention is made of secular music, but the whole volume is devoted to sacred song.

Sir John Hawkins, who has inserted nearly the whole of the latter part of this MS. in Vol. II. of " History of Music." says "Of the manuscript of Waltham Holy Cross it is to be remarked, that it appears to be a collection of Wylde's making, and that there is reason to believe that the first treatise, consisting of two parts, the one on Manual and the other on Tonale Music, was composed by Wylde himself. In the latter of these we meet with the term Double Cantus, and an example thereof in the margin, by which is to be understood a cantus of two parts.

" Wylde's tract comprehends the precepts of practical music, and may be considered as a compendium of that kind of knowledge which was necessary to qualify an ecclesiastic in that very essential part of his function, the performance of choral service.

" The Cotton manuscript and that of Waltham Holy Cross, which seems to contain all of music that can be supposed to

---

* Tallis' " Order of Daily Service," edited with historical introduction by E. F. Rimbault, LL.D., F.S.A.

have been known at the time of writing them, make but a very inconsiderable part of those which appear to have been written between the time of Guido and the invention of printing ; and innumerable are those who, in the printed accounts of ancient English writers in particular, are said to have written on various branches of the science. That the greater number of these authors were monks is not to be wondered at, for not only their profession obliged them to the practice of music, but their sequestered manner of life gave them leisure and opportunities of studying it to a greater advantage."

The choristers of the ancient church of Waltham in the middle age appear to have been quite equal to those of other Abbeys in musical proficiency, notwithstanding what the writer under the name of St. Bernard has said. In Wylde's time, and up to the brighter days of the Reformation, the "chaplenes and clerks" serving in the church greatly assisted in the service of song ; as we have before observed, they were required to be "shewinge in descant, clear voyced, well relished and pronouncynge, and suffytente in organes playing" The instrument used by Wylde, and later musicians in the church of Waltham, was probably a kind of portable organ called the Regal, or Regale ; Hopkins says that "musical writers have not explained the nature of the *Regal*, which was evidently to give out and sustain the melody of the plain-song." Mr. Carter describes the Regal as "having one row of pipes giving the treble notes, and the same number of keys." The early monastic organs or regals were very small. (See Lucinius's Musurgia, sen Praxis Musicæ, 1536). An instrument "with broad keys" was used very early in the continental churches, a description of which will be found in the "Theorica Musica," published in Milan in 1492. The Regal was used in Germany till a very recent period.

It might be observed here that early in the seventeenth century the parishioners of Waltham Abbey sold to the church-wardens of Cheshunt an old organ which would only play five tunes. And it appears that from that time to the commencement of the present century the Church of Waltham had no organ of any sort. The service of song was performed by a number of very able singers, who occasionally introduced into the orchestra a full band of wind instruments, such as the hautboy or oboe, bassoon, trombone, clarionet, flute, etc., which, doubtless, the ear of the present generation would fail to appreciate.

Many years ago, while the organ-loft was in the course of erection in the Abbey Church of Waltham, a self-taught musician of the town played a small spinet, an instrument of the pianoforte kind, which succeeded the virginals, and from which it seems to have differed very little. It consisted of a case, sounding-board, keys, jacks, and a bridge. This feeble instument in a short time gave way to make room for the organ presented by Mr. Leverton. This organ was used on all occasions for upwards of forty years, with very little cost to the parish. For a number of years a lady, known generally by the name of "Polly Thompson," played the old organ. Since then the post has been filled by persons of great musical skill. W. Cummings, Esq., was for some time the gifted organist of Waltham Church; also Messrs. Gibbons and Banks. This last named organist was succeeded by Joseph Chalk, Esq.

THE FONT of the Abbey Church has been entirely changed in shape and character, by successive modern alterations. Originally it was a square bowl* with arcaded sides, the panels sunk about half-an-inch, and a sharp moulding round the lower edge. It was supported on a central pillar one foot four inches in diameter, and four angle columns $3\frac{3}{4}$ inches in diameter. Years ago the angles of the bowl were cut away so as to make it octagonal, and the smaller supporting columns were removed, and the whole font was coated with paint. During the restoration of the church (1859-60), the bowl was further reduced by the removal of the mutilated arcades, still leaving the shape octagonal. It is now considered a fine font of Purbeck marble, but all trace of its original character is gone.†

THE STAINED WINDOWS, IN THE CHURCH.—Before the restoration of the Church the clerestory windows of the chancel were blocked up. They have, however, been opened and repaired, and glazed with tinted glass in various patterns. When the plaster was removed from the north aisle, the four large modern windows were found to have taken the place of a beautiful, two-light, early

---

* A "Pardon bowl" is spoken of in Cranmer's works as being in Waltham Abbey Church (*temp.*) Hen. VIII.

† Essex Arch. Trans. Vol. ii., 44.

decorated window, two Norman windows, and a very large flowing decorated window.

The " Rose " window at the east end is a part of the restoration, and is in the Flemish style of the 13th century. As regards the style of window suitable for this church, most persons agree that it should have been in imitation of Norman or early English. This window is estimated to have cost about £1,000. The stained glass is of the best kind, supplied by Messrs. Powell, of Whitefriars, and the cartoons were designed by E. B. Jones, Esq. The decorations are said to illustrate the divine nature of our Lord; thus, in the centre is a figure of our Saviour, and around are the seven days of creation. The three lancet windows below exhibit the ancestors of Christ and the prophets. The aisle windows represent the instruments by which our Lord was pleased to work out His will upon earth. Under the east window is the annexed inscription—*In memory of Elizabeth, sister of the Incumbent of this Parish, died April,* 1859. Another inscription appears under the last window in the north aisle—*In memory of Lousia, youngest daughter of the late William Banbury, Esq., of this Parish, died at Bournemouth, Nov. 7th,* 1867. In the chancel end of the north aisle is a stained glass window to the *memory of Mr. Charles Carr of this town, butcher, who died August 20th,* 1852. This window was inserted by Messrs. Bell & Co., of London, and the cost defrayed by Mr. James Carr, miller, and one of the Churchwardens during the restoration of the Church. The adjoining window in the north aisle is a three-light stained glass to the *memory of Mrs. Rosabel Saunders, late of Honey Lands, who died August,* 1867. The subject chosen is the three principal incidents in the life of the proto-martyr Stephen. A window (south aisle) in *memory of William Kent Thomas, late of Sewardstone shows us the four Apostles.* Two Norman windows (south aisle) were the gift of the Rev. J. Francis, M.A. These show the four Evangelists. In the same aisle is another to the *memory of Richard Francis, Esq., born June* 23, 1820, *and died July* 19, 1855. In the south-western window are heraldic bearings; also initials within circles—*M.S.-M.N., Obit, Oct. VII., MDCCCLI*—and underneath is *MDCCCLII.* The newly discovered two-light decorated window has been filled up with stained glass, the gift of the late Colonel Edenborough, representing several good women of the Old Testament. A memorial window was proposed some time ago to perpetuate the memory of Joseph Hall, D.D., twenty-two years curate of the Abbey Church, and afterwards bishop of Exeter and Norwich. This proposition has not yet been carried out. The memory of Dr. Thomas Fuller, curate of Waltham for several years after Bishop Hall, is deserving of consideration. Two memorial windows have been added to the Abbey Church, in the west end of the building. The window is stated to be " In loving memory of the Rev. James Francis, for 38 years Vicar of this parish." The window over the small west door represents the works of the Apostles, and is inscribed " To the glory of God and the memory of Sir Philip Francis, who died 9th August, 1876 ; and Colonel Alfred Francis, who died 27th March, 1876, brothers of the Vicar of this parish."

THE HISTORY OF A WINDOW.—There is a very interesting piece of history extant in connection with an early stained glass window which adorned the church prior to the dissolution of the Abbey in 1540. The window is now in St. Margaret's, Westminster. The characters represent the crucifixion. A copy was taken in 1768 by Basire, for the London Antiquarian Society.* The letter press at the foot of the plate expresses the following :—" The great east window of the parish church of St. Margaret, in Westminster, was made by order of the Magistrates of Dort in Holland, and by them intended as a present to K. Hen. VII. for his chapel at Westminster, but he dying before the window was finished, it was set up in the church of Waltham Abbey, and there remained till the dissolution, when it was removed to New Hall, in Essex, part of the estate of Gen¹ Monk ; and was there by his vigilance preserved from injury during the Civil Wars. Some years since, John Olmius, Esq., the then possessor of New Hall, sold this window to Mr. Conyers, of Copt Hall, in Essex, from whom the inhabitants of Saint Margaret, Westminster, purchased it in the year 1758, for the sum of 100 guineas.

The figures kneeling at the bottom of the two side panels represent Henry the VIIth. and his Queen, and were taken from original pictures sent to Dort for that purpose. Over

* _Vide_ Vetusta Monumenta.

the King is the figure of St. George, and above him a white rose within a red one; over the figure of the Queen stands that of St. Catherine of Alexandria; and in a panel over her head appears a pomegranate. " *Vert* in a Field *or* the Arms of the Kingdom of Granada." Another version of the window is, that it was removed by the last Abbot, Robert Fuller, to a private chapel at New Hall, an ancient seat belonging to the Earls of Ormond, of Wiltshire. The duke of Buckingham afterwards bought it, and to guard against imputations from his party, caused it to be buried under ground during the civil wars, and it was afterwards replaced in the chapel of New Hall by General Monk. After that when the chapel was demolished the window lay for some time cased up in boxes, till Mr. Conyers purchased it for his chapel at Copt Hall near Epping, and paid Mr. Price, a great artist, a large sum of money for repairing it. There it remained till his son John, building a new house at some distance from the old seat, sold it to the committee appointed for the repairing and beautifying of St. Margaret, Westminster, in 1758, for 400 guineas (Vide " Ornaments of Churches," 1761.) On the re-opening of St. Margaret's Church after the window had been inserted, a fine anthem was composed for the occasion by Dr. Dwyer. Soon afterwards the window got into Chancery, a bill being filed by the Dean and Chapter of Westminster, to restrain the parish authorities of St. Margaret's from exhibiting that which the capitular body declared to be "a superstitious image or picture." But after seven years' litigation the bill was dismissed, in memory of which Mr. Churchwarden Pierson presented, as a gift for ever to the parish, a silver gilt cup weighing nearly one hundred ounces, which remains to this day the loving cup produced with great ceremony at the parochial entertainments.

TOMBS IN THE ABBEY CHURCH.*

Some of the greatest noblemen of this country have found a resting place within the sacred precincts of the Abbey Church. The body of Harold, the founder of the building, was interred in an eastern choir which was destroyed in the Pre-Reformation

---

* For a fuller description of the tombs, see " Our Parish Registers," by W. Winters.

times. Hugh Nevil, Lord Justice of England, was buried in the Church, in 1222, in a splendid sarcophagus, and in 1245 the body of his son John Nevil was buried near his remains; also the favourite of Hen. III., Robert Passelew, archdeacon of Lewis, was buried in the Abbey, June 6, 1252. No monumental remains of the above noblemen exist at the present day. It is possible the tombs suffered much damage during the Commonwealth, as there were no less than forty-six old tombs in the Church at the dissolution of the Abbey, temp Hen. VIII., many of which covered the remains of Abbots, Earls, Knights and other notable personages. Bishop Hall once said that the church was the place for the living and not for the dead. The tombs are arranged thus :—

WEST END OF THE CHURCH.—John Halfhide, died 14th Oct. 1814, aged 82. Also Mrs. Jane Halfhide, his wife, died 13th May, 1827, aged 76. Edward Halfhide died 4th Sept., 1764, aged 72. Also Ann Halfhide, his wife, died 3rd Jan., 1784, aged 80. Elizabeth Powell, died 29th August, 1750, aged 55. George Fawbert, died 22nd April, 1821, aged 68. Also Sarah Fawbert, his wife, died 19 April, 1828. Mrs. Mary Denton, wife of Mr. Robert Denton, died 4th June, 1795, aged 44 years. Also Mr. Robert Denton, died July 18, 1811, aged 73 years; Mors Janna Vitæ. Susan, wife of John Chase. Esq., only daughter of the above, who died at St. Heliers, Jersey, Nov. 6, 1841. Epson Middleton, Esq., dep. 17 June, 1825, aged 59. Edward Hillersdon, Esq., died 4 Jan., 1784, aged 67. Louisa Sophia Charlotte Harcourt, 3rd daughter of Henry Harcourt, Esq., of Pendley co. Herts, by whom he had issue three sons and three daughters. Also Louisa Sophia Charlotte Hillersdon, relict of the above Edw. Hillersdon, dep. 26 May, 1798, aged 80. Also Sophia Hillersdon, daughter of the above Edward and Lousia Hillersdon, dep. Nov. 6, 1801, aged 57. Fredrick Jessopp, who died at the island of St. Vincent, 9 June, 1820, in the 20th year of his age.

> By Strangers honoured,
> And by Strangers mourned.

John Utterton, Esquire of Cobbin House, in the Parish of Waltham Abbey, dep. 22nd May, 1797, aged 52. Also Mary Utterton, his second daughter, dep. 4th May, 1822, aged 54; and Lt. Col. John Utterton, of Heath Lodge, Croyden, Surrey, eldest son of the above John Utterton, Esq., died March, 1843, aged 67. Elizabeth Harrison, wife of William Harrison, Esq., of Lincoln's Inn Fields, London, and of Cheshunt, Hertfordshire. His eldest daughter dep. 25 July, 1827, aged 62. Also Ann Saunders, wife of Thomas Saunders, dep. 21 May, 1811, aged 68.

SOUTH AISLE.—On the floor of the south aisle is a slab bearing the following initials :—E. H., 1791. L. S. G. H., 1795. Mr. John Birks, dep. June 1st, 1765, aged 48. (South West Corner) *Armorials'* Richard Naylor, M.D. dep. 23 June, 1683, aged 63. Ann Pordage, daughter of Benjamin Pordage, and Elizabeth, his wife, dep. 20 Oct., 1682. Lionel Goodrick Pordage, son of Benjamin Pordage* and Elizabeth, his wife, dep. August 30, 1684. Elizabeth Pordage, wife of Benjamin Pordage, departed this life Novemb. ye 9, 1687, in her 43rd year, left Behind her Rachel Elizabeth and Edward Pordage of which she died.† Francis Wollaston, the onely son of William Wollaston of Shenton in ye County of Leicester, Esq., and Elizabeth his wife ye onely daughter of Francis Cave of Ingorsbie in the said county of Leicester, & the Lady Viliers of Brooksbie in ye said county of Leicester. Hee was born on ye 3rd July, 1668, and dep. ye 28th Nov., 1684. He died aged 17, Nov. 28, 1684. There is an ornamental slab to the memory of Francis Wollaston over the porch door, in the tower of the Abbey. The *Arms* of Charles II., dated 1662, were fixed on the porch wall. The Wollastons and Foxes of Waltham were related. Alexander Ruddall and Elizabeth his wife.

The 29th April Anno Domini 1683, Ætat suœ 90—Oblitibus ero. [The above stone is broken and turned the wrong way.]

Near the Font is a black and white marble slab. Mrs. Sophia Wood (wife of Mr. John Wood) dep. 26 June, 1841, aged 66. Also Mr. William Clark, brother of the above Mrs. Wood, died 20th Jan., 1847, aged 66. Mr. John Wood

---

* Benj. Pordage made an application to the Lords of the Treasury for the property of three men who were hanged at York, for counterfeiting the King's coin.

† This family was related to Samuel Pordage, the barrister and dramatist, whom the poets, Oldham and Dryden, severely satirised ; the former as "the wretched bard," and the latter as "lame Mephibosheth, the wizard's son."

died Sept. 10, 1854, and was interred in the Churchyard at the east end of the church. Likewise Mrs. Salley Page, sister of the above Mrs. Wood, and Mr. Clark, died 16th March, 1856, aged 83. There are a few brasses which have escaped the hands of the spoiler. On the south wall is a mural brass of the Stacey family, headed by two lines in Latin. The son is kneeling behind his father, and on the table are two books. (*Legend*) Edward Stacey of Waltham Holy Crosse countie of Essex, gent. of ye age of lxxii yeares died ye 17th Marche 1555, leaving one sonne, Francis Stacey. Katherine, his only wife of the age of threescore and eyghtene dyed xxiiiith daye of Febrvary Anno 1565.

Near the above is another brass in black letter. To the memory of the Colte family.

"Here under lyeth Buryed near to this Pillar the bodyes of Thomas Colte Esquyre and Magdalene his Wyfe who had isshue betweene them bi sonnes & iiii Daughters Which Thomas deceased the xxix day of June ano. mcccclix and the sayd Magdelen Who was the Cavser of this monnment, deceassed the last daye of Nobembr. ano. mcccccxci whose bodes and soules god send joyfull resvrrection. This was made 1576."*

Small brass—Robert Rampston, of Chingford, in the county of Essex, gent., deceased. As he was carefull in his Life-tyme to reliebe the Poore soe at his ende by his last Testament he gabe xrii£ yerely for eber to the Poore of dvis Pishes and Prysons, whereof to the Poore of this Pishes of Waltham Holy Cross he hath giben yerely for eber xls. To be paid in the Moneth of Nobember. He departed this Mortall life ye third day of Angust m.cccc.lxxx fibe.

THE CHANCEL END.—Flat Stone. Master Walter Grenfall Chinnery son of William and Margt. Chinnery of Gillwell House, Sewardstone. He died 19 Nov. 1802 aged 10 years 7 months. Near the Denny tomb is the effigy of Lady Greville, of Harold's Park. At one time this effigy was in a recumbent posture, under a canopy supported with two marble pillars, over which were the Denny arms and the annexed inscription—Heere lyeth buried the Body of Elizabeth Ladie Grevill Daughter of the Lord John Graye Brother to Henry

---

* Above this inscription appears the family group, in a devotional attitude before two reading desks with books opened. The males on one side and the females on the other are surmounted by three shields bearing the arms of the family. A curious tale is told by Dr. Fuller of Sir Thomas Colte catching a Waltham monk in a "buckstall."

Lord Graye Duke of Suffolk, Sonnes of Thomas Lord Graye of Grooby, Marques of Dorset, &c.

Another old tomb is also gone. To the memory of Ion and Ione Cressy. James Cressy, Esq., of Waltham Abbey, was living in 1574. He was the son of William Cressy, who by marriage was related to Archbishop Cranmer.

In the south-east corner of the church is the effigy of Lord Edward and Lady Margaret Denny, beneath a canopy of veined marble, and surmounted by armorial bearings of the family. These effigies are life size. Lord Denny is dressed in armour, and rests in a recumbent posture, leaning on his left arm. His lady is placed in the same attitude, in a black dress, with a ruff and veil. Under them are the effigies of their six sons and four daughters, kneeling. Above the effigies is a lengthy inscription.* Several members of the Denny family have visited this tomb, and proposed to restore it.

NEAR COMMUNION RAIL.—Mrs. Susan Holmes, the wife of Mr. Thomas Holmes, who dep. 10 March 173½ in her 43rd year. Mr. Thomas Holmes who dep. 12 Jan. 173⁵⁄ in his 63rd year. Thomas Leverton, Esq.,† dep. 23 Sept. 1824. His wife died August 4th, 1833, aged 76. John Walton Esq. second son of William Walton of Surrey Esq. by Philippa Bourchier 4th daughter and Co-heiress of John Bourchier M.D. formerly of this county. He married Hester Jacobsen eldest daughter of the two daughters and Co-heiresses of Sir Jacob Jacobsen of Walthamstow. He died on the 19th July 1757 Ætatis 58.

---

* Farmer states, that underneath one Pillar of the said Monument on a black marble pedestal is the following:—

> Learn curious Reader how you pass,
> Your once Sir Edward Denny was
> A courtier of the Chamber
> A soldier of the Field:
> Whose Tongue could never flatter,
> Whose Heart could never yealde.

There is no trace of the above lines on the Denny tomb at the present day.

† Thomas Leverton was the founder of the Leverton School. This school is kept up by the interest of £6,000, left by the founder.

Ann Walton second daughter of William and Philippa both late of Balam in the parish of Streatham and County of Surrey. She died unmarried 29 May 1772 in her 66th year.* William Sworder Walford eldest son of W. Walford of High Beech dep. 11 Sept. 1823, aged 25.

The Travers' tomb (with Heraldic bearings) has been very roughly used. James Travers, buried August 5, 1707. Near it is the tomb of the Thomas family, late of Sewardstone. Carolettœ suæ mærentes posuerunt Gulielmus et Eleanor Thomas, Parentes Nata die vii Septemb A.D. 1816. Obiit die xvi Aprilis A.D. 1820.—Eleanorae optimæ Conjugi Gulielmus Kent Thomas mæreus posuit Obiit die xix Aprilis A.D. 1826, armos nata xlii. John Skirrow of Leppits Hill in this parish and of Gilstead in the parish of Buigley co. York, dep. 11 Jan. A.D. 1794 aged 59. Also William Skirrow youngest son of the above, dep. 21 Jan. A.D. 1801 aged 7. Also Elizabeth, wife of the above John Skirrow Esq., dep. 27 Feb. 1832 aged 77. Also of Bridget Skirrow youngest daughter of John and Elizabeth Skirrow, dep. 31 July A.D. 1838 aged 49. The following is on a Brass in the chancel. Henry Austin, servant to the Right Honourable Iames Earle of Carlile, and gentleman of his Horse, who departed this life the 6 of November Anno Dom: 1638. James Smith gent of Honey Lane in this parish Dyed August ye 18 1725 aged 58. Also Mrs Lucretia Smith wife of the above said James Smith who died June ye 27 1726 aged 41. Mrs. Mary Smith died 3 Oct. 1731, aged 27. Near the Denny Tomb is a stone slab partly hid by the floor boards. Coll. Peter Floyer son of ye late Sir Peter Floyer Knt. and Alderman of the City of London Obt. 17 Jan. 1724. Also Mrs Mary Floyer wife of Capt. Charles Floyer Ob. 3 Jan. 1725, and Capt. Charles Floyer son of Sir Peter Floyer, Obt. 23 March 1732. Also William Woolley married Leitia sister of Coll. and Capt. Floyer died August, 1762 aged 70.

Flat Stone with armorials (east end) Mr. Henry Arcourt dep. 1704, and Hannah his wife dep. 1735, and their nephew James Arcourt dep. 1769. The old iron rails which formerly enclosed the communion table were " finely gilt," and brought from Copt Hall. They once surrounded a royal bed on which

---

* John Walton, Esq., was proprietor of the Powder Mills in this town.

some of the Kings of England have reposed. Near the communion rails at the end of north aisle is a stone which at an early period contained the brass effigy of an abbot. There is also a massive Purbeck marble slab within the communion rails. The inscription round the verge of this incised stone in Lombardic metal characters has long been destroyed, but the matrix of the letters still remains. Another stone adjoining it, and partly hid by the rails, bears the following inscription :—*Hic Haroldi ; in Cœnobio Carnis Ressurrectionem. Expectat Jacobus Raphael, Gallus, Demum Scotus, demum Anglus, Denique nihil. Anno ætat,* 70 *Obit Mar.* 30 *Anno* 1686. "Here lyeth Mr. Swynefield." The epitaph has been Englished thus :—Here in Harold's tomb James Raphael, a Frenchman, claimed both by Scotland and England, but now nothing, awaits the resurrection of the body. Died March 30 1686 in the 70th year of his age. The register records the burial of James Raphael April 1st, 1686. Flat Stone Francis Atkyns gentleman servant to ye Right Honourable Edward Earl of Norwich, and after his decease to the Lady Mary Countess of Norwich, and after her decease to the Right Honourable James Earl of Carlile. Buried July 6, 1640.

The North Aisle.—In the north cast corner of the church is an early black marble body stone on the centre of which is a floriated cross in relievo. A marble urn surmounting a pillar.—To Caroline Chinnery, died in the twenty-first year of her age on the 3rd April, 1812. Caroline is inscribed on the centre of the urn and on the base of the pillar is written—Walter Grenfell Chinnery lies interred in the same tomb. (See south aisle). Black marble tablet—James Austin of High Beech in this county Esq. formerly of Kingston in the Island of Jamaica and late of London merchant dep. 4th June 1803 aged 50. Miss Mary Austin died 16 July, 1827, aged 50, also Ann daug. of the above died 28 April 1828 in her 46th year. Brass plate (near the robing-room). In the faith of our Lord Jesus Christ in which S. Stephen lived and fell asleep. This window is inscribed to the memory of Rosabel the devoted and beloved wife of H. W. Demain Saunders, 16th August 1867. The finest tomb in the church is one of black and white marble, near the vestry-room door (north side), to the memory of Robert Smith, a naval officer. The tomb is

adorned with angels and coats of arms at the four corners,
and on the front is represented a ship under full sail with her
name on her side, INDUSTRIA, surrounded with carved mathe-
matical naval instruments, fire arms, and cutlasses, under one
of which is inscribed the word "Socordia." The black marble
slab above bears a lengthy inscription in Latin. On this tomb
stands the marble bust of Henry Wollaston justice of the peace
temp Charles II. Tablet. Thomas Leverton Esquire of Bedford
Square London many years architect and surveyor to His Majesty's
land revenue and other public offices, and in the commission
of the peace for the city of Westminster and for the counties
of Middlesex, Surrey, and Kent. A benefactor to this parish
the donor of its organ and the founder of its Charity Schools.
He departed this life on the 23 day of September 1824 aged
81 years. Also of Rebecca his wife, Obt. the 4th day of
August 1833 Æt. 76.*   Francis John Birthwick Cole wife of
    * It is probable that the Jones and Edmonson charity dated 1756 for
educating six poor boys led to the foundation of the Leverton School.
John Cole of the Inner Temple, London, Gent. dep 11 August
1822 aged 35; and was interred in a vault under the vestry
of this Church.

Black and white marble tablet in memory of the Thomas
family of Sewardstone (Latin inscription). Underneath is a
brass plate—Annie Thomas youngest daughter of William
Kent and Eleanor Thomas of Sewardstone died June 5th 1851
aged 28. The window to the west of the plate is to the
memory of her father. Sarah wife of Robert Wellham Citizen
and grocer of London and daughter of Charles & Elizabeth
Warner of this town died Nov. y^e 17 1722 aged 29. Sarah
daughter of Robert & Sarah Welham died March y^e 23 171$\frac{7}{8}$
aged 8 months. A beautifully ornamented stone on the lower
part is the profile of two heads. James Spilman Esq. F.R.S.
many years one of the directors of the Bank of England and
a commissioner of Greenwich Hospital. He died Nov^r· 1st
1763 in the 83 year of his age. And also of Hester his wife
one of the sisters & co-heiresses of Sir Wm. Willys of Fen
Ditton Co. Cambs, Bart. She departed August 23rd 1761 aged
72. This monument was erected by their only child Julia
wife of George Richard Carter of Chilton co Bucks & Warlies
in this County Esq. Near the north door, north aisle Tho.
Jones Gent, Obiit 7 die D[ec.] A.D. MDCCLIII.

THE CRYPT.—In the Crypt under the Lady Chapel are several stones with only the surname upon them, viz., CLARKE, BELLAS, COLE and also a large upright slab. A part of the Crypt, south west, was presented by the parish to Richard Morgan Esq of Warlies Park as the burial place for him and his family. The usual fees for burying in the charnel house were one third less than in the church. Mr. Thomas Pickthall, curate of Waltham, had a family vault in the crypt, but his remains were interred in Broxbourne Churchyard. James Webb born in this town and a citizen of London died 28th April 1794 aged 78. Also Elizabeth Dingle granddaughter of the above James Webb died 20th Jan. 1812 aged 26. Also John Orlton father of Elizabeth Dingle and son-in-law of the above James Webb died 24 Feb. 1818 aged 78. Also Mrs. Sarah Orlton widow of John Orlton and daughter of the above James Webb died 19 July 1827 in her 79th year. Also James John Orlton son of the above died 7 May 1837 aged 58 years. James Andrews departed April yᵉ 20 1709 aged 60. William Clarke died 26 March 1815 aged 39 years. Also Martha daughter of the above who died 19 Oct. 1810 aged 6 years.—In memory of Mrs Jane Richfield who died 3rd Dec. 1775 aged 54. Also Mr. John Richfield who died 15 April 1778 aged 63. Also Miss Temperance Richfield youngest daughter of the above who died 3 Oct. 1780 aged 25. This stone and the Orlton Tablet formerly stood in the little south vestry and was removed to the Crypt when the vestry was demolished in 1875. In the Crypt are the remains of Mrs. Sophia Wood who dep. June 26 1841, and her brother Mr. William Clark who died 20 Jan. 1847 aged 66 years. There are other tombs mentioned by *Farmer.* Ann Warton daughter of Sir George Warton Bart. died Sep 2 1708.* Ann wife of Edward Parker dep 1780. Edward Parker Esq born 1736, died 1780.†

---

* The Parish Registers, give Mrs. Theophilis Wharton daug. to Sir Polycarpus Wharton, Baronet, Bur. 13 May 1706. Also Mr. Richard Wharton son to Sir Polycarpus Wharton, Bart., Bur. 10 June 1709. Also Susan Wharton, Bur. 8 Jan 1719-20

† Richard Brinsley Sheridan, resided for some time with Mr. Parker, of Waltham Abbey. See *English* Illustrated Mag. (April) 1887.

INVENTORY OF CHURCH GOODS, A.D. 1540.

NVENTORY of Church Goods belonging to Waltham Abbey, taken at the dissolution of the Abbey by Sir Richard Riche,Chancellor of the Augmentation, and other Commissioners, March 24, 31 Henry VIII.* The original *Inventory* of the Abbey goods is preserved in the Public Record Office. Several portions of this inventory with other Waltham inventories were published some years ago by the Rev. M. E. C. Walcott, all of which in detail are here given from original MSS., as also those noted by Dr. Fuller and John Farmer. The value of the following inventory is considerable, as it shows the number of sacred and domestic buildings and their furniture connected with the Abbey, Temp. Henry VIII., nearly all of which buildings have long since been demolished:—

Thinner Parlor.†—Item the hangings of the same of olde grene saye, v$^{s.}$ Item a table borde wth ii trestelles and ii formes ii$^{s.}$ iiii$^{d.}$ Item an olde carpett of verdure xvi$^{d.}$ ‡ Item a turned cheyer & a joyned stole, viii$^{d.}$ Item a plane cubborde, viii$^{d.}$ Item a portall of wainescott.

---

* In one copy of MS. is mentioned—THE GRETE HALL first, with iij grete table bordes, with iij formes the same filed about with wainescott and a portall of the same and ij old cubbords. THE ABBOTS UTTER PARLOR Item table bordes with peir of trestells. Item iij formes a ioyned stole and old cubbord, and the same parlor filled with wanescott. Item ij old gentish (Kentish) carpetts are in the wyndowe & the other on the cubbord, valued at vs. viii$^{d.}$ THE STONE PARLOR, wainscotted, with a portal of the same.

† The Inner Parlour.

‡ Verdaur, a hanging on the wall. Add. MSS. 24, 529, fol. 215.

⁎ The Rev. M. E. C. Walcott says—"The Inventory beginning at this end speaks of the Lady Chapel [which was built 1188] and the choir built c 1242 [Matt. Par. iii. 286], and then of the chureh [that is the nave], and my Lady Roos Chapel, which no doubt was the chapel of decorated date still existing. [W. Burges Report, 6.] The Roos family lived at Chingford, and I find two Chantries at Waltham, one of the Charnel in which the priest helped in serving the cure, and the other Our Lady's, with a fraternity called Our Lady's Brotherhood. [Certif. of Chantr. xix., 45, xxx. 61.] [See view of the Minster in Gents. Mag. with its southern chapel horribly mutilated, 1798]. I also met with an order for the repair of the Minster-nave as the parish church of Waltham, dated 6th Sept. 1286, *in viridario*

The Grete Somer Chambor.—Item ii table bordes wth ii peir of trestells and iiii short formes. Itm an old carpet of turkey-worke. Itm an olde carpet of verdure. Itm ii flaundres cheyers & iiii. turned cheyers.* Itm vii olde white cosshions ii olde cussh. of vdure, and vi w^t armes and myters. Itm one Aundyron & iii olde carpetts in the wyndow w^t a longe white olde cusshion. Itm a cubbord w^t an old gentish [Kentish] carpet.

The Abbotts Chambor.—Itm a fethurbed a bolster a pelowe A peire of blanketts a peir of shets and a Covering off verdure. Item a folding counter a plaine new cofer ii trusfing cofers vi cosshyones and a trussing beddestede.†

The Abbotts Inner Chambor.—Item a materes a fetherbedde a bolster a coving of Imagerie & a new coser.

The Warderobe.—Item xii cosshyons of verdure. Item iii other olde cosshyons. Item iii grete chests bovnde w^t yron. Itm a peir of aundyrons. A fire pike and a peir of tonges.

The Kings Chambor.—Item hangings of grene saye‡ w^t borders of painted cloth xxxiii^s· iiii^d· Itm. a trussing bedstede wth Silor and testor of white bustyan olde embrondered with fflowres w^t corteuins of grene and red saye ii fetherbedds ii bolsters ii pelowers a peir of fustyans & a courlet of the said bustyan iii *li.* Itm a litle square table a cubbord ii olde turkey carpetts ii gentish carpetts a flaunderes cheyers iii olde white cosshios and ii ioyned fformes, xx^s·

---

prope inferiorem aulam quæ camera abbatis appelatur. [Land. Reven. Papers 1277.] The various chambers of the Abbot's Lodge and the Monastic buildings are mentioned in the inventory. It is satisfactory to find how completely in many particulars it corresponds to the official notices of receipt of the plundered treasures. A guard we find was set to keep watch over the sacrilegious plunder until it was removed. A few vestments were reserved to the church use, and given to the neighbouring parishes. Organs were neither large or very common before the Reformation, but we find here ' a greate large payer above one the northe of the quyre, and a lesser payer beneth in the choir, and a lytell payre in the Lady Chapel.' Two 'Gospels in the Saxon tongue' which would be now prized as invaluable, are mentioned; and among rarer articles of furniture, a folding table, the materials of lether gold, and crystal glasses."

* Richly carved like Flanders chests.

† A folding bedstead used in travelling.

‡ Green silk. Royalty frequently slept in the Abbey in a chamber especially prepared.

The Abbotts Chapell.—Item a table on the aulter* peinted xxi^d. Itm an old carpet, ii. other olde cosshyons iiii^s. Itm olde hanging of thaultes with a diaper cloth and a litle dexte,† ii^s. viiii^d.

The Grete Chambor called the Wintor Chambor.—Item olde hangings of blew and white throde, iii^s. iiii^d. Itm a trussing bedstede with a testor of like threde and corteins of grene buckeram vii^s. Itm a mattres a fethurbed a bolster ii blankets an old couyng viiii^s. Itm aundyron a cheyer a cosshion & ii formes xii^d.

The next Chambor.—Item the hangings of red and yolowe buckeram a trussing bedestede w^t testor of the same buckeram and corteins of blew buckeram, xvi^s. viii^d. Itm a matres a fetherbedde a bolster a peir off blanketts & a countrpoint of olde Imagerye, xiii^s. iiii^d. Itm a trundell bedstede a fethurbedde a bolster and an old coulet, vi^s. viii^d. Itm a cubborde an olde carpet a turned cheyer, xii^d.

The Quenes Chambor.—Item hangings of olde woven Aris, xxvi^s. viii^d. Item a trussing bedstede w^t an olde testor and corteins of threde colored, x^s. Itm a matres a fetherbed a bolster a peire of fustyans a peir of shets an olde coulet of tapestrie and a pelowe, xxvi^s. viii^d. Item a cubbord with a gentish carpet a korven stole a turned cheyer, iiii^s. Itm a trundell‡ bedstede a fethurbedde a bolster a peir of shets and a coverlet, iiii^s.

The Master§ of the Childernes Chambor.—Item olde hangings of peinted cloth a matres a fethebedde a peire of blanketts a bolster a peir of shets and an other olde matres, xiii^s. iiii^d.

Pratts Chambor [to Pratte].—Item a matres a flockebed an olde coverlett with a bolster.

The Bakers Chambor.—Item a matres an olde coulett a course peire of shets and a bolster. given to the said Pratt and Baker.

The Buttrye.—P. Abbe, Item v diape table clothes old woren. xxx^s. Itm i double and vi sengle towells of diapr xx^s. P. Abbe, Item a Dosem of Diap^r napkyns. Itm a cubbord cloth and a coupane of diapr xvi^d. Itm vi Plaine clothes for thabbotts table, xvi^s. viii^d. P. Abbe, Itm viii coser table clothes for side bords

---

* Altar   † Desk, a lectern *i.e.*, Litany-desk.
‡ A truckle, rolled back under a standing bed. § Schoolmaster.

x^{s.}   Itm xii towells and vii cubbods clothes plaine xxiii^{s.} iiii^{d.}
Itm v Dosem & vii plaine napkins, xi^{s.} P. Abbe, Itm viii necke
bandes. Item xii candlestickss of brasse x^{s.} P. Abbe, Itm vi
Candlesticks of pewter. Itm iiii Pewter pettell potts, iii^{s.} iiii^{d.}
Itm v saltes off tynne, ii^{s.} For the Abbott, Item ii chafinge
dishes of brasse, iiii^{d.}

The Kechyn [*Kitchin.*]—ii P. Abbe, Item iiii grete brasse potts
and iiii other lesser potts of brasse xiiii^{s.} Itm one posnet pott,
xii^{d.} P. Abbe, Itm one chafron with eares. P. Abbe, Itm an
other chafre wth a stele. Item a grete panne wth ii eares, ii^{s.}
Itm vii other pannes with eares, ix^{s.} Itm a grete and a litle
kettell xvi^{d.} Itm ii Skomers and ii Ladells, xii^{d.} i P. Abbe,
Itm ii litle brasse morters w^t iii pestells xx^{d.} Itm one Collender
& i frying pane iiii^{d.} Itm ii gredyrones, xii^{d.} ii P. Abbe Itm
x spitts grete and small, xvi^{s.} Itm iii peir of rackes, viii^{s.} Itm
iiii kachyn knyves ii peir of pothoks one fire shouell & vi yron
wedges, iiii^{s.} Itm a grete pot standing in a furneys in the grete
kechyn, xiii^{s.} iiii^{d.} Itm an Iron pyle, ii^{d.} Itm a grete brasse pott
broken iiii^{s.}

The Scullery.—P. Abbe, Itm iiii Dosem di of good platers &
viii olde xxxvi^{s.} viii^{d.} no. ii platts lackyng. Itm ix chargers and
ii Slats, x^{s.} Itm iiii Dosem potyngers xvi^{s.} Itm iiii Dosem
& v sawcers, viii^{s.} Item a kettyll of brasse in a furneys. Itm a
cestron of leade wth ii cockes.

The Bakehouse.—Item ii kneding troughes wth a brake and ii
molding bords. Itm a panne w^t a leade to heat water in.

The Brewhouse.—Item ii grete ffatters wth leads on them A
masshing fatte & xxviii Kymnells xxxiii^{s.} iiii^{d.} Itm a grete furneys
of Coper and an other lesser furneys likewise of coper,
xiii£ vi^s viii^{d.}

The Graner there [*Garner*].—Item vii quarters of malt a
iiii^{s.} the quarter, Sum xxviii^{s.} Item a horsemyll. Itm an horse
for the same myll, v^{s.} Itm ii Dragge neats for fysshing.

The Smythes fforge.*—Item ii Andevyles the one the stele
woren out and other trashe for a Smyth, xxx^{s.}

The Graunge† *in the garner there.*—ffirst by estimacon x
quarters off whete at vi^{s.} the quarter, lx^{s.}

---

* The house in the Market Place belonging to the parish is called " The
Forge."

† Probably the Abbey Farm.

The Otebarne[Oat Barn].—Item in ots thresshed by estimacon .v quarters at ii^s· viii^d· the quarter, xiii^s· iiii^d Item in the mowe on thresshed by estimacon xv quarters at ii^s· viii^d· the quarter, xl^s·

The hey barne [Hay Barn].—Item by estimacon xxi lodes besydes iiii lodes for iii Browne hey at v$^£$ xiii^s·

The Plowhouse.—Item iii peir of harrowes and a plowe vi^s· viii^d· Item a litle ffurneys off leade iii^s· iiii^d·   Item ii peir of yron draughts & vii yoks iii^s· iiii^d·   Item the bodies of ii Donge cartes and one lyme cart wt i peire of wheles, x^s·   Item ii carts wt yron bounde wheles, xxvi^s· viii^d·

The Deyhouse.*—Item a cawdron of brasse bounde wth Iron iiii^s·   Item iii brasse potts a kettyll trivett a barre of yron and ii pothangers, vi^s·   Item a litle cawdron in a furneys iii^s· iiii^d·   Item a gredyron and ii spitts xii^s·

The Cattell.—ffirst iiii^{xx} viii shepe wt xii Lambes viii$^£$ Item v^{lxs}· Kyne ii^{xxs}· Bulles ii Bullockes and v$^{xvis. viiid}$ yerelings cxii^s· viii^d· Item vii Oxen vi$^£$ Itm xiii bores and sowes yonge and old with viii Pigges xxiiii^s·   Itm vi carte horses v$^£$ Item vi malte horses iiii   Item xii Oxon in the stall x$^£$ xvi^d·   Sum t. xl$^£$ xii^s· viii^d·

Corne.—Theise done Remityon unsold vntyll the Channellers pleasure be knowen.   Itm in whete in a feld called Cobbefeld† cxl acr at vi^s· the acr.   Itm in the same field in ots c acr at v^s· the acr.   After open measure, made by the Tenants and the Kyngs Officers there was in whete iiii^{xx}· i acr at vi^s· the acre xxiiii$^£$ vi^s·   Itm after measured the oots whiche doth amount to iii acres lxiii at iiii · the acre xii$^£$ xii^s·   Sum Totall of the goods sold to Mr. Deny‡ besydes the Corne in the felds c$^£$ x^s· vi^d·   Whereof Receyued by the Receyuer of geffry gates xl$^£$·   And so re. lx$^£$ x^s· vi^d·   Itm of the corne xxxvi$^£$ xviii^s· Sum Due by Mr. Deny besydes that that ys payed before iiii^{xx}· xvii$^£$ viii^s· vi^d· .   Sum Totall of the ornaments, goods, & chatalls before mentyoned w^t the corne in the fld. ccij$^£$ xvi^s· x^d·

Whereof by Mr. North for iii Copes vestments deacons & Subdeacons xl^d· franc Browne for hey cxiii^s· Mr. Deny cxxxii$^£$ iii^s· x^d·   Receyued by the Receyuor lv$^£$

---

* A place for cooking.

† Cobbing Mead.

‡ Probably Sir Anthony Denny, the King's Chamberlain.

Pensyons & rewards appoynted to the late Abbot of Waltham & to his Co brethere the xxiiii day of marche A⁰ xxxi H. viii by the. Com[missione]rs.—It. to Robert ffuller Clerk late Abbott there for term of hys life [in land and possessions to the yearly value] thereof as doth appere cc. It. to Thos Warren prior ibm xx£ pensyon, iii£ reward; It. Robert Wodleff, ix pensyon, iii£ reward; It. to Ric Rede, vi£ xiiiˢ· viiiᵈ· pensyon, iii£ reward; It. Willm lyllye* Chaunter ibm vi£ viiiˢ· iiiiᵈ· pensyon, iii£ reward; It. Tho hawkyns, ix£ pensyon, iii£ reward; It. to George solye, vi£ xiiiˢ· iiiiᵈ· pensyon, iii£ reward; It. to Ed. Sanders, Subprior, vi£ xiiiˢ iiiiᵈ· pensyon, iii£ reward; It. to Robert Pker† Sexton ibm, vi£ xiiiˢ· iiiiᵈ· pensyon, iii£ reward; It. to Edward Story, viii£ pensyon, iii£ reward; It. to Hege Yonge‡ vi£ xiiiˢ· iiiiᵈ· pensyon, iii£ reward; It. to Humfry Martyn, vi£ xiiiˢ· iiiiᵈ· pensyon, iii£ reward; It. to Miles Garrard, vi£ xiiiˢ· iiiiᵈ· pensyon, iii£ reward; It. p John Norreys, vi£ xiiiˢ· iiiiᵈ· pensyon, iii£ reward; It. to John Sanders, v£ pensyon, iii£ reward; It. to John Holmested, v£ pensyon, iii£ reward; It. to Robert Hall§ v£ pensyon, iii£ reward; It. to Edmund ffreke,¶ v£ pensyon, iii£ reward. [Signed] Richard Ryche, Wyllyam petre‖ Sum cccxxvi£ Nicholas Gate, John ap Rice, Thomas Myldemaye, ffrances Jobson [auditors].

---

* A friend of Thomas Tallis, the Organist.

† Robert Parker.   ‡ Hugh Young.   § Justice of Peace.

¶ Edmund Freke, a scholar of high repute; made Bishop of Norwich in 1584, and died Bishop of Worcester in 1590.

‖ Sir William Petre was principal Secretary of State for many years. He died in 1571 and was buried at Ingatestone.

It was thought at one time to make a Bishopric of Waltham Abbey. The scheme of the intended Bishopric here comprised a Bishop, a president xxiij£ vjˢ. viijᵈ. [B for the corps of his promotion ix£ and xvjᵈ· by day] Book 24 Augm. Off. fol. 7. 58. by prebendaryes every of them by the yere xx£ [the corps 7£ and viijˢ· by day,] a reder of divinite xx£. iv peti canons to sing. [B to keep the quire] in the quire every of them viijˢ· £1. [B. there are 6, one to be Sexton, a Gospeller vj£, a Pisteler cˢ.] [B. like the peti canons they were to have £1.] vj layemen to sing and serve in the quere, every of them vj£ xiijˢ· iiijᵈ. viij Choresters every of them v marks; a Master of the children x£. iiij Students of divinite, ij at Oxenford and towe at Cambrydge, every of them xl£; xx Scholars every of them v marks.

Wages and *Rewards.*—Itm. Edward Stacy,* xiii$^{s.}$ iiii$^{d.}$; xiii$^{s.}$ iiii$^{d.}$ John Henghaie, xiii$^{s.}$ iiii$^{d.}$; xiii$^{s.}$ iiii$^{d.}$ It Cristofer Cressey,† xiii$^{s.}$ iiii$^{d.}$; xiii$^{s.}$ iiii$^{d.}$ Thomas Talys‡, xx$^{s.}$; xx$^{s.}$ John Buck, x$^{s.}$; x$^{s.}$ Itm. Henry Smyth, x$^{s.}$; x$^{s.}$ John Herde, vi$^{s.}$ viii^{d} ; vi$^{s.}$ viii$^{d.}$ Willm Corbyn, vi$^{s.}$ viii$^{d.}$; vi$^{s.}$ viii$^{d.}$ Rogr Gyttones, x$^{s.}$; x$^{s.}$ Richard Wallenger, viii$^{s.}$ iiii$^{d.}$; viii$^{s.}$ iiii$^{d.}$ John Corbey, vi$^{s.}$ viii$^{d.}$; vi$^{s.}$ viii^{d} Richard Marten, vi^{s} viii$^{d.}$; vi$^{s.}$ viii$^{d.}$ James Pratte, viii$^{s.}$ iiii$^{d.}$; viii$^{s.}$ iiii$^{d.}$ John Mombrey, viii$^{s.}$ iiii$^{d.}$; viii$^{s.}$ iiii$^{d.}$ Anthony Pynnock, x$^{s.}$; x$^{s.}$ Humfrey Barrett, xiii$^{s.}$ iiii$^{d.}$; xiii$^{s.}$ iiii$^{d.}$ John Palmer, vi$^{s.}$ viii$^{d.}$; vi$^{s.}$ viii^{d} John Childe, vi$^{s.}$ viii$^{d.}$; vi$^{s.}$ viii$^{d.}$ John Forman, viii$^{s.}$ iiii$^{d.}$; viii$^{s.}$ iiii$^{d.}$ Aleyn Heyne, vi$^{s.}$ viii$^{d.}$; vi$^{s.}$ viii$^{d.}$ John Peycock, v$^{s.}$; v$^{s.}$ Raff Matres, vi$^{s.}$ viii$^{d.}$; vi$^{s.}$ viii$^{d.}$ Thomas Blakenam, vi^{s} viii$^{d.}$; vi$^{s.}$ viii$^{d.}$ Mathew Pek, vi$^{s.}$ viii$^{d.}$; vi$^{s.}$ viii$^{d.}$ the wyff lauunder, xiii$^{s.}$ iiii$^{l.}$; xiii$^{s.}$ iiii$^{d.}$ Robt Buck, x$^{s.}$; x$^{s.}$ John Grey, v$^{s.}$; v^{s} John Bennet, v$^{s.}$ x$^{d.}$; v$^{s.}$ x$^{d.}$ Robt Curteyss,§ v$^{s.}$ x$^{d.}$; v$^{s.}$ x$^{d.}$ Richard Pratte, vi$^{s.}$ viii$^{d.}$; vi$^{s.}$ viii$^{d.}$ George Spruce, v^{s} ; v$^{s.}$ Willm Robts, vi$^{s.}$ viii$^{d.}$; vi$^{s.}$ viii$^{d.}$ John Nevelock, x$^{s.}$; x$^{s.}$ John West, x$^{s.}$; x^{s} Richard Werbeck v$^{s.}$; v$^{s.}$ Lawerence Mune, vi$^{s.}$ viii$^{d.}$; vi$^{s.}$ viii$^{d.}$ David Hedley, xiii$^{s.}$ iiii$^{d.}$; xiii$^{s.}$ iiii$^{d.}$ Raff Smyth, vi$^{s.}$ viii$^{d.}$; vi$^{s.}$ viii$^{d.}$ Lawrance Mody, vi$^{s.}$ viii$^{d.}$; vi$^{s.}$ viii$^{d.}$ Willm Morice, v$^{s.}$; v$^{s.}$ Richard Curteys, v$^{s.}$ x$^{d.}$; v$^{s.}$ x$^{d.}$ Willm Stacy, v$^{s.}$; v$^{s.}$ Robt Brooke, v$^{s.}$; v$^{s.}$ John Bosten,‖ iii$^{s.}$; iii$^{s.}$ Richard Wyldborne, x$^{s.}$; x$^{s.}$ Xpofer Godfrey, v ^{s} ; v$^{s.}$ Isaac Benyngton, x$^{s.}$; x$^{.}$ John Barbor, x$^{s.}$; x$^{s.}$ John Jawdry, v$^{s.}$; v$^{s.}$ Thomas Bennett, vi$^{s.}$ viii$^{d.}$; vi$^{s.}$ viii$^{d.}$ v children in the church, xx$^{s.}$; xx$^{s.}$ Willm Shelley x$^{s.}$; x$^{s.}$ Willm Parrett, x$^{s.}$; x$^{s.}$ Richard Rawlynes, viii$^{s.}$ iiii$^{d.}$; viii$^{s.}$ iiii$^{d.}$ John Syredd, ix$^{s.}$ iiii$^{d.}$; ix$^{s.}$ iiii$^{d.}$ xpofer Brymyngton viii$^{s.}$ iiii$^{d.}$; viii$^{s.}$ iiii^{d} x Thomas Muffett, vi$^{s.}$ viii$^{d.}$; vi$^{s.}$ viii$^{d.}$ Richard Herte, v$^{s.}$; v$^{s.}$ John Bedwell, v$^{s.}$; v$^{s.}$ Willm Byrke, v$^{s.}$; v$^{s.}$ John Westwood, v ·^{s}; v$^{s.}$ John Tybbs, iii$^{s.}$; iii$^{s.}$ Hugh Busshe, iii$^{s.}$ iiii$^{d.}$; iii$^{s.}$ iiii$^{d.}$ Robt Cley, iiii$^{s.}$ viii$^{d.}$; iiii$^{s.}$ viii$^{d.}$ Richard Bossewell, iiii$^{s.}$ iiii$^{d.}$; iiii$^{s.}$ iiii$^{d.}$ Willm Soresby, v$^{s.}$ iii$^{d.}$; v$^{s.}$ iii$^{d.}$ The wyff of the Bayly of the Graunge, v$^{s.}$; v$^{s.}$ Elizabeth Plume,

---

* Edward Stacy, gent., see Tablet in South Aisle of the church.
† The Cressys resided in the Romeland, and were buried in the church.
‡ Thomas Tallis, celebrated Musician and Organist in the Abbey Church.
§ Robert Curteyss, [Curtis] ancestor of the Pilgrim Fathers of that name.
‖ John Boston, organist.

ii⁸· vi^d·; ii⁸· vi^d· Henry Chideley, v⁸·; v⁸· The nurse of the howsse takyng no wages in Reward, x⁸· Sum liii^£ xvi⁸· ii^d·

INVENTORY OF MINISTER'S ACCOUNTS OF WALTHAM taken in the 31st and 32nd of King Henry the Eighth, 1540-1 [Exchequer Office Pub. Rec. Office]*
Terri & possession imp *Monaster de Waltham* ptm.

Maner sive Somum de Waltham cu Membris.—Compus Johms hyghine [Heigham] Ballun et Collects & ffirmitrum ibm ₽ tempus pdcm.

Arrerayia.—Null qr prumus Compus impius Compits ad usum dui Regis (no arrears) Sum null.

Reddies Assis libor et Custum tenen in Waltham.—Scd rd. Compm de xxxviii£ vii⁸ v^d· ob de Redd Assis tam libor qui Customiorum tenents in Waltham pdca pvt ₽ diuers septiler Rentalia mde de pticulis ffacts sub hunc compu exam & prat pleums liguet & apparet Soluend ad ffest Aunnciaconis velete Marie virginis et St Michis Archi equaliter ₽ annum. Sum xxxviii£ vii⁸· v^d· ob.

Ffirma. Terrar admuss divers psons ad Volunt Domini in Waltham.—De xxiiii£ v · ix^d· de firmat dins terri ibm dumss dinsis psonis ad volunt dm vt Pr Rentlea Pdia sumliter sup hunc compm examinat & pbat Soluend ad ffesta pdia equaliter ₽ ann. Sum xxiiii li. v⁸· ix^d·

Ffirma Terra in Waltham dunnfs dudf pson. Indentur ₽ termino.—De xxx£ xix⁸· defirma divers terr dumff duis psons ₽ Indentur ₽ termino Annor vt Pr Rentlia pdia ₽ Annm Soluend ad ffest pdia equal Pann. de vi£ de ffirma dms terr ibm dumff Edwards Stacye ₽ termino Annor ₽ Annum Soluend ad terminas pdios de vi£ de ffiim de le *Sheppecottefelds* de *Scrutehills* ibm dimss dco comput av anno Ann Soluend ad pdca equalit ₽ ann. Sum xlii£ xix⁸·

Ffirma V ^may *pratorma in Holyfeld et Waltham.*—De lxvi⁸· iii^d· de ffirma x ^may pratorum ibm dumff dms psons de anno in Anr soluend ad ffesta pdia equaliter ₽ ann pvt Pr Rentlia pdia Sum lxvi⁸· iii^d·

Reddus Assis liborum qui Custum tenin Halyfield memb dm de Walthme.—De vii£ vi⁸· od. de Redd Assis tm liborum qui Custum Tenens ibm ₽ ann Soluend ad ffesta pdca Aunciacoins

---

* From land in the four Wardships in the Parish.

vte marie virguns & sc Michs Archi equaliter ℣ ann prt Pr Rentlia pdca sumlit sup hunc Compm. examiatr. Sum vii£ vi⁸· oᵈ·

Ffirma Ter in hallifeld.—De xiii⁸· iiiiᵈ· de ffirma certs terr in tennia ad termuos pdcos equaliter ℣ ann.   Sum xiii⁸ iiiiᵈ·

Reddus Assis tam liborum qui Custumunonr Teneno in Uppeshire hamlett de Waltham.—De xv£ xvii⁸· viᵈ· de Redd Assis tam liborum qm Custum Tenen ibm ℣ ann., Soluend ad pdia ffesta Annunciaconis bte marie virgnus et Sc Michs Archi equaliter ℣ ann., Pvt. ℣ Rentlia pdca   Sum xv£ xvii⁸· viᵈ·

Ffirma Terra ad voluntatem dm in Vppeshire.—De xxi⁸· de ffirma cert terr ibm dumff dms psons ad Voluntatem dm ℣ ann., Soluend ad eosdem terminos vt ℣ Rentlia Pdca. Sum xxi⁸·

Reddus Assis Custum Tenemum Sydwardstoun Hamlett de Waltham.—De xxxiiii⁸· iᵈ· ob ov de Red Assis Custum Tenem ibm ℣ Ann. Soluend ad ffest pdca equal ℣ Ann pvt ℣ Rentlia pdca.   Sum xxxiiii⁸· iᵈ·

Ffirma Terra in Sydwardstoun ad volunt.—De xxvii⁸· iiiiᵈ· de ffirma cert terr ibm, &c.

Domim.—De vi.£ xiii⁸ iiiiᵈ· de ffirma cert terr ibm dumss Jacobo Sutton, &c.

Redd Mobilin in Sidwardsto.—De iiii⁸· ii⁻ˡ· de Redd mobili xxv gallmarum recept de Tenen ibm &c.

Firrma Moli ffulloms in Waltham.—De xl⁸· de firma moli ffollonis* ibn dumss ℣ Indentur Robert Cressey† ℣ termino Annor Soluend ad ffesta Aunciacoins ble marie virgine sc Michis Archi equal ℣ Ann.

A LIST OF PIECES OF GOLD PLATE, &c., which accrued to King Henry VIII,, "as well by the surrender as Visitations of Religious Houses and Cathedrals. The original signed by the King's owne hand.   By John Williams Maister and Treasurer of the King's Jewells."—(Glastonbury Monastery) 1539.   Hereafter ensuithe, as well all suche Somes of Money as have ben delyvered unto the King's majestie by the saide John Williams master of our saide soveraigne Lorde juells as also dyverse and sondry percells of plate newe made and bowght by the saide John Williams, sythens the saide first daye of Octobere Anno xxx.   That is to say—Furst delivered unto his majestie

---

*A *Fulling Mill* for scoureing cloth.   † Of the Romeland.

the furste day of November. An. supra, by thande of Anthony Deny one of the Gentlemen of the King's privey Chamber, the some of three thowsand fyve hundrethe fifty three pounds— sterlinge.—iii^m· v^c· liii$^£$ *Item*, delyvered more unto his majestie the same daie, and yere by the ands of Frauncys Jopson, of suchestuffe as came frome the late dissolved howse of Walt..ame, a pair of gilte Cruetts, weinge one and twentie unces. xxi oz. *Item*, delyvered more unto his maiestie the same daie, of Waltham stuffe, a Bason and an Ewer, parcell gilte* weinge four score and one unc. $^{xx}_{iiii}$ — i oz. *Item*, delyvered more unto his maiestie the same daie of the same stuffe a Cuppe of Serpentyne, garnished with silver and gilte, weinge with the Serpentyne, seven and thirtie unces. Sum. xxxvii oz. *Item* delyvered more unto his maiestie the same daie, of the same stuffe, a Sconnse with an handle of silver, weinge fyfteyne unces. Sum. xv oz. †

DETTS PAYDE AT THE DISSOLUCION OF THE SAID HOWSE [OF WALTHAM].—Payde to Sir Thomas Hawkeynes‡ as apperyth by a byll of pcells, lxxii^s· ii^d· Signed wt th Chauncellor hand. Itm more payed by the Channcellors Commandment Willm Dune, xiii^s· iiii^d· Itm more payed xp ofer Colte§ for his wages and Rewards, viii^s· Itm more lykewyse payed to Richard Kyrby by the Chauncellor's Commandement, viii^s· vi^d·

The Charges of the Comissioners at the tyme of Dissolucion the xxvth Daye of Marche An^o xxxi. (Hen. VIII.)—

To the Clerkes for ther paynes, xlv^s· viii^d· Item to the twoo p^{r}cevaunts attendyng of the Chauncellor at Walthame, vii^s· vi^d· Itm payed to Mr. Gates, svant for Watchynge in the churche,‖ v^s· Itm to Doctor Peter, xl^s· Item to Price, xl^s· Itm to Solocitor, xl^s· Itm to Auditor, iiii$^£$ Item to Receyor iiii$^£$ Item to horsekepers for their charges in towne, v^s· iiii^d· Coste for the carrage of the plate. Itm to a Carter for carrying of the Kyng's plate and Juells from Walthame to

---

* Parcel gilt means gilt inside only, or partially gilt.

† Dugdale's Monasticon, Vol. I. pp. 63-7.

‡ Thomas Hawkins, one of the Officers of the church, ejected at the dissolution.

§ The Colte family were buried in the church, see tablet in the south aisle.

‖ Guarding the plundered ornaments.

London, iii^{s.} Itm to ii men for weytynge upon the same place from Walthame to London, vi^{s.} viii^{d.} Itm for vi ells of Canvas to stuffe the Coopes and vestments resquyd fr the Kyngee, ii^{s.} Itm for iiii boundells of Ropes to stuffe the Chests w^{t.} plate at vii^{d.} the bundle, ii^{s.} iiii^{d.} Itm for the carage of the plate to the Courte and home agayne to the the Juell howsse xx^{d.} Sum xxiii[£] ii^{s.} ii^{d.}

This bill made the xxvii day of Aprill An° 32 Hen xxxii wittensseth that I Nycolas Brystowe have receyved of ffracnis Jobson the Kyngs Rec^{rs} of . . . with the . . . of harteford* the pcells following Itm. ii Coppes of Redde coursse tissue with v woonndes.† Itm. A coppe of couse Redde tissue with vesture deacons & subdeacons sorted with ther Albes. Itm vi coppes of blew tissue with vestments deacon & subdeacon sorted with ther albes. Itm a vestment of olde turkey sylke the oferers of goold garnished‡ with purle & counterfett stone. Rec all pcells aforesaid by the Kyngs Commandement and to his graces only use. Menst Aplis An° Regeni xxxii^{d.} ⅌ me Nich Bristowe.

THE LATE MONESTRY OF WALTHAM.—*This Indenture made* the xviiith day of Marche in the yere of the Reigne of our souaigne Lorde Kyng henry the viiith Witnesseth that I Sir John Williams Knight master and Treasorer of our said souaigne Lords Juells have Received and hadd the day and yere above said of ffrancis Jobson Gentleman one of the Kings particular Recevors of his Courte of Augumentation and for the Dyssoluying of the late monestery of Waltham in the Countie of Essex. Alle such pcells of plate as cam to the use of our said Souaigne lord by the Dyssoluyng of the said late monestery of Waltham aforesaid. The particulars whereof herafter ensuyth. *In Witnese* whereof the pties above said to thise Indentures have setto there names and seales. The day and yere above written.

Church Plate Delyuered to the said Sir John Williams these pcells of plate defaced and broken, ffurst a Crosyer wt iii pecs

---

* Hertford, see Inventory of Parish Churches in Hertfordshire by *J. E. Cussans.*

† Wounds of Christ.

‡ Oferers or Orfrays, two bands about eight inches in breadth, reaching f.... ....

of a staff of syluer & gylte [xxiiij oz:] Item iiii tables [of
Or Lady]* plated wt sylver and gylte eny one of them wt ii
folding leves [qr pacell pent]† It. v Gospeller‡ wt sylur &
gylte. It. one Crosse plated sylur & gylte. It. one Arme
plated wt syluer & gylte. It. a Crosse of Wodde plated wt
syluer & gylte and a staffe broken plated wt syluer for the
same. It. a myghter [mitre] wt ii labells garnished wt syluer
& gylte smalle plees. It. a pyxe of sylur gylte.§ It. iii Chalices
with there patents gylte. It. iii. chalices of sylur white wt there
patents. It. a holywater stock wt a sprynkyll white. It. iii
Sensors of sylur pcell gylte. It. A Shypp for franckensens
pcell gylte. It. A nother shypp for franckensens pcell gylte.
It. ii smalle candillstycks of syluer pcell gylte wt small
buryalls.|| It ii Cruetts gylte. It. ii smalle Cruetts of
Syluer whyte one lacking a cover. It. A paxe of syluer white.
It. a smalle Bason for the Altar. It. a Scons¶ of syluer white.
It. a monstrance of syluer gylte. It. ii Crystall glasses typped
wᵗ Syluer.**

Householde Plate.—Item a stonding Cuppe wᵗ a cover wᵗ a
pounde garnett enamyled in the top of the cover ℞ oz. It. a.
standing Cuppe wᵗ a cover and a Dolphin enamyled in the toppe
of the cover. It. a Goblett wᵗ a cover haueing in the toppe of the
cover the Image of Saint John. It. one smalle salte wᵗ a Cover
hauyng on the same a Roose in the toppe. It a Spyce plate wt
oute a cover. It. a nutt of Buryall garnysshed wᵗ syluer gylte.
Item a Sarpentyne Cuppe ffassheon wᵗ a cover of a masor
garnysshed wᵗ sylver. Item a stonding masor wᵗ a cover

---

* The chapel formerly called "Our Lady's," because there was founded
in it a Chantry of that name, and under it is a very fair arched charnel
house to which belonged a gild." Morant's Essex, vol. i, 45.

† "An other foldynge Table [A dyptych for an altar] with ij leves plated with
sylver gilt with Reliques An other Table with foldynge leves plated with
sylver gilt hayng therein the crucifix. An other Table with ij foldynge leves
the myddle pece plated with sylver havynge therin iiij Crossys and the leves
plated with sylver gilte sett with counterfett stones.

‡ Gospels, probably Saxon.

§ *Pax* a small plate on which was represented our Lord's Passion. It was
kissed by the priest and congregation.

|| Beryls, precious stones.

¶ A sconce fastened to the wall.

** For relics.

garnyshed wt sylur gylte. It. v masors garnysshed wt syluer gylte. Item one Bason wt an Ewar of syluer enamyled in the myddes of the bason and in the toppe of the cour wt Crosses pcell gilte. It. ii Goblets wt one cover haueyng in the top of the cover a lyon graued. One geven to the Abbott. It. a Salte of syluer wt a cover graven wt flowres. It. [vi. geven to the Abbott.] iii potts of syluer whyte. It. xxv Spones of sylur whyte. Whiche parcells of plate above written and mencioned so defaced and broken waiyng in maner and fournne folowing, that is to say:—In plate Gylte—cccclxxix oz. In plate pcell Gylte—ccli oz. In Whyte—ccccxxxix. oz. By me John Williams.

LAND IN ST. PANCRAS BELONGING TO THE ABBEY OF WALTHAM, 27 HEN. VIII.—This Indenture made by Robert, Abbott of Waltham holy crosse on the oon ptye and John Palmer of Kentyschtown on the other ptye Wytnessth the said Abbot & convent by their hole assent &c., demysed granted and to ferme, all that their lands & tents medowys, wodes, &c., in the pyshe of Seynt Pancras-in-the-ffyelds togeder lying on the south syde of Caenwode & Gyllys Haute comonly now callyd Millefeyld or Canewode feylds and also otherwise callyd. Mylleffeyld, huntffeyld, &c., lately in tennor of oon Nicholas Grey. The said John Palmer his assigns, &c., to have and to hold the said premises for the term of forty and oon years, paying yerely the some of ffyve pounds sterlyng at too usual times in the yere, &c. In wytnes whereof eyther of the seid ptes to these psents indenturs enterchaungeably have put the Seales geven in the Chapyter howse of the seid Abbott & Convent the day & yere as aforseid. [*Vide* Conventual Leases.]

THE VESTERY STUFF.—iii copes ffurste a pryst deacon and sub-deacon of blewe satten of bridges with albes to the same xxx⁵· ii copes of white satten of bridges xiij⁵· iiij⁴· a cope of olde white damaske, with a vestment pryst, deacon and sub-deacon to the same, with albes geven to the parrysshe of Walthame xiij⁵· iiij⁴· Itm. ii copes and vestment deacon and sub-deacon, with albes to the same of redde old Turkey silke xx⁵· a cope of olde redd satten of bridges, with vestment deacon and sub-deacon lakkinge albes, vj⁵· viij⁴· iiij copes of old braunched saye [silk] black, with vestment deacon and sub-deacon, with albes xv⁵· geven to the pysshe of *Walthame.* Itm. a vestment deacon and sub-deacon, with albes of old dovnyxe v⁵· geven to the pore churches ther abouts, a vestment deacon and sub-deacon, with albes of old dornixe v⁵· a pryst deacon and sub-deacon of whyte colyn [Cologne] bawdekyn with albes v⁵· a vestment deacon and sub-deacon of grene and blewe torne sylke with albes to the same v⁵· a vestment deacon and sub-deacon of olde red damaske, with albes, v⁵· prieste, deacon and sub-deacon of whyte bustyan, with albes iij⁵· iiij^d· a syngle vestment of whit and blewe sylke xx^d· an old cope of ymagery, with flowres xiiij⁵· iiij^d· a cusshen of crymsen velvett, with the leteres of C and R, x⁵· *Res pro Rege.* iij copes of redd purple tyssue, with v wondes* a cope of course† redde tyssue, with vestment deacon and sub-deacon of the same sorte,‡ with albes, vj coopes of blewe tissue, with a vestment deacon and sub-deacon of the same sorte, with vj albes lackinge iii. . . . Mr. North—iii coopes, vestment, deacon and sub-deacon of redde bawdekyn, with flewers and albes to the same x⁵· DAT' *Louton* [Loughton] æ *Chygewell*—ii coopes of redde sylke, very olde wherof one with faukouns and another with swannes, with a vestment deacon and sub-deacon, with albis to to the same lxvj⁵· viij^d· an old coope of lether gold§ iiij^d· *Broxbourne and Wormley*—iiij coopes of olde yellow sylke vestment deacon and sub-deacon, with albes to the same iiij£. v coopes, a vestment, deacon and sub-deacon, of white damask with albes l⁵· iij coopes of greene damaske, with albes xxvj⁵· viij^d· iiij coopes of redd bawdekyn xl⁵· *Nasyng.*—A tunicle of white bawdekyn, with coper gold.‖ Itm. ij coopes of grene sylke, wroughte with byrdes and floures xiij₃ ij coopes of redd counterfett sylver x⁵· *Wormeley.***—iij coopes of lether gold, ij grene and

* The heart and pierced hands and feet of our Saviour.
† "Course," in the ' receipt " a vestment of cowers silk.—MS. Inv. Augm. Off 309, 40.
‡ Sortly or agreeably.
§ Probably wall hangings made of thin pliant leather, a tapestry, painted by hand.
‖ Gold of the colour of burnished copper.
** The Abbot of Waltham Lord of the Manor of Wormley was annually wont to send (to the cross erected at Wormley West End) some of his canons, who on the 3rd of May and 14th September, walked in solemn procession with the parishioners singing a litany. This place retains the name of Holy Cross. This seems to be a kind of processioning to keep the lands that join to the kingdom of Mercia distinct from the lands of the Abbey of St. Albans which were in that kingdom, and contiguous to Wormley. See Salmon's Hist. Herts, p. 14,

one blewe, with vestment deacon and sub-deacon, with albes to the same xx^s· ij tunicles of greene silke with albes to the same iij^s v coopes of blewe velvet, wherof one with aungels of gold and crosses and the vjth with aungells in cloudes, with vest-ment deacon and sub-deacon, and albes to the same xiiij£. *Broxbourne.*—iij coopes with vestment deacon and sub-deacon, and albes of white bustain xiij^s· iiij^d· a coope vestment deacon and sub-deacon with albes to the same of redd silk wrought with byrdes x^s·

GEVEN TO THE CHAPPELL IN WALTHAME.—A vestment. deacon and sub-deacon of grene and white bawdekyn with albes vj^s· viij^d· [at S. John's altar] a syngle vestment of olde redd velvett iiij^s· on other single vestment of white bustain xxj^d· *Pro rege*, a redd velvet coope, a white coope of sylke a coope of blewe bawdekyn and a vestment sett with perle, given to Mr. Pope By Mr. North.   Summa Ornamentorum ^{c}xxv£ cum x li superplus Edward North.   a Gospeler plated with sylver having upon the same a Crucifixe and Marye and John, gilte (nil), a crosse, plated with sylver gilte with a large long bone in the same, a Gospler, plated with sylver gilte havinge in the myddes the Ymage of Cryste with the iiij Evangelysts nl. an other Gospler plated with sylver gylte havinge the crufixe, Mary and John in the myddes, and ij Teth* a GOSPELER OF THE SAXON TONGUE, having thone syde plated with sylver parcell gilte, with ye ymage of Cryst nl, an other GOSPLER OF THE SAXON TONGE, with the Crusifixe and Mary and John having a naked man holding up his hands of sylver gilte, nl.an Arm† with relyques garnysshed with counterfett stone, plated with sylver gilte, nl. a crosse of wood plated with sylver gylt garnysshed with counterfett stone, and a staff, broken, plated with sylver for the same, nl.‡

OUR LADY CHAPPELL.—A Table of ymagery of the xij. apostells x^s· a lytell payre of organes xx^s· §

---

* Teth, probably of Mary and John (?).   In the Inv. of Sarum is an ampul. of chrystal containing a tooth of St. Anne."

† "Reserved for the King."

‡ The Rev. M. E. C. Walcott says, "Another receipt is appended for vestments for the king's use, marked with this addition, a vestment of olde Turkey Sylke, the orferes of goold garnesshed with parls and counterfeit. stone." These may have been beads or artificial pearls.

§ A pair of organs simply means an organ having more pipes than one.

IN THE QUYRE.—A greate large payre of Organes above, one the northe of the Quyre, a lesser payre beneth. ij smalle candelstyks of tynne xxij^d iii smale lamps of brasse.

IN THE CHURCH.—xlvj Gravestones and Tombes in sundry places of the churche

IN MY LADY ROES CHAPPELL.*—Geven iii syngle vestments, with ij albes, very olde vi^s· viij^d· The Abbot received a stondynge cuppe with a cover, with a crowne ymperial in the toppe of the covei, twoo Saltes, with one cover of a sort, with a rose graven in the top of the cover, ij Nutts, with one cover garnysshed with sylver gylte. ix Masors, garnysshed with sylver gylte. Parcell gylte, ij basons of sylver, with ij ewers enamelyd in the myddes of the basones in the toppe of the covers with crosses, white ix potts of sylver xxvi spones of sylver, x spones of sylver with knoppis gilte. *Nomina* [vi.] *Juratorum aa verè et indeferenter appreciandum omnia singula mobilia dicti nuper monasterium electorum et juratorum.* Signed Johnes Cocks gent., Robertus Cressy, Johnes West, Rolandus Raunson, Willm Roche, Willm Woodleffe.

CHURCHWARDENS' ACCOUNTS OF THE ABBEY, A.D., 1540-2.— The progress of destruction (according to Dr. T. Fuller) with which the Abbey was visited after the dissolution, was great. Part of the church, with the offices, &c., were demolished for the sake of the materials, the nave only being reserved to the inhabitants to serve as a parish church.

Dr. Thomas Fuller writes—Item, know, then, there were six ordinary obits which the churchwardens did annually discharge, namely, for Thomas Smith, and Joan his wife, on the 16th of January; for Thomas Friend, Joan and Joan his wives, on the 16th February; for Robert Preest, and Joan his wife, on the 10th April; for Thomas Towers, and Catherine his wife, the 26th April; for John Breges and Agnes his wife, the 31st May; for Thomas Turner, and Christian his wife the 20th Dec. The charge of an obit was 2s. 2d., and if any be curious to have the peculiars thereof it was thus expended, viz., To the parish priest, 4d; to Our Lady's priest 3d.; to the charnel priest 3d.; to the clerks 4d.; to the children (choristers) 3d.; to the sexton 2d.; to the bellman 2d.; for two tapers 2d.; for oblation 3d. To defray the expenses of these obits, Thomas Smith bequeathed a tenement

---

* See my history of Our Lady Chapel, restored 1875.

in the corn market, and others gave lands in Upshire, called Paternoster Hills; others ground elsewhere, besides a stock of 18 cows which the wardens let out yearly to farm for 18s.

Anno 1542.—*Imprimis.* For watching the sepulchre, a groat. *Item,* paid to the ringers at the coming of the King's grace, six-pence.—"Yet Waltham bells told no tales every time King Henry came hither, having a small house in the Romeland to which he is said oft privately to retire for pleasure." *Item,* paid unto two *men of law* for their counsel about the church leases, 6s. 8d. *Item,* paid the attorney for his fee, 20d. *Item.* paid for ringing at the prince's coming 1d.

Anno. 1543.—*Imprimis*—Received of the executors of Sir Robert Fuller given by the said Sir Robert to the church, £10. Abbot Fuller bequeathed to the church a chalice, silver and gilt, which they afterwards sold for £7.*

Anno. 1544.—Received of Adam Tanner the overplus of the money which was gathered for the purchase of the bells, £2 4s. 11d. *Item.* Received of Richard Tanner, for eight stoles, 3s. These very rags of popery sold for 4½d. each. *Item.* Paid for mending the handbell 2d. This was the "saint's bell," carried by the sexton at the "circumgestation" of the sacrament, the visita-tion of the sick, &c. *Item.* Paid to Philip Wright,† carpenter, for making a frame in the belfry, 18s. 4d.

Anno. 1546.—*Item,* for clasps to hold up the banners in the body of the church, 8d. *Item.* Paid to John Boston‡ for mending the organs 20d.

The Abbey Flour Mills.—The two flour mills near the Abbey were let by the Abbot of Waltham *temp.* Henry VIII. to James Blount, miller, for £26 13s. 4d. per annum, to be paid quarterly (*Vide* Conventional Leases Aug. Off. Essex, No. 209, Pub. Rec. Off.)‖.

---

* *Vide* Churchwarden's Accounts, *Anno* 1556.

† The author possesses the original list of subscribers towards buying the bells; and in which occurs the name of Philip Wright (See "Our Parish Registers," p. 136.)

‡ John Boston, organist, a pensioner at the dissolution of the Abbey.

‖ This Indent. made xxviii. day of Septembre the twenty yere of the Reign of Kyng henry the viii. bytweene Robert Abbot of Waltham holy crosse on the one pt, and Jamys Blount of Waltham afsd myller, on the other ptye, Wytnesseth that the afsd Abbott and Convent have dymysed lettyn and

This Cedull wytnessyth that hereafter ensuying bene specyfyed certene Implements and necessaryeas beyng wthyn the saide mylle that is to say:

a ffyrst a payer of mylstons for the whete myll a Byn and a hoper.

a Item. A payer of mylstons for the malte myll a Byn and a hoper. Item. oon drage hoke w tyngs.

a Item. ij Bushel basketts ij tryndells vii tryndells heds viii sett of Coggs vi Trindells savye vii^{oz.} fetherbords iiii Plancks oon fane oon cable vi hopys of yron for the tryndell heds, oon grett hamer, oon Crowe of yron, oon small Crowe of yron, oon hadds, oon shave, ii chesells xii myll bylls, oon Pecke, oon half pecke And oon sherynge hoke.

KING EDWARD THE SIXTH, A.D., 1547—1553.—Extracts from Certificate of Colleges and Chantries, taken by the Com-

betakyn to ferme unto the afsd Jamys Blount, there two Water millis in Waltham afsd, under one Ruffe *stondynge and beynge next unto foresayd Abbey*, durying the terme of sex and ten yeers, to have and to hold the afsd two mills wth all, &c., from the feast of seynt michell the archnngell next comyng unto yeldyng and payinge therefor yerely unto the afsd Abbot & Convent &c.. twenty-sex pounds threttyn shillings and four pens at four term:s in the yer, That the sayd James Blounte his executors at there proper cost shall there cutt and cleanse all the Weds in Ryus whereby the water may have his full course to the afsd mylls. Also the afsd Jamys Blount couenutythe (covenanteth) unto the afsd Abbott that when the sayd Abbott shall send unto the afsd mylls any manor of corne As whete or malte to be grounde there, that then the sayd Jamys Blount shall not make no delay for the gryndyngy of the same corne, and on that the afsd Jamys Blount shall suffer the afsd Abbott to enter ynto the afsd mylls or ynto any grounde to the sayd mylls. And there to cast at there liberty wth a castynge nett ynto all the waters there bynge And all suche ffyshe as they shall take at any time to have yt to thire owne use Also the afsd Abbott couentith for him and his successors to susteyne and kepe all the Repacons of the afsd two mylls and to fynde all man of milestons and Cogke tymber to the same mylls with the caryage of the same And so to be contynewed at the proper cost and charge of the afsd Abbott durying the afsd time. And also the afsd Abbott and his successors grauntyth to the afsd Jamys Blount to have yerely owt of the forest xii loods of fewell callyd ffyerwood so that the afsd Jamys Blount shall paye the charge for the fellynge and caryage of the wood durynge this psent terme. And where the afsd Jamys Blount & Thomas Waren of Waltham, bocher by these wrytinge obligatorye and either of them be bounde under the afsd Abbot in the sum of forty pounds sterlynge, &c., in witness.

Robert Cressy rented a fulling mill in Waltham of Lady Joan Denny 7 Ed VI per annum xl^{s.} *Vide Particulars for Grants*, Augmentation Office.

missioners *temp* Ed. VI. A.D. 1547-53.—Reditt vuns Shoppe sine Stall in le butcherye in tennis Thome fletcher p. Anum. v[s.]

Eddford St.—Redit vuns Tenti voc in *Eldfforde Stret* in Tenu Thome blackman p. Anum iiii[s.] iiii[d.] *Honey Lane.*—Reddit vuns Croft terr cont p estimac 11 Acre terr vacen in honey lane in tenn Johis West p Ann. v[s.] *High Street.*—Reddit vums Tenti jacent in *high strete* in teun Radulphi Smith p. Ann. xii[d.] Reddit vums horrei in pormar iacent in Eldforde Stret in tenn Willm Sponer p Anm. vi[s.] viii[d.] *Freshing Lane* Reddit 11 pec prati cont p estimac 1 Acr et iac in *freshing lane* in tenur Willm Aylewarde p Ann. vi[s.] viii[d.] *Elford fields.*—Reddit vuns Croft terr cont ℘ estimacon ii Acras et di iac in *Elfforde ffeldes* in tenur Anne bright vidue ℘ Ann. v[s] *Avey lane.*—Reddit vums Croft terr cont p Estimac 111 Acr iac in *Alvre lane* in tenur Johis Pecoke ℘ Ann vi[s] *Holyfield.*—Reddit vums di Acr prati iac in *holyffeld* meade in tenur Johis Cavill ℘ Ann. xviii[d.] *Edmundsey.*— Reditt 11 Acr prati iac in *Edmudsaye* in tenur. . . . Curteis vidue ℘ Ann. vi[s.] *Shermans Mead.*—Reddit vuins Acr prati iac in *Sherman's-meade* in tenur Johis Peacock ℘ Ann. iii[s.] iiii[d.]

Guilds sine ffraternitas voc to Charnell in Waltham sce cruc.— *Padrpool.*—Reddit vunis di acre prati iacent in *Padypoole* in tenur Mich Stocke ℘ Ann. xviii[d.] *Town Mead.*—Reddit vuns di Acr prati iac in *Tunne meade* in tenura Willim Aylewarde ℘ Ann. xx[l.] *Roydon.*—Reddit vums di Acr prati iac in *Roydon* in tenur Ann viii[d.] *Town mead.*—Reddit vums Acr prati iacen in *Tune meade* in tenur William Aylewarde ℘ Ann. iii[s] *Fowlley.*— Reddit iii Rodap prati iacut in *ffowlley* in tenur Martyn ℘ Ann. xx[d] Reddit resolut duo Racri put Manerio suo de Waltham Sce Crucis ℘ Ann. iiii[s] viii[d.] ob. *Cobmead.*—Ptaclers del to one of the sumptors of the Kyngs howssehold in one coll.—Reddit vums Tenti cu di Acr prati iac in *Cobmeade* in tenur Thome Walleys reddend in dep Ann. xx[s.] *Highbridge Street.*—Reddit vums Cottag jac in *West Strete* in tenur Robti Postays redd inde ℘ Ann ii[s.] *Cobmead.*—Reddit di Acr prati iac in *Cobmeade* in tenur. p Ann. xvi[d.] *Elderstreet.*—Reddit vums tenti iac in Elderstrete in tenur Willim hill p Ann. v[s.] Reddit tenti iac 1 in fforo ibm in tenur—Jenkynson Showmaker p Ann. viii[s.]

FRATERNITAS.—Voc o[r] ladyes brotherhoode in Waltham. Sce Crucis   Pticlers del to Williams Mr. Deny Sumter in one collection.—Reddit di Acr prati iac in *bunttyngsay* in tenur p Ann xx[d.]

Reddit di acr prati iac in *Roymny* in tenur William Stephin reddend inde p Ann. xxi^{d.} Reddit vums orti iac in *highe streate* cont vuam acr et di p. estura in tenur Alic Turner p. Ann. vi^{s.} viii^{d.} Reddit vums Tenti iac in *Ellford Strete* in tenur Alc Birde p. Ann v^s Reddit vums Shopp in fforo ibm in tenur Thome Dudley p. Ann. iii^{s.} Reddit iiii Acr ter iac in communibus Campis ibm in tenur John Peacocke p Ann. iii^{s.} iiii^d Reddit umus Tenti iac Apud *Shepcotstreate* tenur Rici Mrter p Ann iii^{s.} iiii^{d.} *Marsh gate.*—Reddit vums Tenti iac Apud *mshe gate* in tenur Johis Hacrells p Ann. xii^d *Langrege Holyfield.*—Reddit cert ter iac in *Nasing* voc *langrege* in tenur Johis Porteis reddend inde p Ann xxxvi^{s.} viii^{d.} *Reeps.*—Reddit resolut duo Regis prt mano suo de Waltham p Ann v^{s.} iiii^{d.}

ANNO 1549.—*Imprimis.* Sold the silver plate which was on the desk in the *charnel* weighing five ounces, for 25s. This desk was inlaid with silver. *Item.* Sold a rod of iron, which the curtain run upon before the rood, 9d. *Item.* Sold so much wax as amounted to 20s. " More light and fewer candles." *Item.* Paid for half of the book called *Paraphuse*, 5s.* *Item.* Spent in the visitation at *Chelmsford*, amongst the wardens and other honest men, 14s. 4d. Nicholas Ridley, then newly Bishop of London.

ANNO 1550.—*Imprimis.* Received for a knell of a servant, to the lady Mary her Grace 10d.† *Item.* Lost 40s. by reason of the fall of money by proclamation. *Item.* Received for 271 ounces of plate, sold at several times for the best advantage £67 14s. 9d. In this church there appears to have been two chantries and six obits. In the Certificate of Colleges and Chantries, 1 Ed. VI. Augmentation Office is the following account:—Lands and tents put in ffeoffm^t by diverse and sundrie p'sons to the maintenance of a prieste callide o^r Lady prieste in *Waltham Holy Crosse*, the seide pryest to saye dyvine s'vice in the pishe

---

* On the 6th May, 33 Henry VIII., a new impression of the Bible was finished and the king commanded that all curates and parishioners should set up in every parish church a Bible of the greater volume, that the people might read therein before All Hallowtide, under penalty of forfeiting 40s. a month after that time. Bishop Bonner immediately issued an exhortation that the people were not to gather multitudes together by reading the Word aloud. One of these Bibles was then chained to one of the south pillars of the church.

† Princess Mary, afterwards Queen Mary, frequently visited Copt Hall, probab'y during the time Sir Thomas Heaneage was resident there.

church of Walth'm aforesaid. The said chantry is now vacant & wth out anye incumbent. The seid town of Walth'm is a gieat towne, having in it to the number of . . . housling people. The yerely valewe of the same doythe amount to the sum of iiii£ xiiii^s. Rent resolute v^s. iiii^d. The value of the plate, juels, p'cell &c., viz., One chalice of silver gilte, poysant ix oz. at per oz. . . . v vestments, viii clothes, one corparas xxvii^s. ii gilte candlesticks w'th other implements p'ysed together at . . . And so remayneth cleare to the king's ma^ties use iiii£ xii^s. Lands and tents put in ffeoffment by diverse and sundrie p'sons to the maintenance of a priest callide the *charnell* p'st in *Waltham Holy Crosse;* the seide priest to say dyvine s'vice in the church of Waltham aforesaide, & to helpe s've the cure their. The saide chantry is now vacant & wth owt enye incumbent, and haythe been this . . . yere and more. The yerely valewe of the same doth amount to the sum of lviii^s. Rent resolute iiii^s. viii^d. The valewe of the plate, juells, &c.,. viz., one chalice of silver p'cell gilte poisant ix oz at per oz. . . Vestments & fyve altar clothes, price vi^s. iii^d And so remayneth cleare to the King's ma^ties use liii^s. iii^d. (See list *temp.* 2 Ed. VI., Feb. 7th.)

QUEEN MARY, A.D., 1553-58.—*Imprimis.* For a cross with a foot, copper and gilt, 25^s. *Item.* For a cross-staff, copper and gilt, 9^s. 4^d. *Item.* For a pax, copper and gilt, 5^s. *Item.* For a pair of censers, copper and gilt, 9^s. 8^d. *Item.* For a stock of brass for the holy water, 7^s. *Item.* For a chrismatory of pewter, 3^s. 4^d. *Item.* For a yard of silver sarcenet for a cloth for the sacrement, 7^s. 8^d. *Item.* For a pix of pewter, 2^s. *Item.* For Mary and John, that stand in the rood loft, 26^s. 8^d. *Item.* For washing eleven aubes and as many head clothes, 6^d. *Item.* For watching the sepulchre, 8^d. *Item.* For a processioner and a manual, 20^d *Item.* For a corporas-cloth, 12^d. *Item.* To the apparitor for the bishop's [Bonner] book of articles at the visitation, 6^d.

ANNO. 1556.—*Extracts from 32 A Book of Corrodies and Anuities to divers Religious Houses, temp. Philip and Marie.* Formerly preserved in the stone *Tower Westminster*, and now deposited in Room c 10, of the Public Record Office. Annuit. Edwardi Stacie Ᵽ ann liii^s iiii^d. Hugoine Yonge Ᵽ ann vi^£ xiii^s. iiii^d. Georgu Solye Ᵽ ann vi^£ xiii^s. iiii^d. Edwardi Storye Ᵽ ann viii[£] Johnes Saunders ℈ ann . . c^{s.} Milions Gerarde ℈ a nn vi[£] xiii^{s.} iiii^{d.} Johnes Norrys ℈ ann vi[£] viii^{s.} iiii^{d.} Thoms Hawkins ℈ ann ix[£] Thoms Warren ℈ ann xx[£]

The above list corresponds with the pensions assigned to the officers of the Abbey on March 24, 1540.

Imprimis. For coles to undermine a piece of the steeple which stood after the first fall, 2^{s.}

QUEEN ELIZABETH, A.D. 1558-1603.—*Imprimis.* For the taking down of the rood-loft, 3s. 2d. *Item.* Received for a suite of vestments being of blew velvet, and another suite of damask and an altar cloth, £4. *Item.* For three corporasses, whereof two white silk and one blew velvet, £2 13s. 4d. *Item.* For two suits of vestments and an altar cloth, £3.

ANNO, 1562.—*Item.* For a cloth of buckeram for the communion table, and the making, 4s. *Item.* For lattices for the church-windows, 15s. *Item.* Paid for a bay nagge, given to Mr. Henry Denny for the Abbey wall, £3 17s. *Item.* To labourers which did undermine the said wall, 45s. 9d.

ANNO, 1563.—*Imprimis.* For an old house in the old market place, £13 6s. 8d.—This tenement let at 9s.per annum. "The Parish sold it and another house in *West Street.* Such bargains made a famine for posterity." *Item.* For the old timber in the vestiary of *St. George's chappel*, 15s. "In vain," says Fuller, "have I inquired for the situation hereof long since demolished." *Item.* Received of Mr. Denny, for one cope of cloth of gold, £3 6s. 8d. *Item.* For two altar-cloaths of velvet and silk, £2. *Item.* Received of Mr. Tamworth* twenty loads of timber ready hewed which he gave to the parish. *Item.* For taking down the stairs in the Abbey, 7s. 8d. *Item.* For taking down the lead from the charnel-house and covering the steeple, 18s. † *Item.* For the archdeacon's man coming for a record of all the inhabitants of the parish, 4d.

---

* In the "*State Papers, Foreign,*" appears under date March 2, 1561 a letter from Marco Antonio Erizzo to John Thornworth. He was justice of the peace in 1532. (See the Author's History of the Royal Gunpowder Works.)

† Fragments of old masonry were taken from the Abbey Tower in Sept., 1887, to make way for the new clock—the gift of John Parnell, Esq. The ancient stone work consisted of portions of the elegant western arch, the clerestory, and the lost zigzag column. Some of the surface stones had distemper paintings upon them.

LADY CHAPEL AND CRYPT.*

T̤HIS Chapel is situated south of the Abbey Church, similar to most chapels of the kind dedicated to the Virgin, and is perhaps one of the richest specimens of mediæval architecture to be found in this county, although, of course not so rich in its historical associations as the Abbey itself. In 1875 the Lady Chapel was restored at the expense of Sir Thomas Fowell Buxton, Bart., of Warlies Park, in this Parish. The date of the foundation of this Chapel still remains a mystery; its style, however, resembles the work of the middle of the 14th century. Matthew Paris suggests that it was built when Henry III. "re-dedicated" the church. It may have been erected then, but the church was never "re-dedicated" by the Third Henry. The late Mr. W. Burgess, architect, adopted the year 1316 as the probable date of the foundation of the Lady Chapel; he also considered it to be even older than that. Before the Reformation there were several Chapels existing in connection with the Abbey Church of Waltham. There was the Chapel of *St. Thomas the Martyr's* (possibly the one now existing in the Abbey Garden) founded, 1188; *St. Sepulchre's Chapel*, erected in 1347; the *Abbot's Chapel*, existing in 1547 (now unknown), and *St. George's Chapel* of which nothing could be found in 1655.

THE CRYPT, OR CHARNEL HOUSE.—Beneath *Our Lady Chapel* is a Crypt or Charnel House, "the fairest," says Fuller, "that I ever saw," and which was originally approached (as now) by a small doorway at the west end. The Crypt consists of two bays of quadripartite vaulting. The windows looking south are small and unglazed. The crypt at one time was

> " O'er covered quite with dead men's rattling bones,
> With reeky shanks and yellow chapless skulls."

To this Crypt was anciently a Guild endowed with houses and lands. In early days the Lady Chapel was used as a Chantry in which priests sang masses for the repose of departed souls. The crypt is still beautiful to one who has an eye for architectural

---

* See History of The Lady Chapel, by W. Winters.

design. Built of chalk, the roof is still almost perfect. Here once stood an altar, but in the days of Charles II. it was turned into a prison for Quakers, several of whom had their goods taken away by the Justice of the Peace, and deposited in the Lady Chapel for not attending church. This Crypt now is little better than a coal-hole or cellar. The floor has been raised some ten feet by rubbish. The arches are hidden by hideous brick graves. The well once used by the monks is now utilised by a common pump. Where service was once held a heating stove for the Abbey now stands. All that was once beautiful is now obscured, made dirty, and put to base use. To improve this ancient Crypt it needs nothing but the pulling down of a few brick walls and the removal of some insanitary rubbish to make its proportions evident. Mr. Ayrton once called St. Stephen's crypt a vault. But, says a writer, "Waltham Crypt is a vault for the dead, a cellar for coal, a cupboard for a pump, and a mere furnace-room. Perhaps some Quaker, like him who gave the new Bishop of Newcastle a palace a few years ago, will restore it as a memorial to the Quaker martyrs who, according to local tradition, were tortured therein." In old prints of the Abbey is seen a small building east of the Lady Chapel. This belonged to the Lord of the Manor, and was demolished sixty years ago. The Lady Chapel had very costly furniture, as is seen in my history of it. It had also a "lytell payer of organes" (an organ having more pipes than one). John Boston was organist in 1540, as was also the renowned old musician Thomas Tallis.

In 1563 the lead from the roof of the Lady Chapel was appropriated to the covering of the new steeple! The chapel has been repaired at various times. At the restoration of the chapel in 1874-5, fragments of polychromatic work were discovered on the interior of the east wall, showing heads of angels, mitred abbots, spires of churches, and Hades. It was considered by some archæologists that these distemper paintings represented the "Last Judgment," and that the building was originally called, "*The Chapel of the Resurrection.*" At the south-east corner of the chapel there is a *piscina* or *benatura*. The original ceiling was no doubt flat and painted; and the lower part of the east end was occupied by an altar, above which the old Norman lights were seen to advantage when the plaster was removed.

These windows were used for lighting the south transept of the church before the chapel was erected. On the north wall portions of zigzag mouldings are now visible, and an arch opposite the chancel of the church, is filled up by the Francis Memorial Screen. Probably access was formerly gained into the church from the chapel by stairs, as the floor of the chapel was much higher than that of the church. In the corner of the chapel is an ancient pulpit which once belonged to the church. The architecture of the exterior west and south of the chapel exhibits great skill and taste. There are well shaped panellings of beautifully cut flints introduced between irregular courses of stone and large red bricks. The masonry of the south buttresses is excellent indeed, as the neatly cut bosses and foliage show. On the east buttress appears to have been a stoup. It is not certain whether the niches in the buttresses were ever filled with effigies. The south front and windows have been carefully restored and made to appear as they did in the 14th century, as also the west end six-light square-headed window.

For many years the Lady Chapel was used as a vestry and a school-room. The parochial schoolmasters were John Matthews, died in 1609-10; Samuel Aire, died 1619; Thomas Wright died in 1656, John Ayres ended his career in 1712. Arthur Herne was schoolmaster early in the present century, and was followed by Mrs. Merrit, Miss Post, Miss Bulbeck, and finally Miss Morgan. A large Board was affixed to the outside of the Lady Chapel some years since, on which was written, "THE PAROCHIAL SCHOOLS." There appears to have been a Sunday School in the town as early as 1811. The Parish Register records the burial of Mary Noon, a Sunday School girl, aged 8, buried 29th May, 1811. The Lady Chapel closed as a Schoolroom and Vestry in 1874.

DEANS, CANONS AND ABBOTS OF HAROLD'S CHURCH, FROM 1060 TO 1540.

THE Church of Waltham, according to Tovi, or "Tofig the Proud," and Harold's foundation, consisted of a dean and twelve *secular* canons; Newcourt and Fuller say only eleven; but documentary evidence goes to prove that Tovi, standard-bearer to King Canute, chiefly known as the beginner of the foundation of Waltham, first established two priests, and to these Harold added ten others, and appointed a dean over them. It is singular to find that neither Newcourt, Stevens, Brown Willis, or the authors of the "Monasticon," mention anything of the dean and canons of Waltham, from the foundation to the year 1144, which reaches over a period of eighty-four years. And nearly all local historians are silent also on this important point. The first canons were called, as before stated, *secular*. The difference between secular priests, or canons, and a monastery of monks, consisted in the fact that the inmates of the former "were ordinary clergymen, bound by no particular vows, but living together on common estates, serving a common church, and under common local statutes. Those of the latter were bound by vows of obedience, poverty and chastity, but were not necessarily in holy orders.

"The multiplication of secular colleges was one of the most likely means of raising up a clergy whose knowledge of mankind, general learning, and thorough sympathy with Englishmen, might improve the character and help to save the souls of the people." (*Stubbs*). It is to be feared that instead of the clergy of that period improving the moral character of the people they did much to corrupt it by their unholy way of living, which was the principal cause of their being ousted in the reign of the second Henry. When Harold increased the number of canons from two to twelve, he then put them in possession of his estates. Portions of these lands were assigned to the canons, in order to supply them with food and clothing, those of which the rents were applied to the latter purpose being distinguished by the name of *shroudland* or *scrudland*—i.e., land allotted to certain communities for the purpose of supplying them with clothing; hence called *clothing-land*. To the dean were allotted four estates, namely, Walde,[1] Alrichsea,[2] Passefield,[3] and Westwaltham.[4]* To each canon a prebend was granted, from which his stall was named. These were probably Nettleswell,[1] Alwaretona[2], Wode-

---

* [1] Southwealde ; [2] Arlsey, in Bedfordshire ; [3] Paslow, in High Ongar ; [4] Westwaltham, in Berkshire. Tovi had property in the last-named place: see Domesday Survey-Book.

[1] Netteswell, near Harlow ; [2] In the hundred of Ongar ; [3] Woodford

forda,[3] Upminster,[4] Luketune,[5] Tippenden,[6] Brichendon,[7] Walcfare,[8] Melnho,[9] Wormeleia,[10] Lambehithe,[11] and Nesing-ham.[12] Each one of the canons had also a portion of North-land. Besides this, each canon had the sum of forty shillings a year from the tithes and offerings of the parish and an allowance of another 40s. a year for dress from the shroudlands in Nazing, Walcfare, and Loughton. According to the founder, the canons of Waltham received extremely liberal rations of food out of the above estates, and which were held subject to a "*feorm fultum*" of a certain number ot weeks each. The dean had to provide for nineteen weeks out of his estates of Pasfield, Walda, and Alrichsea. The prebendary of Nettleswell, seven weeks and two days; Loughton, a week and one day; Upminster, two weeks and two days; Alwartune, four weeks and two days; Woodford, Brickendon and Tippenden, two weeks each. The daily supply of meat and drink to the canons was very liberal; each one had two loaves of very white bread, and one of coarser quality—the three being ample for six persons; six bowls of ale or beer, sufficient for ten men to drink at one time, and six dishes of meat of different kinds each day. In addition to this allowance, on festivals of the first class they were served with pittances of game or poultry, which were esteemed as delicacies. To each canon on the feast of the first dignity was given three pittances; if of the second dignity, he was allowed two pittances; and if of the third dignity, one. At the first-class festivals, such as at Christmas Day and day of Pentecost, and those of the Holy Cross, each one had wine and meat allowed. The remaining proceeds of the prebends were appropriated to the personal uses of the canons, according to their discretion. A pittance from Michaelmas Day to Ash Wednesday consisted of twelve blackbirds, or two *agauseæ*, or two partridges, or one pheasant; during the rest of the year it consisted of one goose or chicken. The main object, it seems, in giving the deans and canons this abundant allowance of provisions was to provide for strangers, and for the poor and needy, the latter receiving each day what was sent away from the Abbey table. It was not unfrequently that the king and his courtiers visited the Abbey of Waltham, and so it was necessary for the canons to keep a good larder. The dean's portion

---

[4] Upminster, in hundred of Chapford ; [5] Loughton ; [6] Supposed to be Epping; [7] In Hertfordshire ; [8] Walchfare, co. Essex ; [9] Melnho, Beds ; [10] Wormley, Herts ; [11] Lambeth ; [12] Nazing, Essex.

being larger than that of the canons, enabled him to deal out more liberally to those persons who depended upon his charity. In early times, when from the want of means of conveyance the produce of the land was necessarily consumed on the land itself, hospitality of this kind was universally practised. Even in the houses of private gentlemen there was the almoner as servant, whose office it was to collect and distribute to the poor at his master's gate what remained of the provision served at the table; and it was customary for the almoner to lay the first loaf in the alms-dish, as an offering to God.*

DEANS OF WALTHAM.—The first Dean of Waltham was *Wulwfin;* he was appointed to this office by Harold, A.D. 1060. For a notice of him see Domesday Survey, under "Berchscire" (Berkshire), vol. i. fol. 58. *Paschal* was the second dean, according to the catalogue of the Durham MSS. (Surtees Soc.), *i.e.*, "6 Id. Jan. *Paschalis Decanus et Radulfus Canonicus, S. Crucis de Waltham.*" *Walter* was third dean, living *circa* 1108; he is mentioned in the same obituary record. *Ernulfus*, fourth dean, *circa* 1144. Roger Wendover mentions the mission of Ernulph, bishop of Lisieux, in 1164. Possibly this is the same man. He is said to have come over to England to make peace between the King and the Archbishop, but was unable to ensure complete success. *Henry of Blois*, fifth dean in 1144, was nephew of William Rufus, and brother to King Stephen. This year was a notable one in the annals of Waltham. King Stephen banished the Earl of Gloucester, and many others of his enemies. Geoffrey de Mandeville died; Geoffrey, Count of Anjou, reduced Normandy.† The canons' houses or conventual buildings in Waltham were destroyed, or partly so, by fire, in an attack made upon the town by Geoffrey de Mandeville and Humphrey de Barrington. The sixth dean was *Richard*, a native of Waltham, probably the same as is mentioned in the Great Roll of the Exchequer as Canon 31 Hen. I. *Wido* was seventh dean. · He is called Guido Rufus, and was an opponent of St. Thomas à Becket, who, in 1168, threatened to excommunicate him. Wido held the deanery of Waltham for ten years—1167 to 1177—and resigned when the Augustine Canons were instituted by King Henry II.

---

* See Beattie's Castles and Abbeys ; also De Invent. S. C. (Stubbs
† Matt. of Westminster, vol. ii.

Canons of Waltham.—*Adelard, or Athelard of Lüttich,** was the first canon. Harold appointed him to office when he founded the minster of Waltham. He was a very learned man, and filled the office of chancellor, or lecturer, besides that of canon, and was also "childmaister" of the college. Harold brought him from Lüttich, or Liege, to be the head of the educational department of Waltham. His son Peter succeeded him in the office of schoolmaster. *Osgod Cnoppe* and *Ailric Childemaister* (schoolmaster) were canons of Waltham when Harold paid his last visit to his much-loved minster, before the great battle of Hastings took place, and these two canons followed him to the field of Senlac, and assisted Eadgyth in finding the body of the King after the battle. We are not certain how long they held office in Waltham after the death of their royal master in 1066. *Aldwin* and *Geoffrey* were canons of Harold's founda tion *circ.* 1108—1118. Geoffrey was chaplain to Queen Matilda, *temp.* Hen. I.

Alwred and *Richard* appear on the list of Canons in 1130. Richard was afterwards Dean of Waltham. *Master Peter*, son of Athelard, was canon of Waltham from 1130 to 1136. The biographer of Harold was brought up under his tuition in the school of Waltham. In 1136 *Brian Bainard* was canon: his name occurs in the "Monasticon" under Walden Abbey. *Rudulphus* is also mentioned as canon at the same time (see Durham Obituary). *Robert filius Walter* was canon *circ.* 1144, and *Adam son of Bruningi* the presbyter. These were followed by Robertus and Walter, canons; they both appear in the Durham registers: *Cal. Aug. Waterius Canonicus de Waltham.* 6 Cal. *Nov. Robertus Canonicus de Waltham.* Thomas de Ware was canon and kitchener of Waltham in 1213, *Vide* Riley's Mem London, p. 105.

The privilege of being exempt from all episcopal jurisdiction was granted to the 1st Abbot Wido, or Guido, by Pope Lucius III. who was the first pope elected by cardinals, A.D. 1181—1185. The Abbot of Waltham was afterwards indulged in the use of the pontificals by Pope Celestine III., A.D. 1191. In the November of 1197, the Archbishop of Canterbury visited the Abbey and

---

* Harl. MSS. 3776, fol. 57.

Convent of Waltham, and expressed his confidence in the abbot's mode of government.*

ABBOTS OF WALTHAM FROM A.D. 1177 TO 1540.—The Abbey of Waltham being a royal foundation was not subject to episcopal jurisdiction,† but only to the "See of Rome and the King." The Superior of the Abbey was one of the twenty-eight mitred Abbots in England, and ranked the twentieth. Four of these mitred Abbots were called "Abbots general, or Abbots sovereign," and sat as lords in Parliament, they were also termed "Abbots exempt,' of whom the Abbot of Waltham was one, the others being those of Bury, St. Albans and Evesham.

Waltham Abbey was ruled from its foundation by Harold, A.D., 1060 until 1540, reaching over a period of 480 years, by several deans, canons and abbots, together with many other officers of a minor class.

Walter de Gaunt was appointed the first abbot of Waltham in 1177; and died in 1201. *Ralph*, a prebendary of Chichester was made prior or canon of Waltham, *temp.* Henry II. 1177.‡

Abbot Richard succeeded Gaunt in 1201. His rule lasted about thirteen years.§

Nicholas de Westminster was abbot of Waltham A.D. 1214.

Walter, in 1217, occurs as abbot in the Waltham Register (Tib. c. ix.)

Richard was abbot from 1219 to 1229, and died 1248.

In 1237 A——— occurs abbot.‖ He is not mentioned either by Willis, Steven or Newcourt.

Simon de Scham (or Soham) abbot in 1248. During his government a serious litigation about the marsh rights occurred between him and the townsmen of Waltham ¶ Simon de Seham died in 1263, and was succeeded in office by

Adam de Witz (or *Wiz*) who governed from August 20, 1263 to 1269.**

---

* Chronicle Ric. I. (Stubbs).
† The Abbey remained free from such jurisdiction until 1854.
‡ Collier's Eccles. Hist. II. 333; also Harl. MSS. 391, fol. 121. *Vide* Bull of Pope Alex. to Prior Ralph of Waltham.
§ Harl MSS. 1520 Cott. MSS Tib. c. ix. fol. 141.
‖ Bp. Kenneth MSS.
¶ Harl. MSS. 3776 (Henricus ex Emwelle)
** Harl. MSS. 7520.

Richard de Harewes (or *Herges*), ruled in the Abbey from 1269 to 1273.

Reginald de Maidenhith received the temporalities Jan. 29, 2 Ed. I. 1273.   In his time the church was restored (A.D. 1286).

Hugh occurs abbot in 1288.

Robert de Elintone was abbot in 1290.   He died in 1301.

John de Babburgham received the assent to his election March 30th, 30 Ed. I., but his temporalities were not restored to him till Feb. 6th, 1303.   He died in 1307.   In the same year (1307)

Richard de Hertford became abbot and died at Canterbury in Nov. 1344.

John occurs as abbot, A.D. 1334.   He also died at Canterbury probably in 1345.

Richard, abbot died in 1345, the same year that he was elected; and was followed in office by

Thomas de Walmersley, who held the temporalities from 1345 to 1371.

Nicholas Morris became abbot on Sept. 6th, 1371.   He was a man of high repute, and died Nov. 17, 1389.

William de Harleton appears 10 Rich. II. 1387, "celler die Abbis de Waltham."   He was probably the same man as died abbot in 1400.

William Harleston, abbot 1397 or 1399.   Probably the same person as is mentioned by Dugdale and the Harl. MSS. 7520, under the term *William*, who died 1 Hen. IV.   William Harleston died of a pestilential fever, *circ.* 1400, and was buried in the Abbey Church.

John Coupe, chaplain at the Abbey in the same year. (1387.)*

William Neel was elected abbot Dec. 29, 1390.†

Michael was abbot in 1397, and died early in the same year.

Walter, abbot in 1408, governed till 1420.   Dugdale affirms that *William* was abbot, May 26th, 7 Hen. V.   This may have been

William de Hertford (or *Hestford*) to whom the temporalities

* Ancient Deeds and Charters Pub. Rec. Off. K. 42, 46.
† W. Neal was rector of Little Ilford in 1364, resigned 1370.

were restored October 12, 1420. Historians are not decided as to whether this *William* is the identical one who ruled in 1439 and 1444.*

John Eld† was chaplain at the Abbey, 6 Hen. VI.

John Lucas occurs abbot in 1460; he held office till his death in 1475. A brass recording the death of his father and mother is preserved in Lofts Wendon Church, Essex.

Thomas Edwards was admitted abbot on the death of John Lucas, August 5, 1475, and was deposed in 1488 for dilapidations.

Gervase Rose received the temporalities May 20, 1488, and governed till 1497 or 1498. The office appears to have been left open for three years.

Alan Rede was made abbot, Nov. 12th, 1500, and died 1507.

John Sharnbroke received the temporalities June 23, 1507.

John Mayln occurs abbot in 1526, but resigned his office sometime in the same year.

Robert Fuller, the last abbot to whom the temporalities were restored Sept. 4, 1526. He was afterwards elected prior of St. Bartholomew's, Smithfield, and held the priorate in commendam with his Abbey, and which he surrendered to the king, March 23rd, 31 Hen. VIII. This abbot wrote a chartulary of the Abbey‡ and died late in the same year in which he was ousted.§

MINISTERS OF THE ABBEY CHURCH FROM 1540 TO 1887:¶

VERY little is now known as to the precise method of conducting divine service in the Abbey Church immediately after the dissolution. When service was held (which was then a rare occurrence) "serving priests" officiated. Dr.

---

* *William*, abbot, according to the Register of London and Canterbury, A.D., 1439.

† Ancient Deeds and Charters, Pub. Rec. Off.

‡ Harl. MSS. 3739.

§ The gross income of the Abbey, 26 Hen. VIII., amounted to £1079 12s. 1d. The clear revenue £900 4s 3d.—*Dugdale*,

¶ Annals of the clergy of Waltham, by W. Winters, F.R. Hist. Soc.

Fuller observes that "the church at Waltham passed from 1547 to 1558 under "four changes in religion, papist and protestant; papist and protestant." It is difficult to determine who were the ministers of the Abbey Church from the time of the last abbot, in 1540, to the beginning of Elizabeth's reign. No doubt the living was vacant for a long while. In 1542 certain charges were paid to the "parish priest," to "Our Lady priest," to the "charnel priest," to "two clerkes," and to the "choristers" of the Abbey. The first parish priest or curate of the Abbey on record, is given by Newcourt as

Robert Rawe. The date of his installation is given under 1561.

John Daniel was minister in 1563 (licensed 30th July, 1580), and died Sept. 18, 1581.

Philip White, minister, is mentioned under date August 7, 1577.

James Day (or *Deys*) was curate in 1583 (licensed July 19, of that year.)

John Webb, A.B., succeeded to the living 23 Feb. 1584.

Thomas Smythe. He is not mentioned by Newcourt, but the register states under date, December 12, 1585, Thomas Smythe, the son of Thomas Smythe, minister of God's worde and preacher was baptised.

Edward Baker, A.M., was incumbent of Waltham in 1592. On the 13th February of the same year he appears as Vicar of Nazing, which living he resigned for that of Waltham. He was buried April 21st, 1604.

George Tipping, minister, married Mary Glascoke of Waltham, Dec. 14, 1608. It is not known whether he was curate of Waltham or not.

Joseph Hall, D.D., was presented to Waltham in 1612. His name occurs in the Register as early as March 12, 1608-9. He was afterwards successively bishop of Exeter and Norwich. His son George was bishop of Chester. Joseph Hall was at Waltham 22 years, and it was here that he wrote most of his great works. The baptism of nearly all his family occurs in the register.

Robert Blinco, curate, probably under Dr. Hall. He died 16th Feb., 1611-12.

Robert Greenough, M.A. was licensed as minister of Waltham (under Dr. Hall) April 15, 1614.

William Pettie, *A.B.* was licensed October 16, 1619.

William Carter is the next on Newcourt's list, and was married at Waltham to Susan Powell, July 6, 1623.

Richard Walmsley was curate of Waltham for many years. His name occurs in the register as early as Sept. 30th, 1627. He was buried at Waltham, June 3rd, 1654.*

John Gibbon (or Guibbon)† incumbent in 1629. His son *John Guibon*, *B.D.*, minister of St. Ann's, Blackfriars, was born at Waltham Oct. 18, 1629, and buried in 1663.

Nathaniel Hatley, curate of Waltham for nearly forty-six years, 1633-1679.

William Price, *B.D.*, first appears in the register as minister of Waltham, March 29th, 1644-5.‡

Thomas Fuller, *D.D.*—In 1648-9, Dr. Fuller was presented to the living of Waltham by James Hay, Earl of Carlisle,§ who resided at the Abbey House. He held the living nearly ten years.

Thomas Reeve, *D.D.*, was curate here (probably) as early as 1660. The Register mentions him in 1662. Dr. Reeve was an author of some repute in his day. During his curacy Dr. Edward Pelling, a great author and who held property in Waltham, buried several of his family in Waltham. (S. T. P. 1660, A. M. 1661.)

John Oliver, *M.A.*, "chaplain at ye Abbey," under the · patronage of the Earl of Kennoul, who was buried March 28, 1676-7. John Oliver was buried at Waltham, March 2nd, 1670-1.

Lionel Goodrick succeeded to the living of Waltham, June 17, 1672. He died June, 1693.

William Mason was curate in 1677 and which office he held many years. (Of Wadham College, Oxon., B.A., March 2, 1679.

Joseph Merrill, *A.M.*, officiated in April, 1668. (Par. Reg).

John Duin (*or Dewin*) officiated in 1690.

Joseph Darby was curate, April 1688, minister in Sept. 1693,

---

* On May 30, 1629, was buried Francis Hill, son of Mr. Percival Hill, rector of St. Catherine, Coleman Street, London.—*Par. Reg.*

† One of the assembly of Divines at Westminster.

‡ Price was one of the Assembly of Divines at Westminster. He was the author of some tracts and sermons.

§ Dr. Fuller wrote most of his works at Waltham. David Leech (or Leigh) vicar of Nazing, buried his wife at Waltham, Jan 1st, 1657-8.   .

and officiated until his death in Sept. 1715. (A.B., 1680, A.M., 1684, of Emmanuel Coll., Cam.)

Francis Phillips curate in 1715.

[*Anthony*] *Lapthorne* possessed the living, Feb. 1716, after a severe contest. Morant says the contest was between John Capon, B.LL. (not Cooper) and Mr. Lapthorne, probably Anthony Lapthorne of Pembroke, Coll, Oxen., B.A., Oct. 17, 1699, and M.A. April 13, 1703.*

Thomas Broadway followed Lapthorne as curate. His name first occurs August 23rd, 1721.† Of St. John's Coll., Cam. A.B. 1716, A.M. 1730.

Robert Swynfen, *B.A.*, curate from 1729 to March, 1732-3. He was much esteemed in the parish and died March, 1732-3. *Christopher Sclater, M.A.*, rector of Chingford, officiated in Oct. 1725; and in Sept. 1733, *Mr. Chapman*, of Cheshunt, officiated.

Robert Fowler, *B.A.*, curate of Waltham for upwards of twenty years, from June 24, 1734, to Sept. 28, 1754. He was afterwards rector of Gt. Parndon. Of Trin. Coll., Cam. A.B. 1733.‡

John Lindsey succeeded Fowler as curate, which office he sustained for upwards of twenty-five years, 1754 to 1779. During his curacy several ministers officiated, viz., *George Farran*, July 24, 1760; *F. Salt*, June 29, 1761, (probably vicar of Nazing). *W. Ramsden*, Oct. 1767; *Matthew Thomas* (curate of Cheshunt) Dec. 6, 1769, August 27, 1770; *G. Smyth*, Jan. 24, 1771; *Bartholomew Booth*, Dec. 30, 1772; *T. P. Slater*, Feb. 3, 1773; *N. Lancaster, LL.D.*, May 11, 1775; *Heneage Diring*, *D.D.*, August 4, 1778.

Samuel Vickers succeeded John Lindsey as curate of Waltham, August 1st, 1779. Of St. John's, Ox. B.D. 1768.

---

* A note in the Parish Register under date Feb. 1716, is as follows: No Register kept during ye contest between Cooper [Capon] and Lapthorne. The contest ended and ye Rev. Mr. Lapthorne to possession of ye Church at ye latter end of February, 1716. Buried the Rev. Mr. Ferdinand Naptin, March 10, 1716-7. Par. Reg.

† The Rev. Mr. Isaac Dalton, of St. Botolph Without, Aldgate, London, buried (in Waltham) Sept. 26, 1722, of Trinity Coll., Cam. A.B. 1677.

‡ Buried Benjamin Waywel, a clergyman, yt had lost his understanding, belonging to St. Catherines, London. April 30, 1736. Par. Reg.

John Boutflower (or Boulflower) followed Vickers, Oct. 3, 1779. Of St. John's, Cam. S.T.P. 1787.

Isaac Colnett, B.A., was curate from March 24, 1786, until his death, which occurred March 2, 1801. During his term of office the following ministers officiated, viz., *Thomas Griffin* (curate of Cheshunt) between Feb. 3, 1780, and Oct. 25, 1784; *James Sloper* (curate of Cheshunt) May 3rd, and June 7th, 1780; *John Festing*, August 15, 1784; *John Sharrar, B.A.*, from 1785 to 1788, *John Procter*, June 5, 1786; *William Towne*, Nov. 5 and 28th, 1788; *James Montgomery*, August 25, 1800, and August 1, 1801; *R. Hughes*, Sep. 27, 1801.

John Mullins succeeded Colnett as minister of the Abbey, Oct. 25, 1801, and continued until Sept. 2, 1806. *William Archibald Armstrong* (curate of Cheshunt) officiated occasionally from 1805 to 1811; also *Richard Smyth, LL.B.*, July 8, 1804; *Reginald Bligh*, June 2, 1805; also *Stephen Thackwell* June 1, 1806; *Charles Lucas Edridge, S.T.P.*, Oct. 1st, 1806.

Thomas Pickthall followed Mullins, Oct. 6, 1806. He was highly respected in the Parish, and resigned for Broxbourne; he was buried in Broxbourne churchyard. *William Cockburn, S.T.P.*, officiated Nov. 28, 1809; *William Batt*, July 28, 1811; *Henry Dixon*, August 11, 1811.

William Morgan Whalley was admitted as curate after Pickthall and held the curacy of Waltham till his death, which occurred in 1846.*

Wiltshire Staunton Austin, "late of Demera" in 1826, served in Abbey as lecturer.

John Lewis Capper, M.A., became curate in 1827 until 1846. *Joseph Clark* officiated a few times after Mr. Capper's resignation.

James Francis, M.A., succeeded Capper in 1846, and sustained his office longer than any other minister since the days of Charles the Second. Mr. Francis was Vicar of the Parish and Rural Dean, and died March 3rd, 1885, aged 68. During Mr. Francis' ministry the following curates have officiated: — *Pugh, F. W. Mann, J. Harman, R. C. M. Rouse, — Hart, C. W. Bond F. G. Batho, A. Workman, F. A. Clark, L. N. Knox, E. Parkinson. Francis Burdett Johnston, M.A.* (curate in 1873) present vicar.

---

* Mr. Whalley was a non-resident for years.

F. B. Johnston, M.A., was curate in charge of the Abbey Church from the time of the death of the late vicar, J. Francis, M.A., in February, 1885, until he was appointed vicar of the Parish of Waltham Holy Cross, in November, 1885. The living, formerly in the hands of trustees, is now under the control of the bishop of St. Albans (Dr. Claughton). J. Francis, M.A., the late vicar, became vicar, in 1868, consequent on the "District Church Amendment Act." *J. B.Stamp*, and *A. Morgan* curates, 1887.

THE CHURCHYARD.

T is not easy to state how long the Abbey Churchyard has been in existence as a burial ground; probably, as in many places, only since the dissolution of the monasteries *temp.* Hen. VIII. Most likely its appropriation for sepulture began with the Abbey itself, as the population of the town in Anglo-Norman times was considerable. Singular to say, no stone coffins of remote antiquity have been unearthed in any of the older portions of the churchyard. Fragments of coffins have been dug from the north-east end of the present church, which, of course, was once covered by the original eastern choir, and which still holds the sacred ashes of the honoured founder of the Abbey—Harold, although as yet hidden from the keen eye of the archæologist.

EARLY CEMETERIES IN WALTHAM ABBEY.—There are two ancient documents, written in Latin, in the Public Record Office, both dated from Waltham, the latest being 20th July, 7 Hen. VI., 1429, which treats of a burial place, or cemetery, at Piner's Green, near High Beech. This may have been for the out-of-town poor during the middle ages, when the aristocracy were interred in the church or churchyard. The poor were generally buried without coffins.

The deed above-named refers to Robert Waltham, son and heir of Walter Waltham, of Waltham Holy Cross, who received for the term of his life in fee simple three tenements, one of which was situated between the house of John Brooks on the east, and a garden looking towards *"Pynest"* on the West, and on the north between the king's highway and the (*Cimitermni*) cemetery and the tenement called the *(Cheker)*, probably an inn on the side of the high road. The parchment is endorsed by very early Waltham names—"Per Robert Waltham and John Gladwin." An earlier document than the above, contains an account of the *cemetery* near Wolmefford, in this parish. This land became church property and known as *Wolmerford*, situated a short distance from the town and is mentioned by Farmer, p. 164. The deed in which this cemetery is mentioned is a contract between John Foot and Sarah Hay, of Waltham, and bears date 7 Edward II. 1314. Walter Maydehethe is one of the witnesses, probably a relative of Reginald de Maidenithe, abbot of Waltham from 1277 to 1288. This is a special item in the history of this parish which has never before appeared in print, and it is interesting inasmuch as it shows that the early parishioners were provided (probably by the abbots) with a quiet resting place near to where they had resided. Thus it is evident that each of the hamlets of this parish had a cemetery, whilst the church and the churchyard were used for interments of the dead of the town.

LICHGATE.—At the south-east entrance to the Churchyard, dividing the "Harp Inn" from the author's own house, is the *Lichgate*, perhaps the oldest existing relic of domestic architecture connected with the Abbey. The folding gates themselves are of no great antiquity. The archway, or Lich gateway, was erected as a covering place for funerals. The coffins and mourners waited under it until the clergyman came to conduct the *cortège* to the Church The path leading to the Church was called the *Lichway*, and which determined the path to be a public thoroughfare as in other places, because the dead had been carried that way. *Lich* is from the Saxon *lic*, a corpse, hence *Lichfield*, the field of martyred Christians. The Lichgate being placed S.E., of the Churchyard shows it to be very ancient. There may have been one at the western entrance of the yard, but no remains of it are left. The Lichgate was evidently the principal way into the Churchyard before the Reformation, when the tower stood east instead of west, and when the Abbey was cruciform in shape. The entrance then into the body of the Church was by the south transept, which ran parallel with the east end of the Lady Chapel. The large ELM TREE in the centre of the churchyard is one of the noblest of its kind.   This *elm tree* measures twenty-two feet round the base and twenty feet round the centre of the trunk, the height from the ground to the head being twelve feet.   The main limbs were lopped off some years ago to prevent danger in the probability of their being broken by storms.   Judging from the size of the tree, it cannot be less than six hundred years old.

A TULIP TREE of great rarity grew in the garden annexed to the Churchyard and bloomed in the months of June and July.   This tree stood for more than 300 years, and several unsuccessful attempts were made to propagate from it.

A large COTTON TREE grew in the centre at the east end of the Churchyard until within the last twenty years.   It bloomed in Midsummer and bore a kind of downy substance like cotton.

The LIME TREES forming the avenue in the Churchyard were planted by Thomas Wilkinson (a foreman in the Government works in this town) early in the winter of 1843.   These trees were the gift of Mr. Joyning, nurseryman, of Waltham Cross, to the then Churchwarden's of Waltham Abbey, namely, Mr. W. R. Clark, Mr. W. Kent Thomas, and Mr. John Griffith, who accepted them and gave permission for them to be planted.   They were given as a freewill offering for the good of the public and out of respect to the parish consequent upon there being no offertory box in the Church.   Other smaller trees appear here and there among the graves, and which, I am happy to find are slow of growth.   When the author last (1868) took a list of the sepulchral monuments in the Churchyard there were no less than 384 grave-stones and wooden rails, and the earliest now existing is a head-stone which stands near the Lady Chapel to the memory of John Streeter, who died 8th February, 1717-18.   In 1870 the Church-yard path was paved and iron railings erected to preserve the graves at a total cost of £272 10s.   Mr. John Bentley was the contractor.

When the ground for the foundations of the houses south-east of the Churchyard and near the Harp Inn was dug out in 1867, nearly the whole bulk of earth was found to be composed of human remains; many of the uncoffined skeletons were quite perfect.   No doubt this ground in early times was connected with the Churchyard, and may have been used for the interment of the poor in the time of the plague.   It also shows that it was open to the highway fronting the Market-place, and may have been the main entrance to the Abbey Mansions occupied by Lord Edward Denny and the Earl of Carlisle. Three of the human skeletons there discovered were lying with their heads north-west, in an angular position, with a square pointed stake through each head. And seven feet below the surface on the same spot was found a dagger blade séven inches long and slightly curved. Probably the persons thus buried were murderers, who were buried with their murderous weapon in a transverse manner in a place where three or four roads met.

In days gone by, from the frequent burials in the Churchyard, a large quantity of human skull, leg bones, &c., were thrown up. They were stored with broken tombstones and rails, in what was then called the "Bonehouse," namely, the Crypt beneath the Lady Chapel. "Old Browney," as he was called, was the grave-digger for many years; and the late Mr. William Carr, the renowned Bellringer, was the " Amen " clerk and sexton.

TOMBS IN THE CHURCHYARD.—At the present day there are not many large monuments in the Churchyard. Various are the emblems of mortality engraved upon some of the older stones, such as hour glasses, angels with trumpets, deaths head, and crossbones, gravediggers' tools, armorial bearings, and other grotesque characteristics of departed worth. There are but few quaint and interesting epitaphs, most of them being in the old stereotyped prosaic style.

In this "God's-acre " are laid to rest the remains of many local personages of note in their day, namely the families of Woollard, Thompson, Colnett, Barwick, Burgoyne, Johnson, Preston, Banbury, Parnell, Jessopp, Buck, Littler, Drayson, Acres, Carter, Pain, Halfhide, Leverton, Mason, Chetwood, Wiggs, Hunnings, Wheatley, Mitchell, Havelock, Edenborough, Woodbridge, Wright, Auther, Bates, Braddock, Dyer, Allen, Law, Helc, Ashcombe, Clark, Chapman, Usborne, Jones, Hilton, Peak, Crean, Parre, Want, Bridges, Ridpath, Pace, Streeter, Death, Gardener, Harvey, Darby, Pigbone, Mills, Jagger, Archer, Carr, Turnham, Evennett, Brett, Smith, Ricketts, &c. For a complete list of the tombs see "Our Parish Register " by W. Winters.

The Churchyard was closed against interments in 1856, except in family vaults by special permission. Mrs. Elizabeth Edenborough was the last interred there. She died December 30, 1883, and her remains were buried with those of her husband in the north-east corner of the Churchyard, January 4th, 1884. Several family vaults have been re-opened since 1856.

"Body-snatching" from Waltham Abbey Churchyard frequently occurred in early days. About fifty years ago the body of George Cook, Veterinary Surgeon of this town, was stolen by Thomas Brace and others from the Churchyard soon after its interment. The body was first taken to a house in Silver Street, and there deposited in a cupboard, and afterwards removed in a sack to Frank Harvey's field and thrown into a ditch. A cart was found waiting for it near the gate in Sewardstone Road, Waltham Abbey, where the Cemetery house now stands, to convey it to London.

A row of old houses standing near the Church and forming the western boundary of the Churchyard, were demolished in 1824. The present brick wall near the road was erected in 1829. In early days portions of the Churchyard were let as small garden plots.* See "Our Parish Registers."

TRUST FOR ENLARGING THE CHURCHYARD.†

This Indenture, made the 21st day of January, in the 54th year of the reign of our Sovereign Lord George III., in the year 1814, between Sir William Wake, of Courteen Hall, in the county of Northampton, Bart., and Dame Janny, his wife, of the first part; Charles Wake, Esquire, a Captain in the Northamptonshire Militia, eldest son and heir apparent of the said Sir W. Wake, of the second part; the Reverend William Whalley, of Upper Slaughter, near Stow-on-the-Woulds, in the county of Gloucester, clerk, minister or curate of the Church, or perpetual curacy of the parish of Waltham Holy Cross, co Essex, of the third part; and Spencer Newman, of the parish of Waltham Holy Cross, Corn Chandler, John Mumford of the same parish, Farmer, and William Clapshew of the same parish, Farmer, the present Churchwardens of said parish of Waltham Holy Cross, of the fourth part. Whereas by Indenture of Lease bearing date the 12 day of April in the 32 of Henry VIII., and made between his said Majesty of the one part, and Anthony Denny Esquire of the other part. His said Majesty did deliver, grant, and to farm let to the said Anthony Denny, Esq., All that Grange called Waltham Grange, in Waltham, to

---

* These houses were last occupied by Messrs. Smart, Mould, Chellis, Woodcock, and Woodbridge.

† Copied from Close Rolls of Chancery, 54 Geo. III., pt. 2, No. 9, Public Record Office.

the late dissolved Monastery of Waltham Holy Cross, co. Essex, then belonging and appertaining, together with all houses, buildings, barns, &c., with divers lands and heredits, in the said Indenture particularly described. All and singular which premises lay and were in Waltham Holy Cross aforesaid, and then lately belonged to the said Monastery, and were commonly called the Demesne Lands of the said late Monastery, and also the Rectory of Waltham Holy Cross with its rights and appurts., together with all Tythes of Corn, Grain, and Hay to the said Rectory belonging. To hold the same unto the said Anthony Denny and his assigns from the feast of St. Michall last past, to the end of the term of 21 years next following under the yearly rent payable in the proportion and manner' therein mentioned. And whereas His said Majesty King Henry VIII., by his letters patent bearing date 28th September, in the 36 year of his reign, did deliver unto the said Anthony Denny the reversion of the said Grange, Rectory, Lands, Tythes, &c., to hold the same, his assigns, from the end of the said term of 21 years to the end of the term of 35 years thence next following. And whereas His Majesty King Edward the Sixth, by his letters patent, &c., bearing date 28th day of June, in the first year of his reign, after taking notice of the said Indenture of demise or lease. He the said King did give and grant to the said Anthony Denny (then Sir Anthony Denny Knight) the reversion and reversions of the aforesaid Grange, Rectory, Lands, Tythes, &c., so as aforesaid demised. And also Scite, Compass, Close, Circuit, and precints of the late Monastery of Waltham, together with all houses, &c., therein described; and in as ample manner and form as the last late abbot of the said monastery of Waltham, or any of his predecessors in right of his said late monastery at any time before the dissolution of the said late monastery had held or enjoyed the same. To have hold and enjoy the same premises unto and to the use of the said Anthony Denny, his heirs, and assigns for ever, to be holden of the same king in chief, by the service of the fortieth part of a knight's fee, and rendering annually to the same king, his heirs, for the aforesaid Grange of Waltham and other premises thereunto belonging. Seven pounds thirteen shillings and eleven-pence farthing, and for the said Rectory of Waltham and other premises to the same belonging, one pound five shillings and sixpence. And whereas by divers acts and deeds or otherwise, the said grange called Waltham Grange, the scite of the said dissolved Monastery, and the greater part of the several lands, tythes, and heredits. mentioned and described in the said Indenture of demise or lease, and in the said letters patent respectively, became afterwards vested in the said Sir William Wake, for his life with immediate remainder. To the said Charles Wake in tail male with divers remainders over. And they the said Sir William Wake and Charles Wake were respectively seized of such estates therein at or immediately before the execution of the Indenture. And whereas under and by virtue of certain Indentures bearing date Nov. 24th, 1812, the release being of ten parts, and made between John Mumford, first part; Richard Hall Clarke, John Bishop, Samuel Ware and Thomas Bowden, therein described as acting devises in trust, named in the will of Ellis Were, Esquire, deceased, of the second part; the said Sir William Wake, and Dame Janny, his wife, of the third part; and the said Charles Wake (therein described as the only child of the said Sir W. Wake by Dame Mary Wake his first wife deceased) of the fourth part; Dame Mary Wake, widow, (therein described as the mother of the said Sir W. Wake) of the fifth part; Isaac Samuel Clamtree, of the sixth part; Robert Bicknell, of the seventh part; William Palmer and Edmund Mumford, of the eighth part; the right Hon. Charles, Lord Barham, and Samuel Gambier, Esquire, of the ninth part; and John Wood, of the tenth part; and of a common recovery suffered in pursuance thereof in Hilary term last, and a declaration of the uses of the said recovery in the said Indenture of release contained the Manor or Lordship of Waltham, otherwise Waltham Holy Cross with the rights, members, and appurts. thereof, the Scite of the capital Messuage and late dissolved Monastery of Waltham Holy Cross, with the court-yard, gardens, &c., thereunto belonging (of which premises the piece or parcel of land hereinafter described and appointed and bargained and sold or expressed or intended so to be, were and are part and parcel) were granted, released, and settled by the said Sir W. Wake and Dame Janny, his wife, and Charles Wake to such uses and for such trusts, intents and purposes, under and subject to such powers, &c., as the said Sir William Wake and Dame, his wife, and Charles Wake, should by any deed or instrument in writing, with or without power of revocation, to be by them sealed and delivered in the presence of two or more credible witnesses, from time to time jointly direct or appoint, and in default of such direction or appointment should extend. To the use, intent and purpose that the said Janny Wake, in case she should survive the said Sir William Wake, and her assigns might receive thereout during her life one annuity or yearly rent-charge of eight hundred pounds, payable in a manner therein mentioned, with the usual power of entry and distress, and of the rents and profits of the said premises for securing payment of the said annuity, &c. To such use, upon trust, under and subject to such power, &c., as the said Sir William Wake and Charles Wake should by any deed in writing, with or without power of revocation, &c., and new appointment, to be by them sealed and delivered in the presence of, and attested by two or more credible witnesses from time to time, &c.

And whereas the Church Yard of and belonging to the Parish Church of Waltham Holy Cross is very inconveniently small and confined for the present number of inhabitants of the said parish, and the said Inhabitants have applied to the said Sir William Wake and Charles Wake, and requested them to give and convey the piece or parcel of land, &c., adjoining to the said Church Yard, to the use for the purpose and in manner hereinafter mentioned, and which they have voluntarily consented and agreed to do. Now this indenture that for effectuating the purpose aforesaid They the said Sir William Wake and Dame Janny his wife and Charles Wake pursuant to and by force and virtue, &c., have jointly directed by this present deed and that all the said piece or parcel of land, &c., shall be to the use of the said Spencer Newman, John Mumford and William Clapshew their heirs and assigns for ever upon the trust. And this Indenture witnesseth that for the consideration aforesaid and for further assuring the said heredits unto and to the said Spencer Newman, John Mumford and William Clapshew upon the trust for the intents and purpose aforesaid. And also in consideration of the sum of ten shillings of lawful money of Great Britain, to each of them the said Sir William Wake and Charles Wake have granted bargained and sold all that piece or parcel of land now part of certain lands commonly called the Abbey Gardens, situate in the Parish of Waltham Holy Cross, being part of or near the scite of the said late dissolved monastery of the yards and gardens belonging thereto and now for several years last past in the occupation of Mowbray Woollard as tenant thereof to the said Sir William Wake. As the said piece or parcel of land lies immediately adjoining to the East end of the Parish Church of Waltham Holy Cross toward the west, and to the present churchyard toward the south from which it is divided now only by a brick wall, and the same piece or parcel of land contains by estimation thirty-two perches be it more or less, &c. Upon this special trust and confidence the said Spencer Newman, John Mumford, and William Clapshaw their heirs and assigns do and shall within six calendar months next ensuing the date of these presents at their own costs as churchwardens, cause the present wall which divides the same piece of land from the present Church-yard to be pulled down and in lieu thereof cause a sub-stantial brick wall of equal height and thickness with the present wall to divide the fence from the said piece of land, which wall is at all times hereafter to be maintained and kept and repaired at the cost of the inhabitants of the said parish of Waltham Holy Cross. And upon this further special trust the said church-wardens, their heirs and assigns do and shall cause the said piece of land to be regularly consecrated as a burying ground, &c. In witness whereof the said parties to these presents have hereunto set their hands and seals* the day and year first above written:— William (L. S.) Wake, Jenny (L. S.) Wake, Charles (L. S.) Wake, William (L. S.) Wake, S. (L. S.) Newman, John (L. S.) Mumford, William (L. S.) Clapshew. Sealed and delivered in the presence of R. W. Wake, Rector of Courteenhall, Edward Appleton, Bailiff to Sir William Wake, Courteenhall. Signed, sealed and delivered in the presence of Edwin Corfield, of No. 7, Lincolns Inn Fields, Land Surveyor, W. Tanner, Clerk to William Bullock, Esq., of Shelly in Essex. Signed, sealed and delivered by the within-named Spencer Newman, John Mumford, and William Clapshew in the presence of us—Jos[h] Jessopp, Jun., Atty-at-Law, Waltham Abbey, Essex; Henry Evans, Clerk to Mr. F. A. Jessop of the same place.

---

* SEALS.—There is a large seal of the Abbey of Waltham Holy Cross " with a secretum at the back. To a letter of procuration by Isabella, Prioress of Haliwell, dated 1392." The seal is in red wax, viz., The holy well, and over it John the Baptist's head in a dish.—" In C. 24 are a number of fine deeds of the 13th and 14th centuries, many with fine seals, and many being grants to and by the Abbey of the Holy Cross of Waltham."

THE CEMETERY*

S situated a short distance S.E. of the town and is slightly elevated on the north of Cobbin Brook. The consecration of the Cemetery for Waltham Holy Cross, by the Bishop of Rochester, occurred on Wednesday, Dec. 17, 1856. A Burial Board was then founded, consisting of the Rev. J. Francis (chairman), Spencer Murch, John Speed Davis, Richard Bates, Thomas Chapman, John Ashcombe, William Roberts Clark, Peter Mills, Charles Pryor, and William Richardson. At the same period James Brown was the first appointed Lodge-keeper, at a salary of £26 per annum. Mr. William Carter, formerly proprietor of the Waltham Abbey and London Stage-Coach, was the first person interred in the Cemetery. John Thompson was Lodge-keeper for some time, and now Mr. Todd (1887) fills the office.

The Cemetery consists of an almost square plot of land, three acres in extent, which was purchased of Sir Charles Wake about the year 1855, for the enormous sum of £150 per acre; and after allowing land for paths, chapels, lodge, fences, etc., the burial space remaining was 2a. 1r. 11½p., or 101,081 square feet, being sufficient for 3,907 graves (see original plan in the Cemetery Board Room). The cost for conveyance of the said three acres of land was £100, and an additional £100 for law expenses, beside £25 to the tenant, Mr. Coxshall, as compensation money, making a total of £675. The cost of drainage, etc., amounted to £605 10s.; the erection of the two mortuary chapels, £1,010, and the fencing and lodge, £1,301 10s. 6d. This was a heavy speculation for the parish, considering the Board had to work on borrowed capital, which money, however, has long since been fully paid. The number of persons buried in the Cemetery up to Nov. 28th, 1884, was 2,568. The rate of mortality in Waltham Abbey is small compared with some parishes of equal number of inhabitants, which speaks well for its healthfulness. In 1884 there were about 168 memorial stones and boards in the Cemetery; this number does not include enclosed family graves which have no inscriptions. The number has greatly

See "Our Parish Registers," by W. Winters.

increased since then.   The Cemetery has recently been enlarged
westward, at the moderate cost of £420.   The dedication of this
new portion of the Cemetery took place on June 1st, 1885, by
the Right Rev. Thomas Legh Claughton, D.D., bishop of St.
Albans.   A procession was formed in the following order:—
Messrs. W. Gardener, P. Mills, and T. Chapman, Junr., churchwardens; the Bishop; F. B. Johnston, E Parkinson, and J. H.
Stamp, curates of Waltham Abbey; W. Jackson, Baptist minister;
Messrs. W. R. Clark (chairman), J. Ashcombe, J. Richards, T.
Chapman, W. Oram, members of the Burial Board; H. Gough,
clerk; and Sir T. F. Buxton and the Misses Buxton, and a
number of ladies and gentlemen.   On arriving at the new ground
the procession slowly wended its way around the paths, the Bishop
and those present reciting in alternate verses the Psalms xlix. and
lxxxviii.   The Bishop then delivered an address, in the course of
which he pointed out the difference between dedication and consecration, the former dispensing with some of the legal formalities
which were required in the latter.

LOCAL AUTHORS.

THE earliest known local author is the ejected canon of
the Abbey, the biographer of Harold, who completed
his work *circa* 1205.*   His name is not handed down
to us, but he was a pupil in the school of Waltham, under
Peter, son of Athelard, who was master from 1130 to 1136.
Of course there were many monks whose work it was to
compose and to transcribe the service books of the Church, as
also certain documents of a historical and biographical character.

Roger de Waltham, a native of this town, born in the latter
half of the 13th century, was a splendid scholar and a man
of high repute in his day.   He was appointed Keeper of
Edward the Second's Wardrobe, and was one of the Canons of

---

* (Vitæ Haroldi). We learn from the writings of this author, that he was
born about the year 1119, and that he commenced his education in 1124;
continued in the College at Waltham fifty-three years, and was expelled in
1177, when King Henry the Second ousted all the *Secular* Canons and
instituted *Regular* Canons in their place. He died at an advanced age.

St. Paul's. Fulke Basset, Bishop of London, was his most intimate friend. Roger of Waltham was the author of a great many learned works, two of which are frequently mentioned as being the most popular of all that he wrote, viz., *Compendium Morale*, and *Imagines Oratorum*.

Hugh de Waltham was Clerk of the City of London in 1312 and in which office he continued many years.*

William of Waltham (1314) and William of Cheshunt are mentioned in the City of London documents.†

Nicholas Morris, Abbot of Waltham, a schoolman of the middle ages, and probably a native of this parish, with fourteen other commissioners, was appointed to examine the miscarriages of Richard II.

John of Waltham, a native of this town, born early in the 14th century, was Bishop of Salisbury, Master of the Rolls, Keeper of the Privy Seals and Treasurer of England. He was a great favourite of Richard II. who sorely mourned his death which took place in 1395. His remains were interred, by permission of the King, in the royal chapel in Westminster Abbey, where a memorial brass with an effigy of this prelate in full canonicals is still preserved, though much defaced. He was rector of Great Berkhampstead *circa* 1369. In the Arundal MSS, 155, is a beautifully illuminated psalter, which was once possessed by John of Waltham, when monk of Christ Church, Canterbury, and who obtained it as a gift from W. Hadley, sub prior.

John Wylde, precentor of Waltham *circa* 1400, was the author of a work on Music‡ which was used in the Abbey.

Thomas Tallis, a celebrated musician, resided in Waltham temp Henry VIII., and was precentor of the Abbey with John Boston and William Lilley. Tallis was buried at Greenwich Church, where a memorial brass once recorded his death, but which has long been destroyed. A verse of his epitaph shows his profession :—

> " Enterred here doth ly a worthy wyght,
> Who for long time in musick bore the bell ;
> His name to shew was Thomas Tallys hyght,
> In honest vertuous lyff he dyd excel."

---

* Riley's Memorials of London, p 105.

† Ibid 110. ‡ Lansd Coll. MSS, 763.

Robert Fuller, the last Abbot of Waltham, wrote a chartulary of the Abbey.* This work is most beautifully written, and contains an account of the possessions of the Abbey at the dissolution.

Edmund Freke, one of the last priors of the Abbey, was the author of several religious works.

John Foxe, wrote a part or the whole of his Book of Martyrs in this town,† and his son Samuel, who resided at Warlies, Waltham Abbey, republished his works in three massive volumes. (See Warlies and its surroundings by W. Winters, F. R. Hist. Soc.)

The Bassano Family, of Waltham, were celebrated musicians to Hen. VIII., Ed. VI., Elizabeth, James I., and the Charles's. This family had large possessions in the parish.

Joseph Hall, *D.D.*, born at Ashby-de-la-Zouch, July 1, 1574, and educated at Emmanuel College, Cambridge, was curate of Waltham Abbey for twenty-two years, where he wrote most of his works and where nearly all his children were born. He became successively Bishop of Exeter and Norwich. He frequently preached before King James at Theobalds.

William Price, *B.D.*, curate of Waltham (1644-49) published several sermons and pamphlets.

Thomas Fuller, *D.D.*, a celebrated historian and divine, was instituted to the living of Waltham by the Earl of Carlisle. Many of his works are dated from Waltham.‡ He resigned Waltham Abbey for Cranford, where he died, Aug. 15, 1661.

Edward Palmer, Greek Professor at Cambridge, afterwards resided at Sewardstone, and was a close friend of Dr. Fuller.

Charles Sackville, *Lord Buckhurst*, the poet, possessed the mansion of Copt Hall.§ (See Warlies and its surroundings.)

Thomas Reeve, *D.D.*, author of several published Sermons and Theological Works, was curate of Waltham from 1660 to 1671-2.

---

* Harl. MSS, 3739, also Eccles. Works of the Middle Ages.
† See Life of John Foxe, by W. Winters, F. R. Hist. Soc.
‡ Annals of the Clergy of Waltham.
§ Johnson's Lives of the Poets.

James Harrington, born at Waltham Abbey about the year 1664, was a learned barrister and author of many excellent works. The preface to the *Athenæ Oxon* was written by him. He was buried at Oxford in 1693.

Edward Pelling, D.D., a great author, held large possessions in Waltham Abbey. He was rector of Petworth in Sussex, in 1683. Most of his family were buried in Waltham.

John Farmer, born in Waltham, studied Law, and was the author of the history of Waltham Abbey, and the history of Abbies from 977 to the reign of Elizabeth, published in one vol., 1735. He was buried in the Churchyard, Oct. 3rd, 1750.

John Auther, the first Baptist minister of Waltham Abbey (1729) was the author of a printed Funeral Sermon, delivered on the death of John Wright of this town, Nov. 15, 1730.

Henry Bridges, a native of Waltham, was an ingenious carpenter, and inventor of a musical clock which took him nine years to complete. His tomb stands near the south entrance to the church. He died June 27, 1754, aged 57.

John Adams, a writer and translator, was a resident of Waltham in 1772. A work originally compiled by Don George Juan and Don Antonio de Ulloa, captains of the Spanish Navy, entitled "A Voyage to South America," was translated from the original Spanish, with notes, by John Adams, Esq:, of Waltham Abbey. John Stockdale published a fourth edition of this work in 1806, dedicated to Sir H. Popham. The work, which is illustrated, displays considerable literary ability and sound taste.

William Sotheby, who held the manor of Sewardstone early in the present century, wrote his "Orestes" in the Manor House. He was a splendid linguist, and entered the field against Alex. Pope by translating the "Iliad" of Homer into English verse.

James Upton, of this town (1776), published a volume of letters on Evangelical Truth. He became pastor of a Church in Blackfriars, and died much respected, September 22, 1834.

R. Coleman, Clerk at Royal Gunpowder Factory, Waltham Abbey, 1790-5, wrote a treatise on the Manufacture of Gunpowder (See Phil. Mag. Vol. ix.)

William Newman, D.D., of Bow, formerly a member of the

Baptist Church, Paradise Row, was the author of several publications. Born at Enfield, May 10, 1773; died Dec. 22, 1835.

Samuel Howell, "Master of the Academy, Waltham Abbey," resided in the large red brick house in Sewardstone Street, now occupied by Dr. Henderson. He wrote a small volume of poems entitled "Village Rambles," &c., in which he styles himself the "Author of Trifles," &c. These poems were printed for the author in 1816. The subject matter of the first poem is drawn from Chingford and its vicinity.

Tom Hood, the Comic Poet, though not a native of Waltham Abbey, was a frequent visitor at the house of his friend James Wright, Esq.,* of Powder Mill Lane, Highbridge Street. It has been stated that Tom Hood recited his "Song of the Shirt" in Waltham with great effect. The late Mr. H. Wright, son of the above, informed me that when he and his brother James (now of Mooresburg, Tennesse) were at school at Cheshunt, a celebrated walker by the name of "Skipper" was walking fifty miles a day for twenty-one days, and these two Master Wrights were anxious to see him perform the last mile, but to do this they had to make a hole in the playground wall to get out of, which circumstance Hood took advantage of and wrote a poem on "Getting a hole holiday;" and on another occasion when Hood was staying at Mr. Wright's, the young Wrights blew up the copper with gunpowder (in order to make it *draw*) and Hood wrote a piece on "Skying the Copper," and another on "Lawk! how the blacks are falling." Hood presented a copy of his "Comic Annual" to Mr. Wright, and on the fly leaf he sketched a pawnbroker's sign, the three balls, and underlined it with the words "To my Uncle." Mr. Hood wrote a description of Epping Hunt, in 1827, as before stated. Another of Hood's acquaintances in Waltham appears to have been the late Mr. F. Joyce, percussion cap manufacturer, Farm Hill, of whom he writes in connection with Mr. Hall, a gunpowder merchant, thus—

> "Percussion cap I dare not snap,
> I may not mention Hall,
> Or raise my voice for Mr. Joyce,
> His wadding to recall."†

And when the great explosion of the Powder Mills occurred on

---

* Government Storekeeper at Waltham Abbey many years.
† Hood's Works (Moxon Ed.) Vol. II., 252.

April 13th, 1843, Hood wrote, not in the most serious manner, *i.e.*, "Talking of Engineering, it is strange that Brunel never calculated on one great use of the Thames Tunnel, namely to give Cockneys at Easter a *hole holiday*, some day I predict the tunnel will become a water pipe, and I'm a prophet, I foretold, in last month's (June, 1843) Magazine that the comet would blow up the Waltham Abbey Powder Mills, July 18th, 1843."

Lord Alfred Tennyson composed his poems, entitled "Talking Oak" and "Locksley Hall," when a resident at Beech Hill House, Waltham Abbey.

John Clare, a poet and the son of *Thomas Campbell* the poet, were inmates (1837-40) of Dr. Allen's Lunatic Asylum at Fair Mead House.

Thomas Sturgeon compiled several hymns for Paradise Sunday School. He went to Fernandi Po, as a missionary with Dr. Prince in 1842.

James Carr, of this parish, wrote during the early half of the present century several parochial pamphlets and broad sheets of local interest. A dialogue on the preaching of Wiltshire Staunton Austin, "late of Demerara, now lecturer at the Parish Church Waltham Abbey, 1826," was probably written by the same hand, as the initials "J. C." are appended to the preface.

Charles Coote, late of New Bond Street, London, a gentleman well known in the musical world for many years, was a native of Waltham Abbey, having been born in Sewardstone Street, in 1808, in the house now occupied by Dr. Henderson.

John Braddock, a resident of Waltham Abbey, compiled a "Memoir on Gunpowder," 8vo. 1832.

James Hargreaves, pastor at the Baptist Chapel, Paradise Row, Waltham Abbey, for 16 years, was the author of a work on the "Divine Decrees," and several religious pamphlets. He died September 16th, 1845, aged 77 years.

R. A. Austin published a work in 1653 entitled "A treatise on Fruit Trees." This work was reprinted by a resident of Waltham Abbey, in 1847, under the title of "The Spiritual Orchard."

Major Baddeley, R.A., of Waltham Abbey, compiled a small work on Gunpowder, 8vo., 1857.

Edmund Littler, a native of this town and a clever draughtsman, wrote several papers on archæological subjects in 1859-60.

W. Burges, Architect, published a report on the state of the Abbey Church, before its restoration, 1859-60.

John Maynard, many years a resident of this town, was the author of the History of Epping Forest, 1860; and the History of Waltham Abbey, 1865. He was a good musician and school-master, and died July 20th, 1871, aged 69. His remains were interred in Theydon Bois Churchyard.

Jesse Upton (living), born in this town author of a poem entitled "Echoes from the Walls of our Ancient Abbey," 1865, two pamphlets on the Book of the Revelation, &c.

Captain F. M. Smith R.A., of Waltham Abbey, wrote an able work on "The Manufacture and Proof of Gunpowder as carried on at Waltham Abbey, 8vo. 1870. Born at Penfont, Dumfriesshire, 1834; died 1873, and interred in Waltham Abbey Cemetery.

Major-General Sir Charles Warren, K.C.M.G., R.E., was for some years Superintendent of the Royal Engineers' department, Waltham Abbey. This occurred after his return to this country from the Holy Land in 1871. Sir Charles Warren, Her Majesty's Chief Commissioner to Bechuanaland, was born in 1840, and received his education first at Cheltenham College, and afterwards at Sandhurst and the Royal Military Academy, Woolwich. He obtained his first commission on December 27th, 1857, being appointed to the Royal Engineers. In 1867, when only twenty-seven years of age, he was entrusted with the command of the exploring party sent out by the Committee of the Palestine Exploration Fund, and greatly distinguished himself by the skill with which he conducted the excavations. He discovered the foundations of the Great Temple of Jerusalem, and completed the surveys of Philistia and the Jordan Valley. Sir Charles Warren is now superintendent of the police force in the place of Colonel Henderson.

William Alfred Gibbs (living), of Gillwell House, Sewardstone, in this parish, inventor of a hay-drying machine, is the author of several volumes of poems of a very high order, published about 1870-6, viz.,—"The Story of a Life," "Battle of the Standard," "Harold Erle," "Kling, Klang, Klong," "Lost and Won," "Church Porch," "World, Press and Poets," "Aslon Grange," &c.

John Holloway (" Defender of Lucknow ") a novel writer, was clerk in the government works in this town several years, and which position he vacated about the year 1876.

J. B. Baynard, pastor of Paradise Row Chapel (1867-72) was the author of a three-volume novel, the heroes in which were thought to be mainly those who had been officers in his Church. He afterwards went over to the Established Church.

Major Wardell, R.A., published a small work on the manufacture of Gunpowder, during his term of office at Waltham Abbey, 1878, 8vo.

William Jackson, pastor of the Baptist Church, Paradise Row, wrote a small history of his Church, from 1729 to 1880.

Robert Tabraham, M.A., a native of Waltham Abbey, gradually rose in scholarship until he became head master of Leamington Grammar School. At Trinity College, Dublin, he was Senior Moderator ; University Gold Medallist in Law, History, &c., and Bishop Stearne exhibitioner for uniform excellence in previous examinations. After his degree, he was for four years assistant master at Worcester Cathedral School, and next for seven years assistant master of Malvern College. These honours, however, he did not long enjoy, for whilst in the prime of life his mental faculties gave way, and he became an inmate of an asylum, where he died. Before this serious calamity occurred he had contemplated publishing a learned work which he had compiled on *Comparative Philology*. Whenever he visited Waltham Abbey he generally preached in the Abbey Church, and was considered an eloquent preacher.

Col. C. B. Brackenbury, R.A., a literary gentleman, and Superintendent of the Royal Gunpowder Works in Waltham Abbey, from 1880 to 1885.

William Winters, a native of Walkern, co. Herts, from which place he removed to Waltham Abbey, at the age of four years ; became a Reader of the British Museum, 1869 ; Member of the Essex Archœological Society, 1871 ; Fellow of the Royal Historical Society, 1874 ; Member of the Anastatic Drawing Society, 1876 ; author of the History of Waltham Abbey ; Boy Life ; Life of Harold ; Pilgrim Fathers ; Annals of the Clergy ; Ecclesiastical Works of the Middle Ages ; Life of John Foxe ; Memoirs of A. M. Toplady; Who was the Author of the

Pilgrim's Progress; Musical Talents of the Wesley Family;
Is the Soul Immortal; Our Parish Registers; Hymns and Poems;
History of the Lady Chapel; Handbooks of Waltham Abbey,
Cheshunt, and Barnet; History of the Royal Gunpowder Works,
Waltham Abbey; History of Warlies and its Surroundings,
&c., &c.; also a contributor to the New England Hist. and
Gen. Register; Royal Hist. Soc. Trans.; Notes and Queries;
Editor of several Christian Monthly Publications, &c.; also
Pastor of Ebenezer Baptist Chapel, Waltham Abbey.*

DISSENTING CHAPELS IN WALTHAM ABBEY.

NONCONFORMITY had taken deep root-hold in Waltham
Abbey, long prior to the existence of
PARADISE ROW CHAPEL.—How the locality surrounding this Chapel obtained the beautiful name of "Paradise Row"
is difficult to tell unless by the Abbots of Waltham holding it,
in the middle ages, as a kind of Elysium. It may have originated
from the erection of the Chapel there, which the founders in 1729
called "Paradise Chapel," and which in after years proved to
many a *Paradise* in the highest sense, namely *a place, or garden
of pleasure*. The cottage property called "Paradise Row"
belongs to Paradise Chapel.

In the middle of the 17th century the Quakers were strong in
this town, many of whom met with much opposition, suffering
themselves for conscience sake to be imprisoned in some instances
in the *Crypt* or *Vestry* of the Abbey Church, and their property
taken by the harsh justices of the peace. In the journal of George
Fox (the founder of the Quakers) under date 1654, he says, "I
went to Waltham Abbey, and had a meeting there; the people
were very rude, gathered about the house and broke the windows."
It appears that he went out with his Bible in his hand and quieted
them. Shortly afterwards a Quakers' Meeting House was erected
in *Quaker Lane*, in which Fox frequently preached. This old
house or Chapel was in later times used as the British School-room,
and was demolished in 1844, when the "the Old Boys' School-

---

* F. Johnson, of Sewardstone, and the late Colonel Palmer, have written
much on the history and rights of Epping Forest. The late Mr. W. T.
Wakefield, of this town, originated *The Waltham Abbey & Cheshunt Weekly
Telegraph*, May 30th, 1863. Bishop Stubbs, and E. A. Freeman have written
largely on the early history of Waltham Abbey.

room" was erected on the spot. Many of the old Quakers appear to have been buried in the meeting ground in Quaker Lane, but no register of them has come down to us.

The first Baptist Chapel in Waltham Abbey was erected in 1729, nearly on the site of the present Paradise Chapel. "The cost of erecting this Chapel," says Farmer, "was £400, and which sum was raised by voluntary contributions." It appears, however, on good authority, that £200 of this money was borrowed at interest of Mrs. Elizabeth Shakerley, and repaid in 1740. The Chapel was opened on May 4, 1729; and on the 16th of the October following *John Auther* was ordained pastor by Messrs. Wallen, Arnold, Richardson, Rees, Rudd and Wilson, and which office he sustained until his death, July 11, 1762, aged 74. His remains were buried in the Churchyard. *John Davis* became pastor June 17, 1764, and was publicly ordained to that office by Dr. John Gill and Samuel Burford, August 15, 1764. Mr. Davis died June 11, 1795, aged 64 years. *W. Brackett,* formerly of Sudbury, became pastor May 29, 1797, and died March 1802, in the 40th year of his age. *George Eveliegh* was ordained pastor December 16th, 1813, and died in office, March 4th, 1820. On February 11th, 1824, *C. T. Keen* was settled as pastor, but owing to certain peculiar religious views held by him the two deacons and nine of the members left and formed a *Strict and Particular* Baptist Church, the present representatives of which now meet in "Ebenezer Chapel," Fountain Square, Waltham Abbey. On February 3rd, 1842, twelve more of the members of Paradise Row Church withdrew on account of the change that had taken place in the order of the church, in allowing unbaptised persons to sit down at the Lord's table. These twelve persons also united with the above *Strict and Particular* Baptist Church.

On May 2nd, 1824, the Paradise Sunday School was founded, Mr. Pugh, Superintendent; Teachers, Mr Davis, Mr. Carter, Jun., Mr. W. Maynard, and Miss Dudley; Scholars, 25. Signed, C. T. Keen. One of the first scholars is now (1887) living, Mrs. Joshua Pegrum. Mr. Keen resigned his pastorate after eighteen months' service. *James Hargreaves* was the next pastor. He was publicly recognised, May 4th, 1829 (just a century from the time the Chapel was first opened) and held office until his death, which took place September 16th, 1845, in the 77th year of his age. During his pastorate the present Paradise Chapel was erected (1836), as also the "Old Boy's School" (British) Quaker Lane. He was succeeded by *D. J. East*, who was publicly recognised May 20th, 1846, and who held office until November 3rd, 1851, at which time he left Waltham Abbey for Jamaica. *Spencer Murch*, of Sudbury, son of Dr. Murch, accepted the office of pastor, on June 6th, 1852, without any public recognition or ordination service, as he did not care for such ceremonies. In 1866 Mr. Murch resigned his pastorate on account of failing health and removed to Bath. After some time he partially recovered and settled quietly down at Goldings Hill, Loughton. In the June of 1867, *J. B. Baynard* of Bristol College, became pastor. He held office for a few years without any apparent success, and eventually resigned and entered the Church of England. Early in 1873, *Mr. Williamson*, from Mr. Spurgeon's College, was recognised as pastor by Dr. Culross and others in the June of the same year. After three years labour Mr. Williamson resigned through ill-health, and removed to Sidney, Australia, where he regained strength and became a successful pastor. The present (1887) pastor, *Mr. W. Jackson*, on leaving his church at Willingham was publicly recognised as pastor of Paradise Row Chapel, in the Autumn of 1876. Within the last hundred years several persons connected with this church have entered the work of the ministry and have laboured in various parts of the world. *James Upton* preached his first sermon (from 1 Cor. xv. 9, 10), in Paradise Row Chapel, February, 20th, 1785, and was for many years pastor of Green Walk, Blackfriars Bridge. *Dr. W. Newman* preached his first sermon in this Chapel, January 13th, 1793, from 2 Cor. ix. 15, and became pastor of a Church at Bow. In the summer of 1806 *Samuel Bligh* preached before this church for the first time and was called to the pastorate at Potters Bar. *John Henderson* preached his trial sermon here, on September 4, 1837, from 2 Cor. v. 1, and afterwards became a missionary in conjunction with W. Knibb. *Thomas Sturgeon* was a very energetic worker in Paradise Sunday School. In 1841, having preached before the Church he was sent as a missionary to Fernandi Po. His farewell address was delivered on December 31st, 1841, in this chapel, from Psalm lxxxvi. 5. *John Upton* and *Samuel Pugh* were called to the ministry, December 14, 1842; they were both members of this Church. W. Claydon, the first master of the Old British School

(1840) was connected with this Church, and in 1841 sailed for Jamaica as a missionary. *Thomas Stephen Baker,* a member of Paradise Chapel, entered Bradford College, and afterwards became pastor of a Church at Maldon, in this county. *G. H. Trapp* went from this Church to Mr. Spurgeon's College, and became pastor of a Church in Norfolk, and afterwards removed to America. There are two branch meeting houses connected with Paradise Row, one at Monkhams Hill, Holyfield, and another at Honey Lane ; the latter MISSION HALL was erected in 1887.

WESLEYAN METHODIST CHAPEL, SEWARDSTONE STREET, was founded about the year 1818.* In 1879 the old Chapel was considerably enlarged, and the new portion brought out to front Sewardstone Street. Previous to this enlargement the entrance to the Chapel was from Quaker Lane. This Chapel is supplied by various ministers. Early in the present century there was a small INDEPENDENT CHAPEL on the right hand side of *Mead Lane* and which was many years ago converted into two small cottages. A Dr. Draper of Cheshunt preached there. The next oldest Nonconformist *Church* in Waltham Abbey, is that now meeting in

EBENEZER BAPTIST CHAPEL, FOUNTAIN SQUARE, which was founded on *Strict and Particular Baptist Principles,* similar to those of Paradise Row Church, when under the pastorate of John Davis. This Church was formed April 18, 1824, by eleven persons, seven males and four females, who separated from Paradise Row Church. John Thompson and James Thompson were chosen as the two first deacons. At this period (1824) John Thompson licensed his house in the *Green Yard* for public worship, and three sermons were preached in it every Lord's day for six months. At the expiration of this term, the house proving too small and inconvenient, an agreement was drawn up between John Thompson and Sarah Dyer, two of the members of the newly-formed Church ; John Thompson then let to Sarah Dyer in trust for the Church a certain building near the *"Baker's Entry"* on a lease for twenty years at a rental of £3

---

* A Chapel was erected, and opened July 13th, 1824, on which occasion Jabez Bunting, M.A., preached in the morning from Col. iii. 4 (The writer is in possession of a copy of this sermon.) W. Martin preached in the afternoon, and J. Gaulter in the evening. The sum of £56 was collected during the day.

per annum. This contract being accepted by the Church, the building was speedily fitted up as a Chapel to accommodate 100 persons at a cost of £110; towards which sum Sarah Dyer, being the most wealthy of any in the Church, gave £40, and the remainder was obtained by voluntary subscriptions. This place of worship existed until the year 1845, when the late Mr. W. Webster, sen., erected a new Chapel on the site of the old one, and called it "BETHEL," and which he let to the Church at £16 per annum. In this place the Church and friends remained until 1868, when after receiving a six months' notice from the landlord to quit the premises, the Church removed with their pastor, Mr. F. Green, into their new Chapel, "Ebenezer," *Fountain Square*, on September 22nd, 1868.* Mr. S. Milner and Mr. J. Hazleton preached the opening sermons. Mr. Green resigned his pastorate in 1869; and in 1876 W. Winters became pastor. In 1879, Ebenezer Chapel was enlarged and a schoolroom added, at a cost of £1,200. Of this money £900 were obtained by the sale of property in Enfield, belonging to the Church, and £300 were borrowed at five per cent. interest to complete the builder's contract. This debt is now paid off.

BETHEL BAPTIST CHAPEL, *Church Street, Baker's Entry*, as before stated, was erected (as the date on the front imports) in 1845; and was hired of the proprietor at a yearly rental of £16 from the time of its erection until 1868 by the Church now meeting in "Ebenezer" Chapel, Fountain Square. For many years after the original Church left "Bethel" Chapel there was no Church formed therein although it was regularly used on Lord's days for divine service. The pulpit is supplied (1887) by various ministers.

A PRESBYTERIAN CHURCH was founded a few years ago at Sewardstone and which continues to worship on Lord's days in the Board School-room; Pastor, Mr. Hunter.

PLYMOUTH BRETHREN meet in a room at the top of Silver Street, near the Market Place. They formerly worshipped in a room in Quaker Lane. This room is now (1887) occupied by

THE SALVATION ARMY, which first appeared in this town in the September of 1885.

---

* A few cottages situated on the left hand side in Quaker Lane belong to "Ebenezer" Baptist Chapel. These were purchased by money realized from the sale of land in Enfield, in 1879.

OLD SCHOOLS IN WALTHAM ABBEY.

EVERTON SCHOOL, *Masters,* since the death of Mr. Leverton; Messrs. J. Braham, Merryman, Hall and Ward. Mr. D. Jones is the present master.

PAROCHIAL SCHOOL (existing a century ago). Arthur Herne, *Master ;* Mrs. Merret, *Mistress* (1800).

NATIONAL SCHOOL, opposite the Church, Mr. Lindeman, *Master,* 1856. The Parochial Schools of Waltham Abbey, have since December 19, 1872, been under the superintendence of the School Board.

BRITISH SCHOOL, Quaker Lane, founded for boys by George Fox in 1667, and re-established 1840, in the old Quaker's Room, *Master,* Charles Clayton. In 1844 a new school-room was erected. The masters who followed Clayton were Frith, Thomas Pugh, and Joseph Upton. This School was abolished on the institution of the Board Schools in 1872.

WALTHAM ACADEMY, Sewardstone Street, *Master,* Samuel Howell (1816), author of a volume of poems. In after years Mr. Thomas Leggett became master and Martha Leggett mistress of a school held on the premises formerly occupied by Mr. Howell. This school was afterwards conducted respectively by Mr. Spencer Carter (an excellent portrait painter,) Mr. Avery, and Mr. Child. Edward Pugh kept a day school in the old timber built house directly opposite the large red brick building in Sewardstone Street, in which many respectable boys were trained between sixty and seventy years ago. Mr. Smith opened a high class school forty years ago, for young gentlemen in Highbridge Street, in what was then called " The Malting Yard." In 1840, Edward Tyler kept a day school in Highbridge Street, also Ann Gibbs.

BOYS' SCHOOL.—A small private school was held, fifty years ago, in an upper room adjoining the Wesleyan Chapel, by Mr. Pardoe (by trade a Brush Maker).

YOUNG LADIES' BOARDING SCHOOL, established late in the last century, probably in Sun Street, *Governess,* Mrs. Ricketts.

A niece of this lady, Miss M. A. Holdsworth, became governess in 1804, or thereabouts, and married in 1811 to Mr. Sherratt. The Misses Dagleys afterwards conducted the School.   The Holdsworth family held "Broomstick Hall" estate in this parish, late in the last century, and became much reduced in position. Early in the present century Mr. Blentcairne kept a respectable school in Sun Street.   His grandson was a military surgeon. Mrs. Littler kept a YOUNG LADIES' SCHOOL for some years in the Market Place.

One of the most noted DAY SCHOOLS for Infants in the town fifty years ago, was that kept by Mrs. ("Old Dame") Parker, in Fountain Square, in which most of the children of that day received their first instructions.   Miss Pegrum kept a respectable day school in Sewardstone Street more than fifty years ago.

Sixty years ago Mr. J. Wilkins kept an evening school at the bottom of Sewardstone Street, nearly opposite the "Three Compasses" Public-house.

A Sunday School in connection with the Abbey Church was founded in 1818-19.   There appears, however, to have been a Sunday School in the town prior to that.   The Parish Register records the burial of Mary Noon, a Sunday School girl, aged 8 years, 29th May, 1811.

In 1824 a Sunday School in connection with Paradise Chapel was founded, consisting of a superintendent, four teachers and twenty-five scholars.   In after years the Wesleyans opened a Sunday School in the town, and one was established in 1876 by the friends of Ebenezer Baptist Chapel, Fountain Square.

ANTIQUITIES FOUND IN WALTHAM ABBEY.* .

A ROMAN coin *Vespasian*, was found a short time since in the old River Lee.

In 1779 a brass coin of *Licinius* was found in Waltham Abbey, legend: IMP. C. VAL. LICIN. LICINIVS P. F. AVGIOVI CONSERVATORI AVG. SMET. B.   Jupiter with a lance and

---

* Unquestionably the parish of Waltham Abbey was known to the *Romans* and *Britons* (not perhaps under its present title) as so many of their ancient relics have been discovered at various times in the neighbourhood.

Victory on a globe, with an eagle and a label over his head. *Vide* Gough, Brit. in Essex. A small earthern figure of a child was found in the Forest by Mr. F. Bird, and was exhibited at the Society of Antiquaries in 1721.

A few fragments of *Romano-British Pottery* were discovered a short time ago in the Ambresbury Banks on the borders of this parish.

A large *Boulder* considered to be of *Roman Cement*, and human bones, were unearthed near the Cock Inn in this town, on opening the ground for the laying of the main water pipes in 1887.

An ancient British Vase was found in Sun Street, in 1851. It was 4½ inches high and 3 inches in diameter.

A water bottle of the mediæval class was discovered in the Market Place, ten feet below the surface, while the men were opening the ground for the Sewage Works. A metal tankard was found in the subterranean passage many years ago.

Portions of green glazed tiles, probably belonging to the ancient Monastery, were found at a considerable depth in the earth.

Several early coins and tokens were found during the restoration of the Lady Chapel in 1875.

In 1855 Mr. Meyrick exhibited a beautiful steel pommel of a sword, of the reign of Elizabeth, wrought in open chain work, richly engraved, found in Waltham Abbey.

About the same time a brass seal, a very ancient lamp, and other items, were found in the town. The seal had a figure of St. Peter, with a key, *circa* 14th century.

Many years ago a half-figure of the Virgin and child, from a brass signet, also a silver ring of the 15th century, were found in the Abbey ground.

A very curious ornamental Flemish tile was found in the roof of the old Baker's Entry, marked 735, with a legend S'IAN SCH. AWI., an illustration of which may be seen in the Essex Archæological Society's Transactions, Vol. II. 52.

A silver coin was found in the town many years ago; legend, C. CONSIDI PAETI. Also a copper coin with ROMA upon it, and a number of others.

During the repairs of the Church in 1860 an axe head was found in the south aisle, about four inches below the surface.

This implement was at once determined by some as being King Harold's battle-axe with which he did such execution at the Battle of Standford Bridge, and on the field of Senlac, where he forfeited his life. An old key and a copper coin, Charles II., were also found under one of the pillars of the Church.

The old lintel of a pointed arch found in the Baker's Entry, with IN DOMINO + CONFIDO carved in relief within the spandrels, is now placed as a lintel in the doorway of the Manse, Paradise Row.

In June, 1867, a dagger blade, seven inches long and slightly curved, was found seven feet below the surface near the Harp Inn. Also several pointed stakes and human skeletons.

A number of Abbey pieces, or Jettons, have been found in the Abbey Garden, and Roadway near the Church. These were used by pilgrims, who travelled from one religious house to another, and were generally of brass or mixed metal.

Trade Tokens have been frequently dug up. Those especially issued by John Hodges, grocer, of Waltham (1666), and Mihill Robinson, grocer. Each of these were worth one farthing. A few other coins have been found in the neighbourhood of Waltham, viz.:—A quarter noble of Edward III., A.D. 1327—1377 *(gold)*; a groat of Edward III. *(silver)*; a groat of Edward IV. *(silver)*; a groat of Mary *(silver)*; and a half-penny of William III. The writer possesses several old coins and tokens that have been found round about the ancient Abbey of Waltham, but few of them are of little worth. In Boyne's Tokens of the 17th century, occur the following, current in Waltham Abbey.

Obverse.—WILLIAM DEANE. = AT = *The King's Arms.*

Reverse.—AT WALTHAM ABBEY, 1668, = His Halfe Penny W.S.D.

O.—IOHN HODGES, = *The Grocer's Arms.*

R.—AT WALTHAM ABBY, I.I.H.

O.—IOHN HODGIS. OF = *A Stick of Candles.*

R.—AT WALTHAM ABBY, = 1666, I.I.H.

O.—MIHILL ROBINSON. = IN = *The Grocer's Arms.*

R.—WALTHAM ABBIE. = M.S.R.

O.—THOMAS TYLAR, His. Half. Penny (in four lines.)

R.—OF WALTHAM ABBY, 1668 (in four lines) *Heart Shaped.*

O.—THOMAS WARRIN, = *Three Pipes in a Triangle.*

R.—OF WALTHAM ABBY, 1668, = His Half Peny, T.S.W.

Tokens were at one time as common as signboards, yet if the following lines be correct they were not always within reach :—

> " For a namesake I gave a token
> To a beggar that did crave it ;
> More he need not me importune,
> For 'twas the utmost of my fortune."

Early in the 17th century it was the custom for partisans of King Charles to carry certain tokens about with them, and if each of the company produced one the conversation became free.

In 1878 a defaced bronzed coin was dug up in Mr. Paul's Nursery, at High Beech. On being submitted, by the Rev. R. Hunter, to Mr. Poole, of the British Museum, that gentleman placed a similar but undefaced one side by side with it, and proved it to be a coin of Antoninus Pius, who was Emperor of Rome from A.D. 138 to A.D. 161.

In 1883 a curious iron ball incased with lead, in the shape of a sugar loaf, was found in a field called " Hungerdowns," High Beech, near " Arabin House." The missile was found about two feet under the surface and weighs about 7 lbs.

On digging near the foundation of the Church, in 1795, a stone vault was discovered; in it was a coffin of thick sheet lead, six feet long, without any inscription thereon. On the left side was the heart enclosed in a double leaden urn, the outer case six inches deep and four inches and a half in diameter; at the mouth it was formed like the bowl of a goblet, when opened the smell was very offensive, but the heart soon evaporated leaving only a white lime like sediment on the lead. The teeth and the bones were but little decayed.*

A few years ago was found in Coleman Street, City, London, a *Stone Mould*, of 12th Century date, used for making religious badgest. The legend, in Lombardic characters, was arranged on the margin, and ran thus : SIGNVM SANCTE CRVCIS DE WALTHAM. This is a most interesting relic, and is noticed by the Rev. Sparrow Simpson, D.D., who states that this was a stone mould incised with a cross, and the legend (as above) appears to indicate that it was intended for the casting of badges to be worn by persons who went on pilgrim-

---

* Gents Mag., 1795.

† Journal of Archœology, Vols. 29, p 421, and 30, p52.

188 HISTORY OF WALTHAM ABBEY

age to the once famous Abbey of St. Cross at Waltham in Essex. Every one knows that a cross with the figure of our Saviour upon it, which had been found at Montacute and had been transferred here, gave a name and sanctity to the place. Dugdale, in the passage just cited, tells us that a cross found at Montacute had a figure of our Saviour upon it, was in fact a crucifix, the pilgrim's sign only exhibiting a cross. The arms of Waltham obviously refer to the cross which was considered one of the chief treasures of the house. There are two coats of arms, viz., I *Argent*, on a cross engrailed *Sable*, five crosslet fitchee *or*; II., *Azure*, two angels volant *or*, supporting a cross Calvary on three grieces *argent*. The stone mould exhibits a plain cross similar to the latter arms.

LOCAL DIRECTORY.

IN addition to the parish Church of Waltham Holy Cross, there is Holy Innocents' Church, High Beech. The Dissenting places of worship are Baptist Chapel, Paradise Row, founded 1729, rebuilt 1836, new school-room erected 1879; Ebenezer, Fountain (Baptist) founded 1824, new Chapel erected in Fountain Square 1868, enlarged 1879; Bethel, Church Street, built 1845; Wesleyan Chapel, Quaker Lane, founded 1818, Chapel erected 1824; enlarged in 1879; and Plymouth Brethren Room, Quaker Lane, in which the Salvation Army meet.

Parochial Registers.—The existing Registers of Christenings, Marriages, and Burials in this parish commenced in 1563. They are in an excellent state of preservation, well bound, and secured in an iron chest.* The Non-Parochial Registers, which by Act of Parliament have become national records, are—(I.) Book of Births, 1799 to 1818; (II.) Book of Deaths, 1770 to 1831; (III.) Books of Burials, 1836 to 1837, at Paradise Row Chapel. (I.) Births and Baptisms, 1818 to 1837, at Wesleyan Chapel. There is a Relieving Officer and Registrar of Births and Deaths.

---

* Copies of these Registers were taken in 1868, and are possessed by the Author.

Town Reading Room, opposite the Church. This room was opened shortly after the old Literary Institution had ceased to exist.

Government Reading Room and Library.—Powder Mill Lane.

High School for Boys and Girls, Harold House, Waltham Lane.

High-Class Boarding and Day School for Girls, Highbridge Street.

Board Schools.—Quaker Lane, Milton Street, Sewardstone, High Beech, and Copt Hall.

School Board.—Instituted in 1873. The first members were Sir T. F. Buxton, Bart. (Chairman), Josiah Norton (Vice-Chairman), T. Chapman, W. R. Clark, J. Claydon, C. Hunt, P. Mills, and H. Gough (Clerk.)

Royal Gunpowder and Gun Cotton Works.

Percussion Cap Factory.—Farm Hill.

Imperial Bank. — Highbridge Street (open on Tuesday and Friday) established 1871.

Benefit Societies.—Benefit Building Society; Oddfellows (M.U.) Providence Lodge; and Ancient Abbey Lodge; Friendly Union Society; and Foresters (St. Lawrence).

Inns in the Town of Waltham Abbey.—Angel; Cock; Green Dragon; Greyhound; Welsh Harp; King's Arms; New Inn; White Lion; Red Lion; Sun; Three Tuns; White Horse; Three Compasses; Ordnance Arms.

Victoria Swimming Bath.—The new bathing place at Rumney Marsh Lock (ten minutes from Waltham Town Bridge) was formally opened on Saturday, 18th June, 1887. George Corble, Treasurer; W. Alps, Secretary.'

RECENT LOCAL EVENTS.—A Fountain erected in the Romeland, and Pump in Greenfield Street. "Clark's Bridge" widened. Sewerage Works removed to south-east of Town Mead after a long litigation and much expense. Tar path made on the causeway bank (Oct. 1884) leading to Small Lea Bridge, which bridge requires to be widened (1887). The almost sudden death of the Rev. James Francis, M.A., occurred March 3rd, 1885, succeeded as vicar by the Rev. F. B. Johnstone, M.A. Essex Agricultural Show held in "Capershott" Field, Sewardstone Road, June 4th and 5th, 1885. This was an immense success. The Government have purchased (1886) Quinton Hill Farm for the purpose of erecting Gun Cotton Works thereon. A plan for making a roadway from Enfield Lock to Waltham Abbey, is under consideration and which, if carried out, will be of great benefit to the town. The East London Waterworks Company have sunk a large well in Canward and are (1887) carrying water pipes through the town to London *via* Sewardstone.

The New Memorial Church Clock.—On Tuesday, October 18th, 1887, the new Illuminated Memorial Clock fixed in the Tower of the Abbey Church was finished. After a short service in the Church, the Rev. F. B. Johnstone, Vicar, led the way to the clock chamber, and behind him immediately followed the Rev. J. H. Stamp, Mr. John Bentley (churchwarden), John Parnell, Esq. (the donor of this handsome gift), and many others. At ten minutes to twelve o'clock the Vicar, who stood facing the company, said: "To the glory of God, and in memory of John Jessopp Parnell and Mary Anne Parnell, I set this clock going;" and having said these words he touched the pendulum, and in a few minutes afterwards the clock chimed and struck the hour of twelve. On the wall near the clock case is placed a memorial tablet of Sienna marble, on which is the following inscription:—

THIS CLOCK

Was Placed in the

ABBEY CHURCH TOWER, .

By John Parnell, J.P.

Oct. 18th, 1887,

In Loving Memory of his Parents,

JOHN JESSOPP PARNELL, Solicitor,

Who died Dec. 28th, 1857, aged 47 years;

AND

MARY ANNE E. J. PARNELL, his wife,

Who died Oct. 18th, 1886, aged 79 years.

The old clock just removed from its ancient position was purchased by the churchwardens of Waltham Abbey, during the ministry of Dr. Joseph Hall. In their accounts, under date 1626, occur the following curious entries:—

"Item, to Frances Arnold for mendinge the leads over the vestrie and for eighteene pound of lead added to the Clocke Waighte, vis. vid. Item to Marmaduke Howe for mendinge the clock diall xd. "To Goodman Dickerson for Oyle for ye Clocke i^{d.} "Item for changeing the olde clocke £iiii. v^{s.}" "Item, for bringinge down the clocke by John Harlows i^{s.} vi^{d.}" "Item, for diet and expenses of the Clockmaker's man while he was setteinge up the clocke vi^{s.}"

The first clock in use in the Abbey was no doubt of contemporary date with the old tower. In the year 1627, the churchwardens of the Abbey paid the following sums:—"Item, for the sextones wages to Jelly (Jolly) and to Goodman Dickerson for keeping ye clocke £1 iii^{s.} November the 1st (1629) paid to Kemp for mending and making cleane the cloke iii^{s.} iiii^{d.}" The old clock was substantially repaired in 1796 when the tower was restored. Mr. J. Clark, of Cold Hall, says that he remembers the old clock being repaired and the dial regilded about forty years ago. Fragments of ancient masonry were removed from the Abbey to make way for the new clock. Several of the pieces I noticed belong to the elegant western arch of the Edwardian period, including other portions taken at some early date from the string course of the clerestory, and from one of the Saxon cylindrical pillars. A small portion of the lost zig-zag column I observed with a heap of pieces of arch moulding, etc., on the roadside near the Church. Some of the surface stones had portions of distemper painting upon them. These fragments I recommended to be placed in some conspicuous part of the old Abbey walls.

Principal Streets in the Town.—Highbridge Street, Church Street, Sewardstone Street, Silver Street, Milton Street, Woollard Street, and Greenfield Street.

Lanes and Yards in the Town. — Powder Mill Lane, Barge Yard (Cook's), North Place, Marshall's Yard (late Cox's), Malting Yard, Romeland, Abbey Lane, Mill Lane, Camp's Alley, Baker's Entry, Backway, Greenyard, Paradise Row, Franchise Place, Fountain Square, Mead Lane, Quaker Lane, Chetwood's Yard (Sun Street.)

Out of Town.—Crooked Mile, Holyfield, Galley Hill, Reeves Gate, Farm Hill, Broomstick Hall, Paternoster Hill, Warlies, Pick Hill, Copt Hall, Woodridden, The Butts, Honey Lane, Pinest Green, High Beech, Fair Mead Bottom, Mott Street, Lodge Lane, Quinton Hill, Sewardstone.

INDEX.

——❦——

The Registrar's Return of the Population and the Number of Houses in the Parish of Waltham Holy Cross from 1801 to 1881.

WALTHAM PARISH.	Inhabited houses.	By how many occupied.	In course of erection.	Uninhabited.	Families chiefly employed in agricul. pursuits	Families chiefly employed in trades, etc.	Families not comprised in the two classes.	Males.	Females.	Total number of persons.
1801.										
Township....	..	..	..	..	..	..	..	1480	1560	1837
Holyfield	..	..	..	..	..	..	..			206
Sewardstone..	..	..	..	..	..	..	..			495
Upshire......	..	..	..	..	..	..	..			502
1811.										
Township....	..	..	..	..	..	..	..	..	..	2287
Holyfield	..	..	..	..	..	..	..	..	..	268
Sewardstone..	..	..	..	..	..	..	..	..	..	583
Upshire	..	..	..	..	..	..	..	..	..	547
1821.										
Township....	422	462	..	15	59	359	44	1021	1076	2097
Holyfield	52	57	..	4	54	2	1	156	137	293
Sewardstone..	120	123	1	5	87	17	19	423	430	853
Upshire......	144	149	..	7	107	29	13	386	353	739
1831.										
Township....	416	455	3	32	35	229	191	1063	1139	2202
Holyfield	62	69	..	3	51	9	9	171	161	332
Sewardstone..	131	133	2	13	69	36	28	385	440	825
Upshire......	151	156	..	13	110	21	25	375	370	745
1841.										
Township....	410	..	2	40	..	..	..	2113	2064	4177
Holyfield	66	..	..	4	..	..	..			
Sewardstone..	144	..	2	9	..	..	..			
Upshire......	164	..	..	12	..	..	..			
1851.										
Township....	461	..	..	4	..	..	..	2143	2160	4303
Holyfield	69	..	..	1	..	..	..			
Sewardstone..	144	..	..	6	..	..	..			
Upshire......	168	..	..	7	..	..	..			
1861.										
Township....	897	..	..	..	..	..	..	..	..	5044
Holyfield										
Sewardstone..										
Upshire......										
1871.										
Township....	978	..	..	..	..	..	..	..	..	5197
Holyfield										
Sewardstone..										
Upshire......										
1881.										
Township	..	..	..	..	..	..	..	2705	2672	5377
Holyfield	..	..	..	..	..	..	..			
Sewardstone..	..	..	..	..	..	..	..			
Upshire.....	..	..	..	..	..	..	..			

In 1815 the annual value of "real property" in the parish of Waltham Holy Cross (as assessed) was £24,886. In 1821 the population of the parish *decreased* from the reduction of the number of labourers employed in the Royal Gunpowder Factory. The return of the population of Sewardstone in 1821 includes a gang of 45 gipsies ! The total number of acres in the parish in 1831 was 11,870. [In 1841 the number of acres is said to have been reduced to "10,876."] The population of the parish in "1870" is said to have numbered "5,700;" according to the *census* taken the year following the return is "5,197." Ratable value of the parish in 1870, £29,839. Number of schools then in operation—six public and one "adventure." Number of children (1870) for whom accommodation then existed at the rate of 10 square   per child—public school, 562 (viz., no returns for two schools); "adventure" schools, 41. The parish contains, according to the last census, 11,870 acres of land ; ratable value, £33,897 ; population, 5,377.

www.ingramcontent.com/pod-product-compliance
Lightning Source LLC
Chambersburg PA
CBHW030822270326
41928CB00007B/848